Paul Lao-Tzu

Lao-Tze's Tao-teh-king: Chinese-English,

With introduction, transliteration

Paul Lao-Tzu

Lao-Tze's Tao-teh-king: Chinese-English,
With introduction, transliteration

ISBN/EAN: 9783337730918

Printed in Europe, USA, Canada, Australia, Japan

Cover: Foto ©ninafisch / pixelio.de

More available books at **www.hansebooks.com**

老子道德經

LAO-TZE'S TAO-TEH-KING

CHINESE-ENGLISH

WITH INTRODUCTION, TRANSLITERATION,
AND NOTES

By DR. PAUL CARUS

報怨以德

REQUITE HATRED WITH GOODNESS
—LAO-TZE, 63

CHICAGO
THE OPEN COURT PUBLISHING COMPANY
(LONDON: KEGAN PAUL, TRENCH, TRUEBNER & CO.)
1898

TABLE OF CONTENTS:

	PAGE
INTRODUCTION: LAO-TZE AND HIS PHILOSOPHY	1
The Old Philosopher	3
The Fundamental Principle of Lao-Tze's Philosophy	9
The Ideal of Lao-Tze's Ethics	17
Taoism Before and After Lao-Tze	30
(Quotations in the *Tao-Teh-King*, 30–34; Lao-Tze and Confucius, 34–38; Taoism After Lao-Tze, 38–41.)	
The Present Edition of the *Tao-Teh-King*	42
Pronunciation	48
LAO-TZE'S TAO-TEH-KING IN CHINESE	49
司馬遷史記老子傳	51
老子道德經	53
ENGLISH TRANSLATION	93
Sze-Ma-Ch'ien on Lao-Tze	95
The Old Philosopher's Canon on Reason and Virtue	97
TRANSLITERATION OF THE TEXT, CHINESE-ENGLISH	139
Sze-Ma-Ch'ien on Lao-Tze	141
The Old Philosopher's Canon on Reason and Virtue	147
NOTES AND COMMENTS	275
INDEX	325

INTRODUCTION

THE OLD PHILOSOPHER.

老子

LAO-TZE,[1] or "the old philosopher," is the designation of one of the most remarkable thinkers of mankind. He was a Chinese who lived in the sixth century B.C., and left to the world the Tao-Teh-King, a small book on Reason and Virtue, which not only exercised a powerful influence upon his countrymen but is also worthy to be compared with the sacred scriptures of the Buddhists and the New Testament. It is on account of the similarities which, in spite of many differences, obtain between the teachings of Lao-Tze and those of Buddha and Christ that the Tao-Teh-King is an indispensable book; and no one who is interested in religion can afford to leave it unread.

*　　*　　*

The date of Lao-Tze's birth[2] is the third year of the Emperor Ting-wang of the Cho dynasty, which corresponds to the year 604 B. C.

Lao-Tze's family name, 李 (Li), means Plum-tree. His proper name, 耳 (Er),[3] means Ear. His appellation was 伯陽 (Po Yang), viz., "Count of the

---

[1] The diphthong *ao* sounds like *ow* in "how," the *e* in "Tze" resembles the short *u* in "but." On pronunciation see page 48.

[2] Mart. Martin's *Hist. Sinica*, p. 133 and Duhalde I., p. 248,

[3] Other transcriptions are *Ur*, *Err*, and *'Rh*.

Positive Principle," representing manliness, the sun, and the South;¹ his posthumous title was 聃 (Tan) long-lobed, long lobes being a sign of virtue. But the people called him simply 老子 (Lao-Tze), the old philosopher. He is also frequently named 老君 (Lao Chün), the ancient sire, master, or prince; and 老兒 (Lao Er), the old child, which means, "he who even as an old man remains childlike." His followers, the Taoists, speak of him as 太上老君 (t'ai shang lao chün), the greatly eminent ancient master, or simply 太上 (t'ai shang), the greatly Eminent One.

Lao-Tze was born in 曲仁 (Ch'ü-Jhren,) a village in 厲鄉 (Li-county) belonging to the 苦縣 (K'u province) of the state 楚 (Ch'u). Abel Rémusat[2] states on the authority of Kwang-Yu-Ki (VI. 15) that:

"*Ch'ü-Jhren* is situated in the vicinity of the present city of *Lu-i*, a town of the third order, belonging to *Kwei-te-foo* of the province *Ho-nan* (lat. 34° north, long. 0° 54' west of Peking)."

Robert K. Douglas, professor of sinology at Oxford, England, calls attention to the strange coincidence that the name of the hamlet *Ch'ü-Jhren*, Lao-Tze's place of birth, means "oppressed benevolence"; *Li*, the parish to which it belongs, means "cruelty"; *K'u*, the name of the district, means "bitterness"; *Ch'u*, the philosopher's native state, means "suffering."[3] He adds:

"If these places were as mythical as John Bunyan's 'City of Destruction' and 'Vanity Fair,' their names could not have been more appropriately chosen to designate the birthplace of a sage who was driven from office and from friends by the disorders of the time." *Society in China*, p. 403.

[1] For *yang* see the *K'anghi*, Vol. 36, p. 10 A.
[2] *Mémoire sur la vie et les opinions de Lao-Tseu*, p. 4.
[3] Professor Douglas's method of transcription is *Chujen, Li, K'u,* and *Ts'u*

Considering the denunciations which Lao-Tze hurled against both "oppression" and "false benevolence"; and the "bitterness" and "sufferings" which he had to endure, the meaning of these names seems startling enough, and were these places not actually in existence they would suggest that Lao-Tze's birth and life were a myth. But Professor Douglas might have added that the coincidence, interesting though it is, is not as remarkable as it appears to Europeans who are unacquainted with the peculiarities of the Chinese language which make such a play of words possible and quite common; for puns are far easier in Chinese than even in French.

Let us look at each name more closely.

曲 (*Ch'ü*) means "crooked" or, as a noun, "a bend," then "scheming," "false," "forced," and finally, in the sense of the German phrase *gebundene Rede*, it denotes "verses," especially "songs, ditties, and ballads." (*K.*, Vol. 17, p. 12 B; *W. S. D.*, p. 458.)

仁 (*Jhren*[1]) means "that which is enclosed, or the kernel of a thing"; then "the essence of man's heart or humaneness"; it also means "the humane or good man." (*K.*, Vol. 6, p. 1 A.) Should the name Ch'u-Jhren be translated according to its proper meaning, it probably ought to be "Good Man's Bend," that is to say, a bend in a valley named after a person whose epithet was "the good man."

厲 (*Li*) means "whetstone; grinding; oppression; danger; disorder." As a verb it means "to grind; to chide; to goad." The name might be translated in English as "Grinding," and *Li Hsiang* would be "grinding county." It may have been called so on

---

[1] *Jhr* is a peculiar *r*-sound. *Jhren* (commonly transcribed *jen*) is pronounced almost like the English word "wren." (See page 48.)

account of being a place where whetstones were found, or made, or sold. (*K'anghi*, Vol. 7, p. 47 A.)

苦 (*K'u*) is the name of the common-thistle. In addition, the word means "bitter; unpleasant; mortifying." As a noun it means "affliction"; as a verb, "to hasten; to be sick." *K'u Hien*, accordingly, might be translated "thistle province." (*K'anghi*, Vol. 29, p. 7 A; *Williams's Syl. Dict.*, p. 436.)

楚 (*Ch'u*) means "a bramble bush" or "a clump of trees." As an adjective it means "full of spines, full of thorns," denoting at the same time "distress" and "pain." If we can translate the name *Ch'u* at all we might call it "the state of the bramble-bush" or "the state of briars." In addition to all these meanings, the word *Ch'u* means "orderly; well done; properly finished."[1] What a choice of allusions cannot be had in Chinese names!

* * *

As to the authenticity of the Tao-Teh-King and the historical reality of Lao-Tze's life, there can be no doubt. 司馬遷 Sze-Ma-Ch'ien, the Herodotus of Chinese history,[2] has embodied a brief account of Lao-Tze's life in his famous 史記 (*Shi-Ki*), or *Historical Records*, which were completed in 91 B. C.

Sze-Mâ-Ch'ien's report of Lao-Tze's life is very terse. It consists only of two hundred and forty-eight words, but is full of interest and very important as the most reliable account that has been handed down to later generations. For these reasons it has been incorporated in the present edition as a kind of preface which will splendidly serve as an authentic historical introduction to the Tao-Teh-King.

[1] See *Williams's S. D.*, p. 94, and *K'anghi*, Vol. 18, p. 28 B.
[2] About 136–85 B. C. See Mayers's *Chinese Readers' Manual*, I., No. 660.

But even before Sze-Ma-Ch'ien, Lao-Tze has been mentioned, commented upon, and largely quoted by a number of his disciples, among whom Lieh-Tze[1] is the oldest, and Chwang-Tze[2] the most ingenious and most famous. Literal quotations from the Tao-Teh-King in the writings of Lieh-Tze, of Han-Fi-Tze,[3] of Chwang-Tze, of Liu-An,[4] of the historian Sze-Ma-Ch'ien himself, and of other authors are so frequent and at the same time so accurate that they verify more than two-thirds of the whole Tao-Teh-King. Professor Legge says:

"I do not know of any other book of so ancient a date as the Tao-Teh-King of which the authenticity of the origin and the genuineness of the text can claim to be so well substantiated."[5]

While the Tao-Teh-King as a genuine production of the age, and Lao-Tze's authorship of the book are beyond dispute, its very existence is a historical problem which has not as yet found its solution. Were Lao-Tze not six hundred years older than Christ, and a hundred years older than Buddha, we should be inclined to believe that he had borrowed his main ideas from either Buddhism or Christianity; but that is a theory which is impossible. Nevertheless, Professor Douglas believes he finds traces of Brahmanical influence in the Tao-Teh-King, and argues that Lao-Tze was a descendant of one of the Western nations of the Chinese Empire, which may have been in con-

[1] Mayers's *Chinese Readers' Manual*, I., 387. His works were edited in the fourth century by Chwang-Tze.

[2] 330 B. C. See Mayers's *Chinese Readers' Manual*, I, No. 92.

[3] Schott mentions him as a contemporary of the Emperor Ngan-Wang (401-374 B. C.), while according to Legge he died 230 B. C

[4] A philosopher on the throne, for he was the King of Hwâi Nan and is best known as Hwai Nan Tze; he died 122 B. C.

[5] *Sacred Books of the East*, XXXIX., p. 9.

nexion with India since olden times. Taking for granted that the name Er, i. e. Ear, was a sobriquet given to Lao-Tze on account of the unusual size of his ears, Professor Douglas says:

"It is remarkable that the description of his large ears and general appearance tallies accurately with those of the non-Chinese tribes on the western frontiers of the empire. His surname, Li, also reminds one of the large and important tribe of that name which was dispossessed by the invading Chinese, and was driven to seek refuge in what is now South-Western China. But however that may be, it is impossible to overlook the fact that he imported into his teachings a decided flavor of Indian philosophy." (*Society in China*, p. 403.)

Douglas goes so far as to find a strong resemblance between Lao-Tze's Tao and the pre-Buddhistic Brahm of the Indian sages, which, however, I am unable to discover. No doubt there are similarities between Indian and Chinese doctrines, but they are too vague and do not prove a common origin; and we must bear in mind that certain similarities of doctrines, nay, also of superstitions, arise naturally in the course of evolution. We must grant, however, that when Lao-Tze resigned his position as custodian of the archives of Cho[1] he went West, which seems to indicate that his sympathies were bound up with those Western people whom his parents may have praised to him as models of simplicity and virtue.

We cannot say that the Brahmanical origin of Lao-Tze's philosophy has been proved. The whole proposition remains a vague hypothesis whose main right to existence consists in the fact that we know too little either to substantiate or to refute it.

---

[1] Other transcriptions are *Chau* (Eitel), *Chow* (Mayers), *Cheu* (Williams) and *Chou* (Wade). See page 48.

THE FUNDAMENTAL PRINCIPLE OF LAO-TZE'S PHILOSOPHY.

道

THE idea that constitutes the corner-stone of Lao-Tze's philosophy is contained in the word Tao, which, however, is so general and comprehensive a term, that his propositions naturally would appear to have existed in a vague form long before him. The universal use of the word gives to his thoughts the appearance of an old doctrine, yet it seems improbable that such an original and extraordinary thinker, as was Lao-Tze, could, like Confucius, have been a mere transmitter of traditions.

The term 道 (*tao*) is a remarkable word.[1] It means "path, way, method, or mode of doing a thing," then also, the mode of expressing a thing, or "word;" and thus finally it acquires its main meaning, which is "reason." As a verb, it means "to walk, or to tread; to speak or to declare; to argue or to reason." Considering the religious reverence in which the term is held, the expression Tao, meaning "word" and "logical thought" at the same time, presents a close analogy to the Neo-Platonic term λόγος. The Buddhists use the word Tao as a synonym of 明 (*ming*), enlightenment,

[1] *K'anghi*, Vol. 34, p. 21 B. Williams, *S. D.*, p. 867. Eitel, *Ch. D.*, p. 743.

to translate the Sanskrit बोधि (*bôdhi*), and the Christians employ it in the version of the New Testament for the term λόγος, "word."

The term "word" in the sense of *Logos* as used in the New Testament occurs also in the Rig-Veda where the fourth hymn is devoted to the *Vâch* (latin, *vox*), "pervading heaven and earth, existing in all the worlds and extending to heaven." Still another striking parallelism is found in the Zoroastrian creed which proclaims that Ahura Mazda, the Lord Omniscient, had created the world by pronouncing the excellent, the pure, and stirring word (*Ahuna Vairyo, Honover*), "the word that existed before everything else."

The same difficulty which translators encounter in their attempts to find a proper rendering of the term λόγος, exists for the term Tao. We might translate it "word," or (as does Stanislas Julien) "path," or (as does Gabelentz) "logos;" or we might (as do Chalmers, Legge, and Victor von Strauss) retain the Chinese word Tao. After a long deliberation the author of the present edition has come to the conclusion that the simplest and most ordinary English analogue for Tao, which is "Reason," would be preferable. But in order to remind his readers of the more comprehensive significance of the word, he has in his translation capitalised it throughout.

The Tao is Kant's "purely formal." Thus it is called 大狀 (*ta chwang*), the great form, and 大象 (*ta hsiang*), the great image[1] (Chap. 35). Other expressions of a similar significance are 寥 (*liao*), vacancy, or a condition of not being occupied, (see Williams, *S. D.*, p. 528) and 寂 (*chi*), noiselessness, or a void of activity. It is the Absolute whose essence is not

[1] Plato's term εἶδος (idea) also means image or picture.

concrete being, but abstract law. To characterise the former, the absence of all the concrete reality, it is called 無 (*wu*), or the non-existent; to characterise the latter, the abstractness of this highest of all generalisations, it is called 冲 (*ch'ung*), hollowness, or 虛 (*hsü*), emptiness, or the void.¹ As the ultimate ground of existence it is called 玄 (*hsüen*), abyss, an expression which reminds one of the Neo-Platonic βυ̃ϑοs, and the *Urgrund* of German mystics.

The terms 狀 (*chwang*), form, and 象 (*hsiang*), image, are commonly used to denote material or concrete forms, but Lao-Tze means pure form, which in his paradoxical mode of speaking is expressed in the terms 無狀之狀 (*wu chwang chih chwang*), the form of the formless, or 無象之象 (*wu hsiang chih² hsiang*), the image of that which has no image, i. e., no concrete shape. In a word, "the form of the formless" means the ideal, the abstract, the universal.

Lao-Tze distinguishes two kinds of Tao or Reason: (1) the Tao that was in the beginning, that is eternal and immutable, the divine presence, which can be on the right hand and at the same time on the left hand, which is bodiless, immaterial, and not sense-perceptible; and (2) the Tao that is individualised in

¹ For *chwang* see *K.*, Vol. 33, p. 6 B; for *shiang*, *ib.* Vol. 22, p. 10 A; for *liao* (a vacuum, or void), *ib.*, Vol. 11, p. 13 B; for *chih* (a state in which no voice is heard, perfect stillness), *ib.*, Vol. 7, p. 10 B; for *wû*, *ib.*, Vol. 21, p. 8 A; for *ch'ung*, *ib.*, Vol. 7, p. 8 B. Compare also *W. S. D.*, p. 109. For *hsü* see *K.*, Vol. 30, p. 2 A. Williams defines *hsü* (p. 227) as "empty; vacant; empty of passions and able to receive, quiet; a vacant, abstracted, contemplative condition such as Buddhists aim to reach; space." Empty space is to both the Taoists and the Buddhists the symbol of absolute rest. (See, e. g., in Samuel Beal's *Catena of Buddhist Scriptures*, p. 157, the simile of the restlessness of dust particles in space, while "the nature of space is rest."

Hsü, vacancy, is a synonym of *k'ung* (*W. S. D.*, p. 464), ecstasy, trance, transport, which is a favorite term with the Buddhists.

² The word *chih* is pronounced „*tze*" in Shanghai, in Canton *chi*. Mr Candlin of Tientsin transcribes it *tzŭ*.

living creatures, especially in man. The latter denotes the reasoning powers of man and is called 人道 (*Jhren tao*), human Reason; the former is characterised as 常道 (*ch'ang tao*), the eternal Reason, or 天道 (*t'ien tao*), Heaven's Reason. It is identified with 玄 (*hsüen*), the mysterious abyss of existence. As the mystery of existence it is called 無名 (*wu-ming*), the Ineffable or Nameless. It is 根 (*ken*), the Root from which everything proceeds and to which everything returns. Although the source of all things, it is itself 無源 (*wu-yuen*), the Sourceless, i. e., Spinoza's *causa sui*.

The difference between the eternal Reason, *ch'ang tao*, and the Reason individualised in man, *Jhren tao*, is emphasised again and again in the Tao-Teh-King; and Chwang-Tze says[1] (Book XI., last paragraph):

"There is the *Tao*, or Way, of Heaven; and there is the *Tao*, or Way, of Man. Practising non-assertion[2] and yet attracting all honor is the Way of Heaven; asserting oneself and being embarrassed thereby, is the Way of Man. It is the Way of Heaven that plays the part of the lord; it is the Way of Man that plays the part of the servant. The Way of Heaven and the Way of Man are far apart. They should be clearly distinguished from each other.'

Says Chwang-Tze:

"The Tao is always one, and yet it requires change."

which means, the Tao is sameness in difference. The same law produces under different conditions different results. The Tao is the world-former, not the world-creator; it is not action but law. Yet it is not merely immanent, it is supernatural and prenatural. It is omnipresent in the world but would exist even though the world did not exist. Says Chwang-Tze (Book VI.):

---

[1] *Sacred Books of the East*, Vol. XXXIX., p. 306.
[2] We replace "Doing nothing," which is a misleading translation, by "Practising non-assertion" for reasons given further on.

"If you could hide the world in the world, so that there was nowhere to which it could be removed, this [Tao] would be the grand reality of the ever-enduring thing." (*Sacred Books of the East*, XXXIX., p. 242.)

The philosophy of Lao-Tze, which places the Tao at the beginning of the world, is the echo of a thinker who was engaged with the same problem as the author of the Fourth Gospel. We read in the Tao-Teh-King that the Tao, far from being made by God, must be prior even to God, for God could never have existed without it, and that, therefore, the Tao may claim the right of priority. Lao-Tze says: "I know not whose son Reason (i. e., the eternal Reason) can be. It seems to be prior to God" (chapter 4); and, following the precedence of the fourth Gospel, Christians will feel inclined to add: "καὶ θεὸς ἦν ὁ λόγος," that is to say, "the Word, the Tao, the Logos, is uncreated, and it is part and parcel of God's being."

What a strange contrast! The Logos or Tao (i. e., the eternal rationality that conditions the immutable laws of the world-order) is, according to Lao-Tze, prior to God; it is God's ancestor or father; but according to Christian doctrines, it is the son of God, not created but begotten in eternity. At first sight both statements are contradictory, but is not after all the fundamental significance in either case the same?

The highest laws of reason are universal and intrinsically necessary; we cannot even imagine that they ever had been or ever could be non-existent or invalid; they have not been fashioned or ordained, they have not been made either by God or man, they are eternal and immutable.

The eternal Reason manifests itself in the laws of nature. Chwang-Tze says:

"When the body of man comes from its special mould [the ever-enduring thing], there is even then occasion for joy; but this body undergoes a myriad transformations, and does not immediately reach its perfection;—does it not thus afford occasion for joys incalculable? Therefore the sagely man enjoys himself in that from which there is no possibility of separation [viz., the Tao], and by which all things are preserved. He considers early death or old age, his beginning and his ending, all to be good, and in this other men imitate him;—how much more will they do so in regard to That Itself on which all things depend, and from which every transformation arises!" (*Ibid.*, p. 243.)

Human reason, *Jhren-tao*, or the reason that can be reasoned, *tao-k'o-tao*, which is contrasted to the *ch'ang-tao*, or the eternal Reason, shows itself in man's interference with the natural course of things. Chwang-Tze says (Book XVII.):

"Oxen and horses have four feet. That is what is called the heaven-ordained. When horses' heads are haltered, and the noses of oxen are pierced, that is called the man-ordained. Therefore it is said: Do not by the man-ordained obliterate the heaven-ordained; do not for your purposes obliterate the decrees of heaven; do not bury your fame in such a pursuit. Carefully persevere in and do not lose it (the Tao). This is what I call reverting to your true (Nature)." (*Ibid.*, p. 384.)

Man's aspiration should not be to follow that which is merely human in him, but that which is eternal; and eternal is alone the Tao, the Reason, the Ultimate Norm of Existence. Thus we find a contrast between 人心 (*Jhren hsin*), the human heart, and 道心 (*tao hsin*), the Rational heart; the former being perverse, the latter a realisation of right feeling, right thinking, and right doing. We read in the *Shu-King*, I., p. 3, 人心惟危 道心惟微 惟精惟一 允執厥中。 *Jhren hsin wei wei, tao hsin wei wei, wei ching wei yi, yun chih chüeh chung,* "the human heart is jeopardised;

but the rational heart is subdued [attenuated]; it is genuine; is unified; thus it keeps its middle (path)."[1]

Lao-Tze's whole philosophy can be condensed in these words: "Men, as a rule, attempt for personal ends to change the Tao that is eternal; they endeavor to create or make a Tao of their own. But when they make, they mar; all they should do is to let the eternal Tao have its way, and otherwise be heedless of consequences, for then all will be well." Christ expresses the same sentiment: "Seek ye first the Kingdom of God and His righteousness; and all these things (the necessities of life) shall be added unto you."

The Tao is not merely a logical principle, it is not "reason" as we commonly use the term; it is clothed with all the awe and reverence of the highest religious idea. Says Chwang-Tze:

"This is the Tao;—there is in It emotion and sincerity, but It does nothing and has no bodily form. It may be handed down (by the teacher), but may not be received (by his scholars). It may be apprehended (by the mind), but It cannot be perceived [by the senses]. It has Its root and ground in itself. Before there were heaven and earth, from of old, there It was, securely existing. From It came the mysterious existences of spirits, from It the mysterious existence of God. It produced heaven; It produced earth. It was before the *T'ai Chi* [the primordial ether]."[2]

[1] This famous passage which is frequently quoted in Chinese literature, is adduced by Victor v. Strauss (p. xxxix) to prove that the ancient Chinese regarded the Tao as a sentient being that is possessed of a heart. He translates "Des Menschen Herz ist gefahrvoll, Tao's Herz ist fein, ist lauter, ist eins. Wollt euch erhalten in ihm." His interpretation of *Tao hsin*, which reflects his theosophical preferences, is against the sense in which the passage is commonly quoted (see the *K'anghi s. v. Tao*, Vol. 34, p. 21 B). The last sentence "Wollt euch erhalten in ihm" instead of "Thus it keeps its middle" is undoubtedly a mistake. Otherwise Strauss's translation is not incorrect. But what shall we say of Legge who (in the *S. B. of the E.*, Vol. III., p. 50) translates this same passage: "The mind of man is restless, prone (to err); its affinity to what is right is small. Be discriminating, be uniform (in the pursuit of what is right), that you may sincerely hold fast the Mean"?

[2] For an explanation of the *T'ai Chi* see the author's article "Chinese Philosophy in *The Monist*, Vol. VI., No. 2.

The Tao is a principle, not a personal being; it is an omnipresent feature of reality, a law fashioning things and events, not a god, nor an essence or a world-substance. Nevertheless, Taoists personify it and use the term as if it were a synonym of God. Thus Lao-Tze himself speaks of the Tao as 天下母 (*t'ien hsia mu*), "the world-mother,"[1] or 萬物之母 (*wan wu chih mu*, "mother of the ten thousand things,[2] and calls it 宗 (*tsung*), the ancestor, and 君 (*chün*), the master,[3] viz., the ultimate authority of the philosopher's words and deeds.

Chwang-Tze speaks of the Tao as "the author of all transformations in whom there is no element of falsehood" (Book V.). Besides, he calls the Tao "the great and most honored Master" (Book VI).

Lao-Tze mentions the word 帝 (*Ti*), God, only once (Chap. 4)[4], calling him 萬物宗 (*wan wu tsung*), "the ancestor" or "arch-father of the ten thousand things." But while Lao-Tze distinguishes God from the Tao and claims that the Tao takes precedence before God, his disciples identify the Tao with God and have coined a special designation 眞宰 (*Chen-Tsai*)[5], i. e., the True Ruler,—a term which is the common appellation of God among Taoists even to-day.

[1] Chapter 52.
[2] Chapter 1.
[3] Chapter 70. For *tsung* see *K.*, Vol. 11, p. 6 B; for *chün* (supreme; one who has land; king; lord; master; a title of respect), *ibid.*, Vol. 8, p. 6 A.
[4] Compare the note to word 40 in the transliteration of Chapter 4.
[5] *Chen* means "true, pure, real" (*K.*, Vol. 24, p. 32 B, *W. S. D.*, p. 15), and *Tsai*, "ruler, responsible master" (*K.*, Vol. 11, p. 9 A, *W. S. D.*, p. 941). The character *Chen* is composed of the signs "upright" and "man," the character *Tsai* shows the sign "bitter," and the sign "roof," which indicate that it means him who bears the burden and cares of the house; its ruler, master, and owner.

THE IDEAL OF LAO-TZE'S ETHICS.

德

UPON his faith in the seasonableness, goodness, and unfailing rightness of the Tao, Lao-Tze builds his ethical system, trusting that through the Tao the crooked shall be straightened, the imperfect shall be made complete, the lowly shall receive abundance as sure as valleys naturally and without any effort of their own fill themselves with water. Thus the Tao resembles water.[1] Lao-Tze demands the surrender of personal ambition and all selfish strivings. His aim is not to fashion, not to make, not to push or force things, but to let them develop according to their own nature.

Virtue, according to Lao-Tze, is simply the imitation of the Tao. The Tao acts, but does not claim; it begets and quickens, but does not own; it directs and arranges, but does not rule.[2] The sage will not make a show of virtue, of benevolence, of justice, of propriety; his virtue is 不德 (*pu teh*), or unvirtue.[3] He will make no pretense of being virtuous, but simply imitate in all things Heaven's Tao. In a word, the ideal of morality consists in realising 無名之樸 (*wu ming chih p'u*), the simplicity of the Ineffable, of the nameless or unnamable Tao.

[1] See Chapters 78, 66, 8.   [2] Chapter 10, 51.   [3] Chapter 38.

Thus, according to Lao-Tze, he who acts a part in the world, as a player does on the stage; he who endeavors to bring about artificial conditions; he who meddles with the natural growth of society, will fail in the end, and virtue is simply 無爲 (*wu-wei*),[1] or "not acting, not making, not doing." Non-action or *wu wei* cannot mean inactivity, for it is with Lao-Tze a principle of action. He never tires preaching 爲無爲 (*wei wu wei*),[2] i. e., to act non-action; he expressly declares that "an able man acts resolutely" (chap. 30); and he assures us (chaps. 37 and 48) that: 無爲而無不爲 (*wu wei er wu pu wei*), "through non-action everything can be accomplished."

Lao-Tze's propositions "to act non-action" and "to accomplish everything by non-action," appear paradoxical, but his idea is simple enough. He who attempts to alter the nature of things will implicate himself in a struggle in which even the most powerful creature must finally succumb. But he who uses things according to their nature, directing their course, not forcing them or trying to alter their nature, can do with them whatever he pleases. Build strong walls and heavy dams to prevent the landslide caused by the waters that sink into the ground, and the waters will break through and carry your dam down into the valley; but provide the under-ground water with outlets in the places where it naturally endeavors to flow, and there will be no danger of a catastrophe.

The same is true of the social conditions of mankind. Lao-Tze requests the government not to govern, but simply to administer. Rulers should not interfere with the natural development of their people, but practise not-acting, not-meddling, non-interfer-

---

[1] *W. S. D.*, pp. 1059 and 1047.   [2] Chapters 3, 10, 37, 57, 63, etc.

ence, or, as the French call it, *laisser faire*, so that the people shall scarcely know that they have rulers. The less laws and prohibitions there are, the less crime will there be. The less the welfare of the people is forced by artificial methods, the greater will be their wealth and prosperity.

Lao-Tze's principle of "not-acting" is accordingly not inactivity; it is simply not acting a part; not doing things in an artificial way; it is not forcing the nature of things. The term 無爲 (*wu wei*) is best explained by its synonym 無欲 (*wu yü*), i. e., "being without desire." Man is requested not to have a will of his own, but to do what according to the eternal and immutable order of things he ought to do. It is the surrender of attachment to self, and the utter omission of 人道 (*jhren tao*), i. e., of man's Tao, the peculiar and particular Tao of oneself and following the course prescribed by the eternal Tao, 常道 (*ch'ang tao*). It is, briefly, not "non-action," but "non-assertion," and this is the translation by which *wu-wei* is rendered in the present translation as coming nearest to the original meaning.

Chwang-Tze, Lao-Tze's most accomplished disciple, characterises *wu-wei*, or non-action, as follows:

"Non-action makes one the lord of all glory; non-action makes one the treasury of all plans; non-action makes one the burden of all offices; non-action makes one the lord of all wisdom. The range of the true man's action is inexhaustible, but there is nowhere any trace of his presence. He fulfils all that he has received from Heaven, but he does not see that he was the recipient of anything. A pure vacancy (of his own and private affairs) characterises him. When the perfect man employs his mind, it is a mirror. It conducts nothing and anticipates nothing; it responds, but does not retain. Thus he is able to deal successfully with all things and injures none."

無爲 (*wu-wei*) is the condition of genuine virtue It leads to 朴 (*p'u*) or 樸 (*p'u*), simplicity, to 虛心 (*hsü hsin*), emptiness of heart, to 質 (*chih*), sincerity to 清 (*ch'ing*), or 清淨 (*ch'ing-ching*), and 淳 (*ch'un*) purity, to 貞 (*cheng*), righteousness, to 素 (*su*), plainness, to 眞 (*chen*), truth,[1] and the application of Lao-Tze's ethics is tersely expressed in the sentence: 報怨以德 (*pau yuen i teh*) "Recompense hatred with goodness." (Chap. 63.)

Lao-Tze further characterises his ethics as 復歸 (*fuh kwei*), "wending home," or 反 (*fan*)[2], "reverting"[3] 歸根 (*kwei ken*), returning to the root. We read in Chapter 40: 反者道之動 (*fan che, tao chih tung*), "returning is the Tao's movement;" and by reverting homeward is meant rest. There is no idea (except perhaps the ideas of simplicity and purity) on which Lao-Tze dwells with more emphasis than upon the ideal of pacification, which he calls 靜 (*ch'ing*), stillness,[4] and 安 (*ngan*), 平 (*p'ing*), 泰 (*t'ai*), i. e., peace, equanimity, and ease.[5] (Chapter 35.)

[1] For *p'u* and *p'u* see *K.*, Vol. 18, p. 2 A; and *W. S. D.*, pp. 710 and 711; for *hsu*, *K.*, Vol. 30, p. 2 A; *W. S. D.*, p. 227; for *chih*, *K.*, Vol. 33, p. 20 A; *W. S. D.*, p. 68; for *ch'ing*, *K.*, Vol. 20, p. 25 B and 27 A; *W. S. D*, p. 995; for *ch'un*, *K.*, Vol. 20, p. 26 B; *W. S. D.*, p. 783; for *cheng*, *K.*, Vol. 33, p. 14 B; *W. S. D.*, p. 73; for *su*, *K.*, Vol. 27, p. 4 A; *W. S. D.*, p. 816; for *chen*, *K.*, Vol. 27, p. 4 A; *W. S. D.*, p. 15.—Williams transcribes *p'oh*, not *pu*; *tsing*, not *ching*; *chan*, not *chen*; *shun*, not *ch'un*.

[2] For *fuh* (to return, to reply), see *K.*, Vol. 13, p. 28 A; for *kwei* (to return homeward), *K.*, Vol. 19, p. 12 B; for *fan* (to revert), *K.*, Vol. 7, p. 38 A. See also *W. S. D.*, pp. 151, 480, 126.

[3] See Chapters 16, 28, 34, etc. Cf. Gen. iii. 19, Psalm xc. 3, Eccl. iii. 20; xii. 7

[4] See Chapters 16, 26, 37.

[5] For *ngan* see *K.*, Vol. 11, p. 5 B; for *p'ing*, *K.*, Vol. 13, p. 1 A; for *t'ai*, *K.*, Vol. 20, p. 15 A. Compare *W. S. D.*, pp. 620, 701, 848; the character *ngan* consists of the radicals "shelter" and "woman," signifying the contentment of being at home, which is the place where a woman is sheltered. *P'ing* (representing scales in equilibrium) means ease, tranquillity, satisfaction, and *t'ai* is composed of "water," and "great," denoting: (1) that which is slippery; (2) that which is in abundance; and (3) that which moves without fric-

The ideal of non-action as the basis of ethics in the sense in which Lao-Tze understands it, is very different from the expressions and moral preachings that the Western people, the energetic children of the North, are accustomed to. Nevertheless, there are remarkable coincidences with Lao-Tze's ethics not only in Buddhism but also in the Bible and the literature of Western saints and sages.

The virtue of the Taoist, which is "tranquillity," "quietude," "rest," corresponds to the Biblical injunction: "Rest in the Lord!" (Psalm, 37, 7) and "In quietude and in confidence shall be your strength!" (Isaiah, 30, 15), or, as the Apostle has it: "We beseech you, brethren, that ye study to be quiet."

This tranquillity, if acquired by all, would become peace on earth to the men of good-will.

The Bible characterises God in words that would have been very congenial to Lao-Tze. We read:

"He maketh wars to cease unto the end of the earth; he breaketh the bow and cutteth the spear in sunder; he burneth the chariot in the fire." (Ps. 46, 9.)

And the ethics of this God, who is the ideal of peace on earth, is stillness. The Psalmist continues:

"Be still and know that I am God."

That God should be conceived as non-action was a favorite idea of Philo, the Neo-Platonist, the same who for the first time used the term Logos in the sense in which it was adopted by the author of the Fourth Gospel. Philo calls God ἄποιος, the non-actor, not in the sense of being passive but as absolute existence,

tion, i. e., a state of ease. Thus *ngan* is peace as opposed to strife; *p'ing* equilibrium, as opposed to an unbalanced state; *t'ai*, smoothness, as opposed to irritation.

as the ὄντως ὄν. Indeed, "activity is as natural to God as burning is to fire" (*Leg. all.*, 1, 3), but God's activity is of a peculiar kind; it is efficiency, not exertion; it is not a particular work that he performs, but an omnipresent effectiveness which Philo finds difficult to characterise without falling a prey to mysticism. Philo was a mystic, and God to him is the Unnamable and Unspeakable, ἀκατονόμαστος καὶ ἄῤῥητος, which is the same as 無名 (*wu ming*).

Stillness, that is to say, self-possessed tranquillity, or quietude of soul is the condition of purity. Anything that agitates the mind disturbs it, for troubled waters cannot be limpid. Chwang-Tze says:

"Sadness and pleasure show a depraving element in virtue; joy and anger show some error in their course; love and hatred show a failure of their virtue. . . . It is the nature of water, when free from admixture, to be clear, and, when not agitated, to be level; while, if obstructed and not allowed to flow, it cannot preserve its clearness;—being an image of the virtue of Heaven. Hence it is said to be guileless and pure, and free from all admixture; to be still and uniform, without undergoing any change; to be indifferent and not self-asserting; to move and yet to act like Heaven:—this is the way to nourish the spirit."

Christianity and Buddhism are classified by Schopenhauer as the religions of pessimism, because they recognise the existence of evil in the world from which we must seek salvation, and in addition to several other similarities the Taoist philosophy would fall under the same category. Chwang-Tze lets the robber Chi express his view on happiness in these words which apparently voice the author's opinion:

"The greatest longevity man can reach is a hundred years; a medium longevity is eighty years; the lowest longevity is sixty. Take away sickness, pining, bereavement, mourning, anxieties, and calamities, the times when, in any of these, one can open his mouth and laugh, are only four or five days in a month. Heaven and earth have no limit of duration, but the death of man has its (appointed) time."

The world is full of anxiety and misery; and salvation consists solely in a surrender of that selfish craving for pleasures which, in common people, is the main-spring of action.

Lao-Tze's ethics of returning, and becoming quiet, remind us of Isaiah's word: "In returning and rest shall ye be saved." (30, 15.)

And the Psalmist says: "Return unto thy rest, O my soul." (116, 7.)

The Taoist term 虛心 (*hsü hsin*), i. e., emptiness of heart, reminds us of the poor in spirit.

Lao-Tze insists on faith as much as St. Paul, saying:

"He whose faith is insufficient shall receive no faith." (17, 23.)

Further Lao-Tze says (Chapters 43 and 78):

"The softest overcomes the world's hardest."
"The weak conquer the strong, the tender conquer the rigid."

St. Paul uses the same expression:

"God hath chosen the weak things of the world to confound the things which are mighty." (1 Cor., 1, 27.)
"When I am weak then I am strong." (2 Cor., 12, 10.)
"My (God's) strength is made perfect in weakness." (*Ib.*, v. 9.)

As the Tao is the same to all people, so the sage is the same to all people. He makes no discrimination. Lao-Tze says: 善者吾善之 不善者吾亦善之 (*shan che wu shan chih; puh shan che wu yih shan chih!*) "The good I meet with goodness; the not-good I meet also with goodness!" (Chapter 49.)

Since genuine merit can be accomplished only through non-assertion, the condition of greatness is modesty or lowliness. As the water that benefits all the world seeks always the lowest places, so the sage abhors self-exaltation. As Christ says, "Whosoever shall exalt himself shall be abased," and "he that shall humble himself shall be exalted," so Lao-Tze compares the Tao of Heaven to a bow (Chapter 77); he says: "It brings down the high and exalts the lowly." Lao-Tze says that the imperfect will be restored, the crooked shall be straightened, the valleys shall be filled (Chapter 20), which reminds one of the words of Isaiah (40, 4):

"Every valley shall be exalted, and every mountain and hill shall be made low: and the crooked shall be made straight and the rough places plain."

Christian philosophers of the Middle Ages, especially the Mystics, present even more striking analogies to Lao-Tze's terminology than St. Paul. As Lao-Tze speaks of "Tao's course" as a "regress" or "a return homeward" (Chapter 40), and of man's necessity of "returning to the root," so Scotus Erigena in his book *De divisione naturæ*, 519 D, declares:

"Deus in unum colligit omnia et ad se ipsum *ineffabili regressu* resolvitur." [God gathers all in one and resolves them in Himself in an ineffable regress.]

Master Eckhart's sermons contain many passages that might have been written by Lao-Tze; so especially his praise of the virtue of simplicity, which he calls *Einvaltekeit* (edition Pfeiffer, II., 600, 31), his recommendation of quietude and rest, which he calls *rouwe* (*ibid.* 601, 4) the importance which he attributes to unity which he calls *eineheit* (*ibid.*, 517 L), and his identification of the highest height with the deepest depth of humility (*ibid.*, 574, 22 and 26).

There is no doubt, the Taoists could claim Eckhart as one of their own.

Johannes Scheffler, called Angelus Silesius, a born Protestant, who was so much affected by mystic sentiment that he turned Roman Catholic, says:

> "Wir beten : 'Es gescheh', mein Herr und Gott, dein Wille,'
> Und sieh, Er hat nicht Will', Er ist ein' ew'ge Stille."
> ["Thy will be done O Lord, my God!" we pray,
> But lo! God has no will; stillness he is for aye.]
> . . . .
> "Ruh' ist das höchste Gut, und wäre Gott nicht Ruh',
> Ich schlösse vor Ihm selbst mein' Augen beide zu."
> [Rest is the highest good; indeed were God not rest;
> I'd turn away from Him, as being no longer blest.]

The Tao-Teh-King exercised a strong influence on Tolstoi.[1] He, too, speaks of non-action, *le non-agir*. Labor, in his opinion, is no virtue; labor is useless, nay, pernicious, for labor, such as keeps men too busy to leave them time for thought, is the curse of the world. Most of us, says Tolstoi, have not time for the consideration of truth and goodness, because we are rushed. An editor must arrange his journal, the general organises his troops, the engineer constructs an Eiffel tower, men of affairs arrange the World's Fair, the naturalist investigates heredity, the philologist must count the frequency of various phrases in certain authors, and no one has leisure enough for a moment of rest; no one has time for finding that peace of soul which the world cannot give. They do anything except that which they ought to do first.

Tolstoi is right, for thinking reforms the world, not laboring. Thought is the rudder that changes the

---

[1] Tolstoi informs the author that he contemplated making a Russian translation of the Tao-Teh-King.

course of the ship of toiling mankind; the energy of the steam that labors in turning the wheels is useful only so long as it is controlled by thought in the right way. For acquiring the right ideal that will guide us in the right direction, we need not labor, nor need we exert ourselves, on the contrary, says Tolstoi, we must abandon all exertion and become calm. If all men would only employ the tenth part of the energy that is wasted on the acquisition of purely material advantages, to settling the questions of their conscience, the world would soon be reformed.

A peculiar parallelism of Lao-Tze's Taoism with Christianity consists in Lao-Tze's belief in an original state of innocence and paradisial happiness. He attributes all the evils that now prevail to a deviation from the original simplicity enjoined by the eternal Tao. The conscious discrimination between good and evil, the studied wisdom of the age, the prevailing method of teaching virtue which does not make men good, but merely induces them to be hypocritical, the constant interference of the government with the affairs of the people are the causes of all disorders. His ideal state would be a return to the paradisial innocence and simplicity, a society of simple-minded people who seek their happiness at home. (Chapter 80.)

There are many more remarkable passages in the Tao-Teh-King, such as the trinity in unity (Chapter 42); the preservation of him who will not perish when he dies (Chapter 33); that the weak conquer the strong (Chapter 43); that we must become like little children (Chapter 28 and 55); that the holy man knows himself as a child of the Tao (Chapter 52); that the Tao can be had for the mere seeking for it (Chapter 63); that the son of heaven (viz., the king or emperor) must bear the sins of the people (Chapter 78), etc.; but we must leave them to the reader who will find enough in Lao-Tze's little book that will set him to thinking.

* * *

The natural result of Lao-Tze's philosophy is the ethical ideal of the sage, the saintly man, 聖人 (*sheng jhren*),[1] who is also called 君子 (*chün tze*), the superior sage, or, as later Taoists have it, 眞人 (*chen jhren*), the Truth-Man, i. e., the man of truth or the true man.

Chwang-Tze says (Book XV.):

"The human spirit goes forth in all directions, flowing on without limit, reaching to heaven above, and wreathing round the earth beneath. It transforms and nourishes all things, and cannot be represented by any form. Its name is "Divinity (in man)." It is only the path of pure simplicity which guards and preserves the Spirit. When this path is preserved and not lost, it becomes one with the Spirit; and in this ethereal amalgamation it acts in harmony with the orderly operation of Heaven.

"There is a common saying, 'The multitude of men consider gain to be the most important thing; pure scholars, fame; those who are wise and able value their ambition; the sage prizes essential purity.' Therefore simplicity is the denomination of that in which there is no admixture; purity of that in which the spirit is not impaired. It is he who can embody simplicity and purity whom we call the True Man." *Sacred Books of the East*, XXXIX., p. 367.

An exhaustive description of the True Man is given by Chwang-Tze in Book VI., where we read:

"What is meant by 'the True Man'?

"The True men of old did not reject (the views of) the few; they did not seek to accomplish (their ends) like heroes (before others); they did not lay plans to attain those ends. Being such, though they might make mistakes, they had no occasion for re-

---

[1] For *Chen*, see p. 15; for *sheng*, p. 773, in Williams's *Syllabic Dictionary*

pentance; though they might succeed, they had no self-complacency. Being such, they could ascend the loftiest heights without fear; they could pass through water without being made wet by it; they could go into fire without being burnt; so it was that by their knowledge they ascended to and reached the Tao.

"The True men of old did not dream when they slept, had no anxiety when they awoke, and did not care that their food should be pleasant. Their breathing came deep and silently.

"When men are defeated in argument, their words come from their gullets as if they were vomiting. Where lusts and desires are deep, the springs of the Heavenly are shallow.

"The True men of old knew nothing of the love of life or of the hatred of death. Entrance into life occasioned them no joy; the exit from it awakened no resistance. Composedly they went and came. They did not forget what their beginning had been, and they did not inquire into what their end would be. They accepted their lot and rejoiced in it; they forgot fear of death and returned to their state before life. Thus there was in them what is called the want of any mind to resist the Tau, and of all attempts by means of the Human to assist the Heavenly. Such were they who are called the True men.

"The True men of old presented the aspect of judging others aright, but without being partisans; of feeling their own insufficiency, but being without flattery or cringing. Their peculiarities were natural to them, but they were not obstinately attached to them; their humility was evident, but there was nothing of unreality or display about it." *Ibid.*, p. 237, 238, 240.

Lao-Tze declares that the True Man is not hurt by fire or water, and that he need not fear either the rhinoceros or tiger, which is explained by Chwang-Tze in Book XVII.:

"Fire cannot burn him who is perfect in virtue, nor water drown him; neither cold nor heat can affect him injuriously; neither bird nor beast can hurt him. This does not mean that he is indifferent to these things; it means that he discriminates between where he may safely rest and where he will be in peril; that he is tranquil equally in calamity and happiness; that he is careful what he avoids and what he approaches;—so that nothing can injure him. Hence it is said: 'What is heavenly is internal; what is human is external.'

"Virtue is in what is heavenly. If you know the operation of what is heavenly and what is human, you will have your root in what is heavenly and your position in virtue." *Ibid.*, p. 383.

The sage is above death; he is one with the Tao:

"Death and life are great considerations, but they could work no change in him. Though heaven and earth were to be overturned and fall, they would occasion him no loss. His judgment is fixed on that in which there is no element of falsehood; and, while other things change, he changes not. The transformations of things are to him the developments prescribed for them, and he keeps fast hold of the author of them."

The same ideas are expressed by Horace in his ode *Integer vitæ* (I., 22) in which the Roman poet praises the perfect and faultless man who needs no arms of any description, who may roam through mountain wildernesses without fear of the wolf and will not suffer from the heat of the desert. Horace exclaims in another ode that the virtuous man would remain firm even if the world broke down upon him: "*Si fractus illabatur orbis, impavidum ferient ruinae.*"

It was natural that in the course of the further development of the Taoist movement the old philosopher was more and more regarded as *the* True Man, beside whom all the others were mere aspirants for saintliness. His life was adorned with tales which remind us of Buddhist legends, and he became the central figure of a triune deity called the Three Pure Ones, which are even in appearance very similar to the Buddhist Trinity of the Buddha, the Dharma, and the Sangha.

TAOISM BEFORE AND AFTER LAO-TZE.

QUOTATIONS IN THE TAO-TEH-KING.

LAO-TZE is commonly called the founder of Taoism, but this is a very doubtful statement, for on the one hand, there appears to have been Taoism before Lao-Tze, and, on the other hand, Lao-Tze's philosophy is too lofty to be identified with the Taoism which at the present day is practised in the innumerable temples of modern Taoism. The Taoists claim Lao-Tze as the revealer of the Tao, the divine Reason, but apparently there are few Taoist priests who are at all able to grasp the significance of the Tao-Teh-King. Lao-Tze is to the Taoists what Christ is to the Christians and Buddha to the Buddhists; but if he came unto his own, those in charge of his temples would not know him, neither would they receive him.

The existence of Taoism before Lao-Tze is evidenced by the numerous quotations, mostly in verse, which are commonly introduced with the word 故 (*ku*),[1] "therefore," which may be translated "for it is said." T'u-T'au-Kien, a commentator (quoted by Stanislas Julien, p. 133) asserts that the passages

[1] Williams, *S. D.*, p. 434.

introduced by the words "Therefore the holy man says," are quoted from the *Fen-tien*. It is a peculiarity of Lao-Tze's that he never quotes an author by name and makes no personal allusions whatever. He is abstract in his thought as well as in his relations to mankind.

We may safely take the existence of a popular Tao-religion and also a current literature of rhymed proverbs and wise saws in the times of Lao-Tze for granted; and the ancient sages of whom he speaks appear to him deep though timid in their expressions (see chapter 15); they were hazy and lacked clearness, yet they were suggestive, and the ideas which their words suggested to him, he is inclined to attribute to them. The main purpose of his book is to make their wisdom, which none could understand, intelligible to the people. But no one who, having perused the whole Tao-Teh-King so as to be familiar with the character of Lao-Tze's thoughts, will, when rereading the fifteenth chapter, fail to understand the situation. The philosophical literature before Lao-Tze probably did not contain anything the loss of which we should have to regret, except for historical or anthropological reasons. It was confused, unintelligible, and full of mystical hints. Its morality appears to have been of a homely character, but not without practical wisdom, such as is found in the proverb literature of all nations as the natural product of the people's experience. Lao-Tze apparently poured new wine into old bottles, and gave to the sages of yore, at whose feet he had sat, more credit than they deserved.

Lao-Tze declares that emptiness is inexhaustible. The motions of the vacant space between heaven and earth do not cease, while the man of many words is soon exhausted. In this connexion he quotes (ch. 5) a Chinese doggerel, probably a proverb of his time:

> "How soon exhausted is a gossip's fulsome talk!
> And should we not prefer on the middle path to walk?"[1]

The sixth chapter contains a curious quotation[2] which (as says the commentator T'u-T'au-Kien) Lieh-Tze attributes to the mythical Hwang-Ti, the Yellow Emperor.[3] The verses may have had reference to the worship of some local deity called "the valley sprite" or "the mysterious mother." She presided over a spring which, because it never ran dry, was supposed to be a direct emanation of the root of heaven and earth. But how much more significant these homely verses become when the ever-enduring, mysterious mother is conceived to symbolise the eternal Tao!

The quotation (in Chapter 1) of the desireless who comprehends the secret meaning of things while the passionate man allows himself to be beguiled by external appearance may have had reference to a popular tale or legend similar perhaps to the story of the three caskets in Shakespeare's *Merchant of Venice*.

The quotation in Chapter 2, which sets forth the co-existence of contrasts and their mutual dependence is, more than to other nations, natural to the Chinese who in their word combinations use compounds of contrasts to denote what is common in both. Thus a combination of the words "to be" and "not to be" means the struggle for life or the bread question;

---

[1] The middle path is the path of virtue.

[2] See Stanislas Julien, p. 133.

[3] Lieh-Tze's full name is Lieh-Yu-K'ow. He belongs to the generation that immediately succeeded the age of Confucius. The Yellow Emperor is commonly assigned to 2697 B. C. See Meyer's *Ch. R. M.*, Nos. 387 and 225.

"the high and the low" means altitude; "much and little" means quantity, etc. But what originally seems to have been the trivial observation of a grammar-school teacher, acquires a philosophical meaning when embodied by Lao-Tze into the Tao-Teh-King.

These are mere guesses at the original meanings of some of Lao-Tze's quotations; they may be right, they may be wrong; who can tell? But the quotations seem to my mind to tell their own story.

Some quotations, such as those in chapters 13, 14, 27, 29, 39, 44, 54, 73, and even the remarkable lines in 78, are simple enough and need no explanation; the quotations in chapt. 12 smack of Chinese schools. The first three lines remind us of sentences contained in the *San-Tze-King*[1] (the classic of three characters), and the other two lines reflect the practical spirit of the Chinese way of moralising. Others (such as in Chapters 2 [the last lines], 4 [repeated in 56], 13, 17, 19, 21, 23, 28, 35, 37, 40, 41, 42, 44, 45, 47) are so peculiarly characteristic of Lao-Tze that we feel inclined to believe that they were either written by the author of the Tao-Teh-King himself, or adapted by him through a slight change in words to their present use, for it is more than probable that the author of the Tao-Teh-King was himself a poet of hymns and of philosophical contemplations. If he shows at an advanced age so much emotion and also love of poetry, how could he in his younger years have abstained from expressing his sentiments in verse? Moreover, the frequent repetitions[1] in the Tao-Teh-King prove

---

[1] Here is a list of the repetitions in the Tao-Teh-King:
"Quickens but owns not, works but claims not," 2, 10, 51, partly repeated in 77.—The verses "Blunts its own sharpness" etc , are quoted twice, 4 and 56.—"Quarreleth (or striveth) not" is repeated with variations in 8, 22, 66, 81.—"Attends to the inner, not to the outer, abandons the latter and chooses the

that he was inclined to quote sayings of his own. However, one of Lao-Tze's most remarkable quotations, found in Chapter 22, is expressly stated to be a saying of the ancients, and Lao-Tze adds that it "was not vainly spoken."

The quotations in the Tao-Teh-King do not prove a lack of originality in Lao-Tze, but they are unequivocal evidences of aspirations before Lao-Tze, which, although less definite, tended in the same direction.

LAO-TZE AND CONFUCIUS.

Taoism is at present, and probably was from time immemorial, certainly long before Lao-Tze, a religion of China. But it is not the only religion; it is one of the three great religions that are officially recognised. Besides Taoism, there is Buddhism and Confucianism. There is a rivalry between Buddhism and Taoism, for Buddhism and Taoism present many similarities; but between Taoism and Confucianism there has obtained since olden times an outspoken antagonism, for Lao-Tze's philosophy stands in strong contrast to the Confucian view of life. We do not speak now of the objections which educated Chinese scholars who hold high offices in the State have to the superstitions that obtain among the less educated

former," 12, 38, 72.—"He whose faith is insufficient shall receive no faith," 17, 23.—"He that makes mars," etc., 29, 64.—"Asserts non-assertion," 3, 37, 48.—"This is called unreason; unreason soon ceases," 30, 55.—"One who has reason has nothing to do therewith," 24, 31.—"If princes and king could keep reason," etc., 32, 37.—"With non-diplomacy he takes the empire," 48, 58.—"Closes his mouth and shuts his sense-gates," 52, 56.—"Thus he becomes world-honored," 56, 62.—"Therefore even the holy man regards it as difficult," 63, 73.

[1] For a translation and exposition of the contents of the *San-Tze-King*, see *The Open Court*, Vol. IX., No. 412. A Latin translation was made by Stanislas Julien, a German translation by Neumann.

Taoist priesthood and also against the religious frauds that are frequently practised in the name of Taoism. We simply speak of the antagonism that obtains between the two sages and their moral maxims.

While 老子 (Lao-Tze) endeavored to reform the heart of the people without moralising or fussing, and left all externalities to fate, 孔子 (K'ung-Tze) or Confucius, proposed to teach propriety. If the people would only observe the necessary rules and ceremonies prescribed by piety and good manners, he expected that all human relations would adjust themselves, and the heart would be reformed by a reform of the habits of life. While Lao-Tze was self-reliant and almost solitary in his way of thinking,[1] Confucius sought the favor of kings and princes. While Lao-Tze stood up for natural spontaneity and independence, Confucius represented paternalism. While Lao-Tze was an anarchist, not in the sense of being against kings, but against governing, Confucius was a monarchist and a regulator of affairs in their details, endeavoring to extend the government into the very hearts of families and the private affairs of the people.

Further, Lao-Tze with all his clearness of thought had a mystic inclination. ⌈He wanted wisdom, not scholarship; Confucius wanted scholarship and hoped to gain wisdom by learning. Lao-Tze wanted simplicity of heart, not decorum; Confucius expected to affect the heart by the proper decorum. Confucius preferred conscious deportment, the product of artificial schooling, but Lao-Tze wanted goodness raised in freedom.⌋

Under such conditions it was natural that there could be but little sympathy between Lao-Tze and

---

[1] Chapter 20 is a pathetic description of Lao-Tze's isolation.

K'ung-Tze, the two greatest leaders of Chinese civilisation, who happened to be contemporaries. Indeed, the Tao-Teh-King contains passages which must be interpreted as direct criticisms of the views of Confucius.[1]

Sze-Ma-Ch'ien's story of Lao-Tze's life which has been incorporated in the present edition of the Tao-Teh-King contains the report of Confucius's interview with the old philosopher, which, for all we know, may be an historical fact. We possess another account of the same meeting by Chwang-Tze (Book XIV, § 6), which, however, although older, can in its lengthier details scarcely be considered more reliable, for Chwang-Tze writes as a litterateur, while Sze-Ma-Ch'ien is conscious of the historian's duties. We need not reproduce Chwang-Tze's account, because it has become accessible through the translations of Victor von Strauss and James Legge.[2]

The Taoist writers are in the habit of censuring bitterly both Confucius and the Confucian scholars, the literati, who down to the present day fill the offices of the Chinese government. The best instances of Taoistic satires are the stories of the madman of Ch'u who rebukes Confucius for his ostentatious manners; the old fisherman who lectures him on simplicity; and the robber Chi who criticises his views on ethics.[3]

The last-mentioned story, viz., of the robber Chi, seems of sufficient interest to deserve a few further remarks. To be brave and courageous and to be a leader of men in battle is, according to Confucius, the

[1] K'ung-Tze's ideal of justice is replaced in the Chapters 49 and 63 by the higher command (which is inculcated by Christ in the Sermon on the Mount) of meeting, not only the good, but also the bad, with goodness.

[2] Strauss, *Tao-Teh-King*, pp. 347-3.7; Legge, *S. B. E.*, XXXIX., pp. 357 ff.

[3] *Sacred Books of the East*, XXXIX., p. 221 ff.; XL., pp. 166 ff., and 192 ff.

lowest virtue, while offering sacrifices to one's ancestors is the greatest merit one can accomplish. The robber Chi rejects the views of Confucius as the arbitrary opinion of an arrogant hypocrite whose lack of success in life proves his inability; and he explains to him that neither he, Confucius himself, nor any one of the old heroes admired by him, were truly virtuous men. Chwang-Tze, in telling the story, claims that the proper procedure in life cannot be laid down in general rules, such as Confucius propounds, but that every creature has its own nature, and every business has its own principles. He only who applies them as suits the peculiar conditions of each case can be successful. He looks upon the virtuous and unvirtuous man of Confucian ethics as an artificial distinction which has no value and is rather a hindrance in real life; at least one prince who followed his maxims lost throne and life. As to principles, however, even robbers must adopt them in order to be successful. Says Chwang-Tze :

"What profession is there which has not its principles? That the robber in his recklessness comes to the conclusion that there are valuable deposits in an apartment shows his sageness; that he is the first to enter it shows his bravery; that he is the last to quit it shows his righteousness; that he knows whether (the robbery) may be attempted or not shows his wisdom; and that he makes a division of the plunder shows his benevolence. Without all these five qualities no one in the world has ever succeeded in becoming a great robber. Looking at the subject in this way, we see that good men do not arise without having the principles of sages, and that Chih could not have pursued his course without the same principles. But the good men in the world are few, and those who are not good are many;—it follows that the scholars (viz., the Confucian literati) benefit the world in a few instances and injure it in many."

Lao-Tze's ethics were rejected by the schools, but

the doctrine of Confucius appealed to the rulers of China on account of its apparent practicability and became thus the established philosophy of the empire. How much different would the development of China have been had Lao-Tze in the place of Confucius exercised the dominating influence upon the thought of the people!

TAOISM AFTER LAO-TZE.

Although the Tao-Teh-King is no popular book, its author, the old philosopher gained, nevertheless, the universal admiration of the masses; but it is natural that the people's Taoism differs greatly from Lao-Tze's Taoism, for while Lao-Tze opposed learnedness and the pretentious show of scholarship, popular Taoism is reported to oppose all learning and with it genuine science and true wisdom.

There is no place in China but has one or more Taoist temples, and at the head of all of them stands the Taoist pope, the vicegerent of God on earth. Professor Legge says:

"Taoism came into prominence under the government of the Han dynasty, and it is recorded that the Emperor Ching (156–143 B. C.) issued an imperial decree that Lao-Tze's book on the Tao and the Teh, on Reason and Virtue, should be respected as a canonical book or *King*, hence its title *Tao-Teh-KING*."

Among the Taoist literature, the books of Chwang-Tze are the most philosophical, while the Book of Rewards and Punishments (*Kan-Ying-P'ien*) and the Book of Secret Blessings (*Yin-Chih-Wen*) are the most popular. Chwang-Tze's writings are a noteworthy monument of deep thought in elegant form, and the two other works are moral injunctions which in the *Kan-Ying-P'ien* are illustrated by stories that bring home to the reader the need of charitableness, piety, universal kindness, and other virtues.[1]

When Buddhism was introduced into China, the Taoists invented legends to prove that Lao-Tze had been the teacher of Buddha, and the Buddhists reciprocated by inventing other legends to prove that Buddha had been the teacher of Lao-Tze. In order to make these claims good they had, however, to alter their chronology, and this is the reason why Buddha's life dates considerably further back according to the Northern traditions than is warranted by the original historical records.

Later Taoists became engaged in the search for the elixir of life, the transmutation of baser metals into gold, and similar aberrations. They were sometimes persecuted by the government, sometimes protected, but they always remained a great power in China on account of the belief of the common people, who never failed to employ and support Taoist priests as soothsayers and astrologers.

When in 208 B. C. the founder of the Han dynasty, Lin Pang, then still the Duke of Pei, took possession of the Empire, he was greatly aided by Chang Liang, who opposed the last successors of the Ts'in dynasty; but when peace was restored Chang-Liang refused to accept any rewards and withdrew, devoting himself to the study of Taoism. A descendant of this hero in the eighth generation became the patron of the Taoist sect. Mayers (in his *Chinese Reader's Manual*, I., No. 35) says about him:

[1] The *Kan-Ying-P'ien* has been translated into French by Stanislaus Julien under the title *Le Livre des Récompenses et des Peines*, etc. Paris and London. 1835. For a good account of both the *Kan-Ying-P'ien* and the *Yin-Tzŭ-Wên* see Prof. R. K. Douglas's *Confucianism and Taouism*. London. 1889. Pp., 256-274.

"He is reputed as having been born at T'ien Muh Shan, in the modern province of Chekiang, and is said at the age of seven to have already mastered the writings of Lao-Tze and the most recondite treatises relating to the philosophy of divination. Devoting himself wholly to study and meditation, he steadfastly declined the offers made him by the Emperors Ho Ti and Chang Ti, who wished to attract him into the service of the State. The latter sovereign ennobled him, from respect for his attainments. Retiring to seclusion in the mountain fastnesses of Western China, he devoted himself there to the study of alchemy and to cultivating the virtues of purity and mental abstraction. His search for the elixir of life was successful, thanks to the instruction conveyed in a mystic treatise supernaturally received from the hands of Lao-Tze himself. The later years of the mystic's earthly experience were spent at the mountain called Lung Hu Shan in Kiangsi, and it was here that, at the age of 123, after compounding and swallowing the grand elixir, he ascended to the heavens to enjoy the bliss of immortality. Before taking leave of earth, he bequeathed his secrets to his son, Chang-Heng, and the tradition of his attainments continued to linger about the place of his abode until, in A. D. 423, one of his sectaries, named K'ow K'ien-che, was proclaimed as his successor in the headship of the Tauist fraternity and invested with the title of T'ien-She, which was reputed as having been conferred upon Chang Tao-Ling. In A. D. 748, T'ang Hsuan Tsung confirmed the hereditary privileges of the sage's descendants with the above title, and in 1016, Sung Chen Tsung enfeoffed the existing representative with large tracts of land near Lung Hu Shan.[1] The Mongol emperors were also liberal patrons of the family, who have continued until the present day to claim the headship of the Taoist sect. In imitation, probably, of the Tibetan doctrine of heirship by metempsychosis, the succession is perpetuated, it is said, by the transmigration of the soul of each successor of Chang Tao-Ling, on his decease, to the body of some infant or youthful member of the family, whose heirship is supernaturally revealed as soon as the miracle is effected."

The Rev. Hampden C. Du Bose says about the Taoist Pope, pages 373, 374:[2]

[1] The Dragon and Tiger Mountains.
[2] Bose, *The Dragon Image and Demon.* New York. 1887.

"The name of Chang, the Heavenly Teacher, is on every lip in China; he is on earth the Vicegerent of the Pearly Emperor in Heaven, and the Commander-in-chief of the hosts of Taoism. Whatever doubts there may be about Peter's apostolic successors, the present Pope, Chang LX., boasts of an unbroken line for threescore generations. He, the chief of the wizards, the "true man" (*i. e.*, "the ideal man"), as he is called, and wields an immense spiritual power throughout the land."

The present emperor respects the rights of the hereditary Taoist Pope and makes all his appointments of new deities or new titles conferred upon Gods or any other changes in the spiritual world through this head of the Taoist sect, whose power is based not only upon wealth, nor upon his priestly army of one hundred thousand men alone, but also and mainly on the reverence of the masses who are convinced of his magical accomplishments and spiritual superiority.

When the reader has finished reading the Tao-Teh-King, so as to have in his mind a clear impression of its grand old author, let him think of the official representative of Lao-Tze's philosophy of the present day. Bose informs us that the scenery of his rural palace is most enchanting; he lives in pomp and luxury, has courtiers and officers, assumes a state whose splendor is scarcely less than that of any sovereign in the world, he confers honors like the emperor of China, and controls the appointments and promotions to the various positions of the Taoist priesthood, many of which are very remunerative, investments being made by written document with official seals.

What a contrast between Lao-Tze and the "vicegerent on earth of the Pearly Emperor in Heaven"! And yet, is it not quite natural? Should we expect it different? It is the world's way of paying its tribute to greatness.

THE PRESENT EDITION OF THE TAO-TEH-KING.

CONCERNING the manuscripts of the Tao-Teh-King, Prof. Stanislas Julien translates the following passage from a Chinese authority:[1]

"The text of Lao-Tze known under the title of *Hiang-in-tsie pen* was found in the tomb of Hiang-in in the fifth year of the period of Wu-p'ing of the Northern T'si dynasty (which is the year 574 A. D.), by an inhabitant of the village of Pong. The text called *Ngan-k'ien-wang-pen* was found by a Tau-sse named Keu-tsien in the period of T'ai-ho of the Wei (which is in our chronology the years 475 and 500 A. D.). The text of the *Ho-shang-kong* was handed down through Kieu-yo, a sage of the kingdom of T'si. Each of these three texts contain 5,722 words. The passages quoted from Lao-Tze by the philosopher Han-fei are found therein exactly and without variations. There was an official text at Lo-yang called *Kuan-pen* containing 5,630 words. The text *Wang-pi* (the commentary of which was composed under the Wei, and according to others under the Tsin), contains 5,683 words, and in certain editions 5,610 words."

Chao-Hong reports that there are sixty-four editions of the Tao-Teh-King. It has been commentated by twenty Taoists, seven Buddhists, and thirty-four literati.

The present text-edition is based upon a compari-

[1] See Stanislas Julien, *Lao Tseu Tao Te King*, p. xxxiv., where he refers to Lao Tseu Tsi Kiaï (ed. Sie Hoeï), Book III. fol. 10.

son of five versions in the translator's possession, the titles of which are as follows:

1. 老子道德經王弼註 宇惠校 須原屋出版 東京
[*Lao-Tze's Tao-Teh-King*, commented by Wang Pi, edited by Ukê, published by Suharaya, Tokio.] Two volumes.[1]

2. 老子道德經 蘇轍註 木山校 松山堂出版 東京
[*Lao-Tze's Tao-Teh-King*, commented by Su Chêh, edited by Kiyama, published by Shozando, Tokio.] Two volumes.[1]

3. 老子諶義 西村著 二書房刊行 東京
[*Lao-Tze Expounded*. By Nishimura, published by the Nishobo, Tokio.] A text-edition with numerous comments.

4. 老子道德經 漢英對照 哲學館發行 東京 Lao-Tze's Tau-Teh-King. [Published by Tetzugaku Kwan, i. e., the Philosophical Institute.][2]

5. *Lao Tseu Tao Te King*. Le livre de la voie et de la vertu, etc. Par Stanislas Julien. Paris. 1842. (Chinese-French, with comments.)

Those chapters which M. Abel-Rémusat quoted in the original Chinese have also been consulted.[3]

* * *

The original text of the old philosopher's life by 司馬遷 (Sze-Ma-Ch'ien), which in the present edition of Lao-Tze's Tao-Teh-King serves as an historical introduction, has been reproduced from Georg von der Gabelentz's edition of this interesting chapter as it appears in his *Anfangsgründe der Chinesischen Grammatik*, pp. 111–115. The sole liberty taken with Gabe-

---

[1] Wang Pi is a famous Chinese commentator who lived 226–247 A. D. under the Wei dynasty, and although he died very young, has the reputation of being a great authority. Su Cheh is one of the two celebrated sons of Su Sun, a prominent author under the Sung dynasty. He lived 1039–1112 and distinguished himself, like his brother Su She, as a statesman and commentator. See Mayers's *Chinese Reader's Manual*, Part I, Nos. 812 and 624.

[2] The Tetzugaku Kwan contains a brief Japanese introduction and Chalmer's English translation, but is otherwise without any comments.

[3] *Memoire sur la vie et les opinions de Laou-Tseu*. Paris, 1823.

lentz's text is the restitution of 蓬 (*p'eng*) to 逢 (*feng*),[1] which obviously is a mere misprint, quite pardonable in consideration of the close similarity of these two words.

* * *

The first translation that was made of the Tao-Teh-King by Western scholars is in Latin. It was made by the Roman Catholic missionaries.[2] Considering the difficulties that had to be overcome, this first venture appears to have been remarkably good, but it is now superseded by the first French translation made by Professor Stanislas Julien.

Julien's edition is very carefully made and may still be regarded as the most diligent and comprehensive work of its kind. It contains the Chinese text mainly based upon Edition E of the Royal Library of Paris. Another French translation has been made by C. De Harlez and is published in the *Annales du Musée Guimet*, Vol. XX. It is based on a careful revision of the text and commentataries. It contains some new interpretations, but enters little into textual criticisms, and as it serves another purpose, it does not render Stanislaus Julien's edition antiquated.

Chalmers's translation is, so far as we know, the first English version. It is very readable and agrees closely with Stanislas Julien's translation but stands in need of a revision. As Chalmers's booklet appeared in a limited edition, it is now out of print, and I could only with difficulty procure a second-hand copy. James Legge's translation, which appeared in the

---

[1] *Feng* means "to meet unexpectedly" (Williams, *S. D.*, p. 158), while *p'eng* is "a species of *rubus* or raspberry, growing sporadically among hemp"; also described as "a weed that the wind roots up and drives across the wastes."—Williams spells *p'ang* and *fŭng*.

[2] Not being in possession of a copy I have not been able to consult it.

Sacred Books of the East, Vol. XXXIX., is no great improvement on Chalmers's translation; on the contrary, it is in several respects disappointing. With its many additions in parentheses, it makes the impression of being quite literal, while in fact it is a loose rendering of the original.

There is a very good German translation by Victor von Strauss, which might be better still had the translator not unduly yielded to his preconception that Lao-Tze was the representative leader of an ancient theosophical movement.

In addition we have two paraphrases of the Tao-Teh-King, one in German by Reinhold von Plaenckner, the other in English by Major-General G. G. Alexander. Plaenckner deviates greatly in his conception of Lao-Tze from all other translators, and is very bitter in denouncing Stanislas Julien especially. Alexander's main contention is to translate the word Tao by God.

For the present translation I have freely availed myself of the labors of my predecessors, to whom I hereby express my gratitude publicly. Most valuable of all has proved to be Prof. Stanislas Julien's work.

Five dictionaries have been used, (1) the *Syllabic Dictionary of the Chinese Language* by Prof. S. Wells Williams, (2) The *Chinese Dictionary in the Cantonese Dialect* by Ernest John Eitel, (3) Kwong Ki Chin's *English-Chinese Dictionary*, (4) Chalmer's *Concise Dictionary of Chinese on the Basis of K'anghi*, and (5) the orginal *K'anghi*.[1] Williams's dictionary, which was in the author's possession from the beginning of his

---

[1] In various references throughout this book the title of Williams's dictionary has been abbreviated in *W. S. D.*, and the *K'anghi* has simply been written *K*.

work, proved most convenient but was in many instances insufficient for the present purpose, in which case the *K'anghi* had to be resorted to.

In addition I am indebted to Mr. K. Tanaka, a young Japanese student of the University of Chicago, and especially to Mr. Teitaro Suzuki, a young Buddhist of Kamakura, Japan, who assisted me in both the comparison of the various editions at my command and in the transliteration of the text. Further, I have to thank Dr. Heinrich Riedel of Brooklyn, N. Y., and the Rev. George T. Candlin of Tientsin, China, for good advice and suggestions.

The purpose of the present translation is first to bring the Tao-Teh-King within easy reach of everybody, and secondly to offer to the student of comparative religion a version which would be a faithful reproduction not only of the sense but of all the characteristic qualities, especially the terseness and the ruggedness of its style.

The translator's ideal was to reproduce the original in a readable form which would be as literal as the difference of languages permits and as intelligible to English-speaking people as the original ought to be to the educated native Chinese. While linguistic obscurities have been removed as much as possible, the sense has not been rendered more definite than the original would warrant. Stock phrases which are easily understood, such as, "the ten thousand things," meaning the whole world or nature collectively, have been left in their original form; but expressions which without a commentary would be unintelligible, such as "not to depart from the baggage waggon," meaning to preserve one's dignity (Chap. 26), have been replaced by the nearest terms that cover their meaning.

The versification of the quoted poetry is as literal as possible and as simple as in the original. No attempt was made to improve their literary elegance. The translator was satisfied if he could find a rhyme which would introduce either no change in the words at all or such an indifferent change as would not in the least alter the sense.

The transliteration of the several words which constitutes the fourth part of this book will enable almost everybody to fall back upon the original Chinese and to verify or revise the translation here proposed.

Comments on the text have been relegated to the critical notes. Observations which on account of their importance should be consulted also by those readers who are not interested in Chinese philology have been marked by a hand, thus ☞. Only a few terse explanatory additions, and such only as are indispensable for an immediate elucidation of the sense, were admitted in brackets into the text.

Standing upon the shoulders of others, and having compared and re-translated the original text, the author feels confident that he can offer to the public a translation which is a sufficient improvement upon former translations to justify its publication.

It lies in the nature of this work that the number of those men who can judge of its merits and demerits is very limited. In handing the book over for publication I crave their indulgence, but, at the same time, ask them to judge of it with all the severity that would be necessary for its improvement in a second edition; for there is a need of a popular edition that will help the English-reading public to appreciate the philosophical genius and the profound religious spirit of one of the greatest men that ever trod the earth.

PRONUNCIATION AND METHOD OF TRANSCRIPTION

It must be regretted that no system of transcribing Chinese sounds has as yet been commonly accepted; nor can any of them be regarded as satisfactory. In the beginning the author of this book adopted Prof. S. Wells Williams's method exclusively, but he has allowed himself to be influenced by Gabelentz, Bridgman, Eitel, Stanislas Julien, and especially by Wade whose system appears to be much used at present. The transcription employed in the Introduction (pp. 3-47) deviates from the traditional methods only where they are positively misleading. For instance, the spelling *Cho* is preferred to *Chou*, because no unsophisticated reader would pronounce *ou* as long *o*.

The diphthong which sounds like *ow* in *how* has been so commonly transcribed by *ao* that Western eyes have become accustomed to the spellings *lao* and *tao*. It would now be difficult to introduce another transcription of the diphthong in *lao* and *tao*, for English readers would be puzzled with either form, *low* and *lou*; the former would probably be pronounced *lo*, and the latter *loo*. If it were transcribed, after the German fashion, *lau*, it would probably be pronounced *law*. For these reasons no change has been made in the traditional spelling of *ao*.

The Rev. Mr. George T. Candlin of Tientsin, China, whose advice was solicited in matters of pronunciation, writes that the vowels of all the systems that follow Wade adopt the continental pronunciation of vowels. However, *o* sounds somewhat like *oah*, and *ou* has the sound of *o* in "alone."

As to the sound which is transcribed by Williams and Wade by *j*, and declared by Gabelentz to be equivalent to the French *j*, (e. g., in *je le jure*, which would be the English *zh*), Mr. Candlin writes: "It is an initial to which I have given much attention, and if I had to choose I would simply write *r* instead of *j*. The fact is, if you listen to a Celestial you hear distinctly the three letters *j*, *h*, and *r* combined into one but the *r* predominant. *Jen* = 'man,' is hardly to be distinguished from the English word 'wren'; *jou* = 'flesh' is nearly 'row,' i. e., to row a boat. But *jhrou* would be right, as there is a suggestion of both a *j* and an *h*."

The Greek *spiritus asper* or an inverted comma is used to denote that strong aspirant which is characteristic of the Chinese language.

The transcription of the transliteration on pages 141-274 follows strictly Professor Williams's method, adding in each case the page of his *Syllabic Dictionary of the Chinese Language* on which the word will be found. The Rev. Mr. Candlin's transcription, wherever it deviated, has been added in parenthesis.

Intonation which plays an important part in the Chinese language has been neglected in transcriptions of the Introduction, where it was commendable to avoid complexities that are redundant for those who speak Chinese and would be useless and unnecessarily puzzling to all the others who do not. In the transcription of the transliteration, however, the intonation has been marked, according to the Chinese fashion, by little semicircles and dashes placed in the four corners of the word, thus: ˌ| the upper monotone and ˌ| the lower monotone; '| the rising tone, |' the departing tone, and |ˌ the entering tone.

As to the printing of the Chinese text we must add that for obvious reasons commonly accepted by sinologues we have followed the usage of arranging the lines, and in quotations the words, according to the Western mode of writing, from the left to the right, not as the Chinese would have it, from the right to the left, nor starting from that page which in Western books would be the last one.

老子道德經

司馬遷史記老子傳

游者可以為綸飛者可以為矰。至於龍吾不能知其乘風雲而上天吾弟子曰鳥吾知其能飛。魚吾知其能游獸吾知其能走。走者可以為罔欲態色與淫志是皆無益於子之身吾所以告子若是而已。孔子去謂累而行。吾聞之良賈深藏若虛君子盛德容貌若愚。去子之驕氣多其人與骨皆已朽矣獨其言在耳。且君子得其時則駕不得其時則蓬曰聘。周守藏室之史也。孔子適周。將問禮於老子。老子曰子所言者司馬遷曰 老子者楚苦縣厲鄉曲仁里人也。姓李氏名耳字伯陽謚

司馬遷史記老子傳

老子乃著書上下篇言道德之意。五千餘言而去莫知其所終。

之見周之衰乃遂去至關。關令尹喜曰子將隱矣彊爲我著書。於是

今日見老子其猶龍邪。老子修道德其學以自隱無名爲務。居周久

老子道德經

上篇

第一章 體道

道可道。非常道。名可名。非常名。無名天地之始。有名萬物之母。故常無欲以觀其妙。常有欲以觀其徼。此兩者同出而異名。同謂之玄。玄之又玄。眾妙之門。

第二章 養身

天下皆知美之為美。斯惡已。皆知善之為善。斯不善已。故有無相生。難易相成。長短相形。高下相傾。音聲相和。前後相隨。是以道沖而用之。或不盈。淵乎似萬物之宗。挫其銳。解其紛。和其光。

第四章 無源

知無欲。使夫知者不敢爲也。爲無爲則無不治。

不亂。是以聖人之治。虛其心。實其腹。弱其志。強其骨。常使民無不尙賢使民不爭。不貴難得之貨。使民不爲盜。不見可欲。使心

第三章 安民

而不恃。功成而弗居。夫惟不居。是以弗去。

聖人處無爲之事。行不言之教。萬物作焉而不辭。生而不有。爲

第五章　虛用

天地不仁。以萬物為芻狗。聖人不仁。以百姓為芻狗。天地之間。其猶橐籥乎。虛而不屈。動而愈出。多言數窮。不如守中。

第六章　成象

谷神不死。是謂玄牝。玄牝之門。是謂天地根。綿綿若存。用之不勤。

第七章　韜光

天長地久。天地所以能長且久者。以其不自生。故能長生。是以持而盈之。不如其已。揣而銳之。不可長保。金玉滿堂。莫之能守。

第九章 運夷

無尤。

第八章 易性

私。

聖人後其身而身先。外其身而身存。非以其無私邪。故能成其

上善若水。水善利萬物而不爭。處衆人之所惡。故幾于道居善

地心善淵。與善仁。言善信。政善治。事善能。動善時。夫惟不爭。故

用。

第十一章　無用

三十輻共一轂。當其無。有車之用。埏埴以爲器。當其無。有器之用。鑿戶牖以爲室。當其無。有室之用。故有之以爲利。無之以爲用。

第十章　能爲

載營魄。抱一。能無離。專氣致柔。能嬰兒。滌除玄覽。能無疵。愛民治國。能無爲。天門開闔。能爲雌。明白四達。能無知。生之畜之。生而不有。爲而不恃。長而不宰。是謂玄德。

富貴而驕。自遺其咎。功成名遂身退。天之道。

愛以身爲天下者。則可以託天下。

第十三章 厭恥

寵辱若驚。貴大患若身。何謂寵辱若驚。寵爲下。得之若驚。失之若驚。是謂寵辱若驚。何謂貴大患若身。吾所以有大患者。爲吾有身。及吾無身。吾有何患。故貴以身爲天下者。則可以寄天下。愛以身爲天下者。則可以寄天下。

第十三章 厭恥

寵辱若驚。貴大患若身。何謂寵辱若驚。寵爲下。得之若驚。失之若驚。是謂寵辱若驚。何謂貴大患若身。吾所以有大患者。爲吾有身。及吾無身。吾有何患。故貴以身爲天下者。則可以寄天下。

此。

第十三章 厭恥

五色令人目盲。五音令人耳聾。五味令人口爽。馳騁田獵令人心發狂。難得之貨令人行妨。是以聖人爲腹不爲目。故去彼取

第十二章 檢欲

與兮若冬涉川。猶兮若畏四鄰。儼兮其若客。渙兮若冰之將釋。古之善爲士者微妙玄通。深不可識。夫惟不可識。故强爲之容。

第十五章　顯德

隨之不見其後。執古之道。以御今之有。以知古始。是謂道紀。
歸于無物。是謂無狀之狀。無象之象。是謂惚恍。迎之不見其首。
不可致詰。故混而爲一。其上不皦。其下不昧。繩繩兮不可名。復
視之不見。名曰夷。聽之不聞。名曰希。搏之不得。名曰微。此三者

第十四章　贊玄

第十六章 歸根

致虛極,守靜篤。萬物並作,吾以觀其復。夫物芸芸各復歸其根。歸根曰靜。是謂復命。復命曰常。知常曰明。不知常妄作凶。知常容。容乃公。公乃王。王乃天。天乃道。道乃久沒身不殆。

第十七章 淳風

太上下不知有之。其次親之譽之。其次畏之。其次侮之。故信不

第十八章 俗薄

大道廢有仁義。智慧出有大僞。六親不和有孝慈。國家昏亂有忠信。

第十九章 還淳

絕聖棄智民利百倍。絕仁棄義民復孝慈絕巧棄利盜賊無有。此三者以爲文不足。故令有所屬。見素抱樸少私寡欲。

第二十章 異俗

絕學無憂。唯之與阿相去幾何。善之與惡相去何若。人之所畏不可不畏。荒兮其未央哉。

足焉有不信猶兮其貴言。功成事遂。百姓皆謂我自然。

孔德之容。惟道是從。道之為物。惟恍惟惚。惚兮恍兮。其中有象。恍兮惚兮。其中有物。窈兮冥兮。其中有精。其精甚真。其中有信。自古

第二十一章 虛心

頑且鄙。我獨異于人。而貴求食於母。察察。我獨悶悶。忽兮若海。漂兮若無所止。眾人皆有以。而我獨我獨若遺。我愚人之心也哉。沌沌兮。俗人昭昭。我獨若昏。俗人泊兮其未兆。如嬰兒之未孩。乘乘兮。若無所歸。眾人皆有餘。而不可不畏。荒兮其未央哉。眾人熙熙。如享大牢。如春登臺。我獨

希言自然。飄風不終朝。驟雨不終日。孰爲此者。天地。天地尚不

第二十三章 虛無

誠全而歸之。

長。夫惟不爭。故天下莫能與之爭。古之所謂曲則全者。豈虛言爲天下式。不自見故明。不自是故彰。不自伐故有功。不自矜故曲則全。枉則直。窪則盈。弊則新。少則得。多則惑。是以聖人抱一。

第二十二章 益謙

及今。其名不去。以閱衆甫。吾何以知衆甫之然哉。以此。

第二十五章 象玄

有物混成。先天地生。寂兮寥兮。獨立而不改。周行而不殆。可以

第二十四章 苦恩

矜者不長。其于道也。曰餘食贅行。物或惡之。故有道者不處也。跂者不立。跨者不行。自見者不明。自是者不彰。自伐者無功。自

亦樂得之。同于失者失亦樂得之。信不足焉有不信。于德。從事于失者同于道者道亦樂得之。同于德者德能久。而況于人乎。故從事于道者道者同于道。從事于德者同

善行無轍迹。善言無瑕讁。善計無籌策。善閉無關鍵。而不可開。

第二十七章 巧用

處超然奈何。萬乘之主。而以身輕天下。輕則失臣。躁則失君。

重爲輕根。靜爲躁君。是以聖人終日行不離輜重。雖有榮觀燕

第二十六章 重德

爲人法地。地法天。天法道。道法自然。

遠遠曰反故道大。天大。地大。王亦大。域中有四大。而王居其一

爲天下母吾不知其名字之曰道。強爲名之曰大。大曰逝。逝曰

器。聖人用之。則爲官長。故大制不割。

第二十八章 反樸

知其雄。守其雌。爲天下谿。爲天下谿。常德不離。復歸于嬰兒。知其白。守其黑。爲天下式。爲天下式。常德不忒。復歸于無極。知其榮。守其辱。爲天下谷。爲天下谷。常德乃足。復歸于樸。樸散則爲器。聖人用之。則爲官長。故大制不割。

之資。不貴其師。不愛其資。雖智大迷。是謂要妙。

物。故無棄物。是謂襲明。故善人者。不善人之師。不善人者。善人

善結無繩約。而不可解。是以聖人常善救人。故無棄人。常善救

以道佐人主者不以兵強天下。其事好還師之所處荊棘生焉。大軍之後必有凶年。善者果而已不敢以取強果而勿矜果而勿伐果而無驕果而不得已果而勿強。物壯則老是謂不道不道早已。

第三十章　儉武

是以聖人去甚。去奢去泰。

敗之。執者失之。故物或行。或隨。或呴。或吹。或強。或羸。或載。或隳。

第二十九章　無爲

將欲取天下而爲之。吾見其不得已。天下神器不可爲也。爲者

道常無名。樸雖小。天下不敢臣。侯王若能守。萬物將自賓。天地

第三十二章　聖德

相合以降甘露。民莫之令而自均。始制有名。名亦既有。夫亦將知止。知止所以不殆。譬道之在天下。猶川谷之於江海。

第三十一章　偃武

夫佳兵不祥之器。物或惡之。故有道者不處。君子居則貴左。用兵則貴右。兵者不祥之器。非君子之器。不得已而用之。恬淡為上。勝而不美。而美之者。是樂殺人。夫樂殺人者。則不可以得志于天下矣。吉事尚左。凶事尚右。偏將軍居左。上將軍居右。言居上勢。則以喪禮處之。殺人眾多。以悲哀泣之。戰勝以喪禮處之。

大。是以聖人終不爲大。故能成其大。

第三十四章 任成

大道汎兮。其可左右。萬物恃之以生而不辭。功成不名有。愛養萬物而不爲主。常無欲可名于小。萬物歸焉。而不爲主可

有志不失其所者久。死而不亡者壽。

知人者智。自知者明。勝人者有力。自勝者強。知足者富。強行者

第三十三章 辨德

知止。知止所以不殆。譬道之在天下。猶川谷之於江海也。

相合以降甘露。民莫之令。而自均。始制有名。名亦旣有。夫亦將

第三十五章　仁德

執大象,天下往。往而不害,安平泰。樂與餌,過客止。道之出口,淡乎其無味,視之不足見,聽之不足聞,用之不可既。

第三十六章　微明

將欲歙之,必固張之。將欲弱之,必固強之。將欲廢之,必固興之。將欲奪之,必固與之。是謂微明。柔弱勝剛強。魚不可脫于淵,國之利器,不可以示人。

第三十七章　為政

道常無為而無不為,侯王若能守,萬物將自化。化而欲作,吾將不居其華。故去彼取此。

識者道之華而愚之始。是以大丈夫處其厚。不居其薄。處其實。不居其華。故去彼取此。

后仁。失仁而后義。失義而后禮。夫禮者忠信之薄。而亂之首前。

爲。上禮爲之而莫之應則攘臂而仍之。故失道而后德。失德而后仁。失仁而后義。失義而后禮。

爲。下德爲之而有以爲。上仁爲之而無以爲。上義爲之而有以爲。

上德不德。是以有德。下德不失德。是以無德。上德無爲而無以

第三十八章　論德

下篇

鎭之以無名之樸。無名之樸。亦將不欲。不欲以靜。天下將自定。

第四十章 去用

反者道之動。弱者道之用。天地萬物生于有。有生于無。

第三十九章 法本

昔之得一者。天得一以清。地得一以寧。神得一以靈。谷得一以盈。萬物得一以生。侯王得一以爲天下正。其致之一也。天無以清將恐裂。地無以寧將恐發。神無以靈將恐歇。谷無以盈將恐竭。萬物無以生將恐滅。侯王無以正。而貴高將恐蹶。故貴以賤爲本。高以下爲基。是以侯王自謂孤寡不穀。此其以賤爲本耶。非乎。故致數車無車。不欲琭琭如玉落落如石。

第四十二章 道化

道生一。一生二。二生三。三生萬物。萬物負陰而抱陽。沖氣以為和。人之所惡。唯孤寡不穀。而王公以為稱。故或損之而益。或益之而損。人之所教。我亦教之。強梁者不得其死。吾將以為教父。

第四十一章 同異

上士聞道。勤而行之。中士聞道。若存若亡。下士聞道。大笑之。不笑不足以為道。故建言者有之。明道若昧。進道若退。夷道若類。上德若谷。大白若辱。廣德若不足。建德若偷。質貞若渝。大方無隅。大器晚成。大音希聲。大象無形。道隱無名。夫唯道善貸且成。

大辯若訥。躁勝寒。靜勝熱。清淨為天下正。

大成若缺。其用不弊。大盈若冲。其用不窮。大直若屈。大巧若拙。

第四十五章 洪德

亡。知足不辱。知止不殆。可以長久。

第四十四章 立戒

有益不言之教。無為之益天下希及之。

天下之至柔馳騁天下之至堅。無有入無間。吾是以知無為之

第四十三章 徧用

名與身孰親。身與貨孰多。得與亡孰病。甚愛必大費。多藏必厚

天下。常以無事。及有事不足以取天下。

第四十八章 忘知

爲學日益。爲道日損。損之又損。以至于無爲。無爲而無不爲。取天下。常以無事。及有事不足以取天下。

第四十七章 鑒遠

不出戶知天下。不窺牖見天道。其出彌遠其知彌少。是以聖人不行而知。不見而名。不爲而成。

第四十六章 儉欲

天下有道却走馬以糞。天下無道戎馬生于郊。罪莫大于可欲。禍莫大于不知足。咎莫大于欲得。故知足之足常足。

夫何故以其無死地。

入軍不避甲兵兕無所投其角。虎無所措其爪。兵無所容其刃。

十有三。夫何故以其生生之厚。蓋聞善攝生者陸行不遇兕虎。

出生入死。生之徒十有三。死之徒十有三。人之生動之死地。亦

第五十章　貴生

天下渾其心。百姓皆注其耳目。聖人皆孩之。

德善。信者吾信之。不信者吾亦信之。德信。聖人在天下慄慄為

聖人無常心。以百姓之心為心。善者吾善之。不善者吾亦善之

第四十九章　任德

致。見小曰明守柔曰強用其光復歸其明。無遺身殃。是謂習常。

第五十二章　歸元

天下有始以爲天下母旣知其母復知其子旣生其子復守其母。沒身不殆。塞其兌閉其門。終身不勤開其兌濟其事。終身不成之。熟之養之覆之生而不有。爲而不恃長而不宰。是謂玄德。之尊德之貴夫莫之命。而常自然故道生之德畜之長之育之

第五十一章　養德

道生之德畜之物形之勢成之。是以萬物莫不尊道而貴德道

觀國以天下。觀天下。吾何以知天下之然哉。以此。

修之于天下。其德乃普。故以身觀身。以家觀家。以鄉觀鄉。以國

修之于家。其德有餘。修之于鄉。其德乃長。修之于國。其德乃豐。

善建者不拔。善抱者不脫。子孫祭祀不輟。修之于身。其德乃眞。

第五十四章　修觀

非道哉。

除田甚蕪。倉甚虛。服文綵。帶利劍。厭飲食。財貨有餘。是謂盜夸。

使我介然有知。行于大道。唯施是畏。大道甚夷。而民好徑。朝甚

第五十三章　益證

不可得而害。不可得而貴。亦不可得而賤。故爲天下貴。

其塵。是謂玄同。故不可得而親。亦不可得而踈。不可得而利。亦

知者不言。言者不知。塞其兌。閉其門。挫其銳。解其紛。和其光。同

第五十六章　玄德

謂之不道。不道早已。

之至也。知和曰常。知常曰明。益生曰祥。心使氣曰強。物壯將老。

而握固。未知牝牡之合而朘作。精之至也。終日號而嗌不嗄。和

含德之厚。比于赤子。毒蟲不螫。猛獸不據。攫鳥不搏。骨弱筋柔

第五十五章　玄符

固久。是以聖人方而不割。廉而不劌。直而不肆。光而不燿。

第五十八章 順化

其政悶悶。其民醇醇。其政察察。其民缺缺。禍兮福之所倚。福兮禍之所伏。孰知其極。其無正。正復為奇。善復為妖。人之迷。其日固久。是以聖人方而不割。廉而不劌。直而不肆。光而不燿。

第五十七章 淳風

以正治國。以奇用兵。以無事取天下。吾何以知其然哉。以此天下多忌諱。而民彌貧。民多利器。國家滋昏。人多技巧。奇物滋起。法令滋彰。盜賊多有。故聖人云。我無為而民自化。我好靜而民自正。我無事。而民自富。我無欲。而民自樸。

第六十一章　謙德

大國者下流。天下之交。天下之牝。牝常以靜勝牡。以靜爲下。故大國若烹小鮮。以道莅天下。其鬼不神。非其鬼不神。其神不傷人。非其神不傷人。聖人亦不傷人。夫兩不相傷。故德交歸焉。

第六十章　居位

治大國若烹小鮮。以道莅天下。其鬼不神。

第五十九章　守道

治人事天。莫若嗇。夫惟嗇。是謂早服。早服謂之重積德。重積德則無不剋。無不剋則莫知其極。莫知其極。可以有國。有國之母。可以長久。是謂深根固蒂。長生久視之道。

罪以免耶。故爲天下貴。

駟馬不如坐進此道。古之所以貴此道者何也。不曰求以得。有
以加人。人之不善。何棄之有。故立天子。置三公。雖有拱璧以先
道者萬物之奧。善人之寶。不善人之所保。美言可以市。尊行可

第六十二章　爲道

各得其所欲。大者宜爲下。
取。或下而取。大國不過欲兼畜人。小國不過欲入事人。夫兩者
大國以下小國。則取小國。小國以下大國。則取大國。故或下以

于足下。爲者敗之。執者失之。聖人無爲故無敗。無執故無失。民
于未亂。合抱之木生于毫末。九層之臺起于累土。千里之行始
其安易持。其未兆易謀。其脆易破。其微易散。爲之于未有。治之

第六十四章　守微

難之。故終無難。
不爲大。故能成其大。夫輕諾必寡信。多易必多難。是以聖人猶
于其細。天下難事必作于易。天下大事必作于細。是以聖人終
爲無爲。事無事。味無味。大小多少。報怨以德。圖難于其易。爲大

第六十三章　思始

江海所以能爲百谷王者以其善下之。故能爲百谷王。是以聖

第六十六章 後已

是謂玄德。玄德深矣。遠矣。與物反矣。乃至于大順。

治國國之賊。不以智治國國之福。知此兩者亦楷式。常知楷式。

古之善爲道者。非以明民將以愚之。民之難治以其智多。以智

第六十五章 淳德

不敗爲。

欲不貴難得之貨。學不學復衆人之所過。以輔萬物之自然。而

之從事。常于幾成。而敗之慎終如始則無敗事。是以聖人欲不

之。

捨後且先。死矣。夫慈以戰則勝。以守則固。天將救之。以慈衞

之。儉故能廣。不敢爲天下先。故能成器長。今捨慈且勇。捨儉且

先。天下皆謂我大似不肖。夫惟大。故似不肖。若肖久矣其細。夫我

有三寶。持而寶之。一曰慈。二曰儉。三曰不敢爲天下先。慈故能勇。

第六十七章　三寶

下莫能與之爭。

民不重。處前而民不害。是以天下樂推而不厭。以其不爭。故天

人欲上民。必以言下之。欲先民。必以身後之。是以聖人處上而

吾言甚易知。甚易行。天下莫能知。莫能行。言有宗。事有君。夫唯

第七十章 知難

相加。哀者勝矣。

攘無臂。仍無敵。執無兵。禍莫大于輕敵。輕敵幾喪吾寶。故抗兵

用兵有言。吾不敢為主。而為客。不敢進寸。而退尺。是謂行無行。

第六十九章 玄用

謂不爭之德。是謂用人之力。是謂配天。古之極。

善為士者不武。善戰者不怒。善勝敵者不爭。善用人者為下。是

第六十八章 配天

勇于敢則殺。勇于不敢則活。此兩者。或利或害。天之所惡。孰知不厭。是以聖人自知不自見。自愛不自貴。故去彼取此。

第七十三章 任為

民不畏威大威至矣。無狹其所居。無厭其所生。夫唯不厭。是以不厭。是以聖人自知不自見。自愛不自貴。故去彼取此。

第七十二章 愛己

知不知上。不知知病。夫唯病病。是以不病。聖人不病。以其病病。

第七十一章 知病

無知。是以不我知。知我者希。則我貴。是以聖人被褐懷玉。

民之饑以其上食稅之多。是以饑。民之難治。以其上之有爲。

第七十四章 制惑

民不畏死。奈何以死懼之。若使民常畏死。而爲奇者吾得執而殺之。孰敢。常有司殺者殺。夫代司殺者殺。是謂代大匠斲。夫代大匠斲者希有不傷手矣。

第七十五章 貪損

民之饑以其上食稅之多。是以饑。民之難治。以其上之有爲。

而自來。繟然而善謀。天網恢恢。疎而不失。

其故。是以聖人猶難之。天之道不爭而善勝不言而善應不召

與之。天之道。損有餘而補不足。人之道則不然。損不足以奉有

天之道其猶張弓乎。高者抑之。下者舉之。有餘者損之。不足者

第七十七章 天道

共強大處下。柔弱處上。

槁故堅強者死之徒。柔弱者生之徒。是以兵強則不勝。木強則

人之生也柔弱。其死也堅強。萬物草木之生也柔脆。其死也枯

第七十六章 戒強

者是賢于貴生。

是以難治。民之輕死。以其求生之厚。是以輕死。夫唯無以生為

德司契。無德司徹。天道無親。常與善人。

第七十九章 任契

和大怨必有餘怨。安以爲善。是以聖人執左契。而不責于人。有德司契。無德司徹。天道無親。常與善人。

社稷主。受國之不祥。是謂天下王。正言若反。

第七十八章 任信

天下柔弱莫過于水。而攻堅強者莫之能勝。其無以易之。弱之勝強。柔之勝剛。天下莫不知。莫能行。故聖人云。受國之垢。是謂社稷主。

欲見賢耶。

餘。孰能有餘以奉天下。是以聖人爲而不恃。功成而不處。其不害。聖人之道。爲而不爭。

聖人不積。既以爲人己愈有。既以與人己愈多。天之道。利而不害。

信言不美。美言不信。善者不辯。辯者不善。知者不博。博者不知。

第八十一章 顯質

不相往來。

食美其服。安其居。樂其俗。鄰國相望。雞狗之聲相聞。民至老死。

舟輿。無所乘之。雖有甲兵。無所陳之。使民復結繩而用之。甘其

小國寡民。使有什伯人之器。而不用。使民重死而不遠徙。雖有

第八十章 獨立

THE OLD PHILOSOPHER'S CANON ON REASON AND VIRTUE

SZE-MA-CH'IEN ON LAO-TZE.

LAO-TZE was born in the hamlet Ch'ü-Jhren (Good Man's Bend), Li-Hsiang (Grinding County), K'u-Hien (Thistle District), of Ch'u (Bramble land). His family was the Li gentry (Li meaning Plum). His proper name was Er (Ear), his posthumous title Po-Yang (Prince Positive), his appellation Tan (Long-lobed). In Cho he was in charge of the secret archives as state historian.

Confucius went to Cho in order to consult Lao-Tze on the rules of propriety.

[When Confucius, speaking of propriety, praised reverence for the sages of antiquity], Lao-Tze said: "The men of whom you speak, Sir, have, if you please, together with their bones mouldered. Their words alone are still extant. If a noble man finds his time he rises, but if he does not find his time he drifts like a roving-plant and wanders about. I observe that the wise merchant hides his treasures deeply as if he were poor. The noble man of perfect virtue assumes an attitude as though he were stupid. Let go, Sir, your proud airs, your many wishes, your affectation and exaggerated plans. All this is of no use to you, Sir. That is what I have to communicate to you, and that is all."

Confucius left. [Unable to understand the basic idea of Lao-Tze's ethics], he addressed his disciples, saying: "I know that the birds can fly, I know that the fishes can swim, I know that the wild animals can run. For the running, one could make nooses; for the swimming, one could make nets; for the flying, one could make arrows. As to the dragon I cannot know how he can bestride wind and clouds when he heavenwards rises. To-day I saw Lao-Tze. Is he perhaps like the dragon?"

Lao-Tze practised reason and virtue. His doctrine aims in self-concealment and namelessness.

Lao-Tze resided in Cho most of his life. When he foresaw the decay of Cho, he departed and came to the frontier. The custom house officer Yin-Hi said: "Sir, since it pleases you to retire, I request you for my sake to write a book."

Thereupon Lao-Tze wrote a book of two parts consisting of five thousand and odd words, in which he discussed the concepts of reason and virtue. Then he departed.

No one knows where he died.

THE OLD PHILOSOPHER'S CANON ON REASON AND VIRTUE.

I.

1. REASON'S REALISATION.

THE REASON that can be reasoned is not the eternal Reason. The name that can be named is not the eternal name. The Unnameable is of heaven and earth the beginning. The Nameable becomes of the ten thousand things the mother. Therefore it is said:

"He who desireless is found
The spiritual of the world will sound.
But he who by desire is bound
Sees the mere shell of things around."

These two things are the same in source but different in name. Their sameness is called a mystery. Indeed, it is the mystery of mysteries. Of all spirituality it is the door.

2. SELF-CULTURE.

When in the world all understand beauty to be beauty, then only ugliness appears. When all understand goodness to be goodness, then only badness appears. For

"To be and not to be are mutually conditioned.
The difficult, the easy, are mutually definitioned.
The long, the short, are mutually exhibitioned.
Above, below, are mutually cognitioned.
The sound, the voice, are mutually coalitioned.
Before and after are mutually positioned."

Therefore the holy man abides by non-assertion in his affairs and conveys by silence his instruction. When the ten thousand things arise, verily, he refuses them not. He quickens but owns not. He works but claims not. Merit he accomplishes, but he does not dwell on it.

"Since he does not dwell on it,
It will never leave him."

3. KEEPING THE PEOPLE QUIET.

Not exalting worth keeps people from rivalry. Not prizing what is difficult to obtain keeps people from committing theft. Not contemplating what kindles desire keeps the heart unconfused. Therefore the holy man when he governs empties the peoples hearts but fills their souls. He weakens their ambitions but strengthens their backbones. Always he keeps the people unsophisticated and without desire. He causes that the crafty do not dare to act. When he acts with non-assertion there is nothing ungoverned.

4. SOURCELESS.

Reason is empty, but its use is inexhaustible. In its profundity, verily, it resembleth the father of the ten thousand things.

> "It will blunt its own sharpness,
>   Will its tangles adjust;
>   It will dim its own radiance
>   And be one with its dust."

Oh, how calm it seems to remain! I know not whose son it is. Before the Lord, Reason takes precedence.

5. THE FUNCTION OF EMPTINESS.

Heaven and earth exhibit no benevolence; to them the ten thousand things are like straw dogs. The holy man exhibits no benevolence; to him the hundred families are like straw dogs.

Is not the space between heaven and earth like unto a bellows? It is empty; yet it collapses not. It moves, and more and more comes forth. [But]

> "How soon exhausted is
>   A gossip's fulsome talk!
>   And should we not prefer
>   On the middle path to walk?"

6. THE COMPLETION OF FORM.

> "The valley spirit not expires,
>   Mysterious mother 'tis called by the sires

> The mysterious mother's door, to boot,
> Is called of Heaven and earth the root.
> Forever and aye it seems to endure
> And its use is without effort sure."

7. DIMMING RADIANCE.

Heaven endures and earth is lasting. And why can heaven and earth endure and be lasting? Because they do not live for themselves. On that account can they endure.

Therefore the holy man puts his person behind and his person comes to the front. He surrenders his person and his person is preserved. Is it not because he seeks not his own? For that reason he can accomplish his own.

8. EASY BY NATURE.

Superior goodness resembleth water. Water in goodness benefiteth the ten thousand things, yet it quarreleth not. Because it dwells in places which the multitude of men shun, therefore it is near unto the eternal Reason.

For a dwelling goodness chooses the level. For a heart goodness chooses commotion. When giving, goodness chooses benevolence. In words, goodness chooses faith. In government goodness chooses order. In business goodness chooses ability. In its motion goodness chooses timeliness. It quarreleth not. Therefore, it is not rebuked.

9. PRACTISING PLACIDITY.

Holding and keeping full, had that not better be left alone? Handling and keeping sharp, can that wear long? If gold and jewels fill the hall no one can protect it.

Rich and high but proud, brings about its own misfortune. To accomplish merit and acquire fame, then to withdraw oneself, that is Heaven's Way.

10. WHAT CAN BE DONE.

He who sustains and disciplines his soul and embraces unity cannot be deranged. Through attention to his vitality and inducing tenderness he can become like a little child. By purifying, by cleansing and profound intuition he can be free from faults.

In loving the people and administering the country he can practise non-assertion. Opening and closing the gates of heaven he can be like a mother-bird: bright, and white, and penetrating the four quarters, he can be unsophisticated. He quickens them and feeds them. He quickens but owns not. He acts but claims not. He excels but rules not. This is called profound virtue.

11. THE FUNCTION OF THE NON-EXISTENT.

Thirty spokes unite in one nave and on that which is non-existent [on the hole in the nave] depends the wheel's utility. Clay is moulded into a vessel and on that which is non-existent [on its hollowness] depends the vessel's utility. By cutting out doors and windows we build a house and on that which is non-existent [on the empty space] depends the house's utility.

Therefore, when the existence of things is profitable, it is the non-existent in them which renders them useful.

12. ABSTAINING FROM DESIRE.

"The five colors the human eye will blind,
The five notes the human ear will rend.
The five tastes the human mouth offend."

"Racing and hunting will human hearts turn mad,
Objects of prize make human conduct bad."

Therefore the holy man attends to the inner and not to the outer. He abandons the latter and chooses the former.

13. LOATHING SHAME.

"Favor and disgrace bode awe.
Esteeming the body bodes great trouble."

What is meant by "favor and digrace bode awe?"

Favor humiliates. Its gain bodes awe; its loss bodes awe. This is meant by "favor and disgrace bode awe."

What is meant by "Esteeming the body bodes great trouble"?

I have trouble because I have a body. When I have no body, what trouble remains?

Therefore, if one administers the empire as he cares for his body, he can be entrusted with the empire.

14. PRAISING THE MYSTERIOUS.

We look at Reason and do not see it; its name is Colorless. We listen to Reason and do not hear it; its name is Soundless. We grope for Reason and do not grasp it; its name is Incorporeal.

These three things cannot further be analysed. Thus they are combined and conceived as a unity which on its surface is not clear but in its depth not obscure.

Forever and aye Reason remains unnamable, and again and again it returns home to non-existence. This is called the form of the formless, the image of the imageless. This is called transcendentally abstruse.

In front its beginning is not seen. In the rear its end is not seen.

By holding fast to the Reason of the ancients, the present is mastered and the origin of the past understood. This is called Reason's clue.

15. THE REVEALERS OF VIRTUE.

Those of yore who have succeeded in becoming masters are subtile, spiritual, profound, and penetrating. On account of their profundity they cannot be understood. Because they cannot be understood, therefore I endeavor to make them intelligible.

How they are cautious! Like men in winter crossing a river. How reluctant! Like men fearing in the four quarters their neighbors. How reserved! They behave like guests. How elusive! They resemble ice when melting. How simple! They resemble unseasoned wood. How empty! They resemble the valley. How obscure! They resemble troubled waters.

Who by quieting can gradually render muddy waters clear? Who by stirring can gradually quicken the still?

He who keeps this Reason is not anxious to be filled. Since he is not filled, therefore he can grow old and need not be newly fashioned.

16. RETURNING TO THE ROOT.

Attain vacuity's completion and guard tranquillity's fulness.

All the ten thousand things arise, and I see them return. Now they bloom in bloom, but each one homeward returneth to its root.

Returning to the root means rest. It signifies the return according to destiny. Return according to destiny means the eternal. Knowing the eternal means enlightenment. Not knowing the eternal causes passions to rise; and that is evil.

Knowing the eternal renders comprehensive. Comprehensive means broad. Broad means royal. Royal means heavenly. Heavenly means Reason. Reason means lasting. Thus the decay of the body implies no danger.

17. SIMPLICITY IN HABITS.

Where great sages are [in power], the subjects do not notice their existence. Where there are lesser sages, the people are attached to them; they praise them. Where still lesser ones are, the people fear them; and where still lesser ones are, the people despise them. For it is said:

"If your faith be insufficient, verily, you will receive no faith."

How reluctantly sages consider their words! Merit they accomplish; deeds they perform; and the hundred families think: "We are independent; we are free."

18. THE PALLIATION OF VULGARITY.

When the great Reason is obliterated, we have benevolence and justice. Prudence and circumspection appear, and we have much hypocrisy. When family relations no longer harmonise, we have filial piety and paternal love. When the country and the clans decay through disorder, we have loyalty and allegiance.

19. RETURNING TO SIMPLICITY.

Abandon your saintliness; put away your prudence; and the people will gain a hundred-fold!
Abandon your benevolence; put away your justice;

and the people will return to filial devotion and paternal love!

Abandon your scheming; put away your gains; and thieves and robbers will no longer exist.

These are the three things for which we deem culture insufficient. Therefore it is said:

"Hold fast to that which will endure,
 Show thyself simple, preserve thee pure,
 Thy own keep small, thy desires poor."

20. DIFFERENT FROM THE VULGAR.

Abandon learnedness, and you have no vexation. The "yes" compared with the "yea," how little do they differ! But the good compared with the bad, how much do they differ!

What the people dread cannot be dreadless! How great is their desolation. Alas! it has not yet reached its limit.

The multitude of men are happy, so happy, as though celebrating a great feast. They are as though in springtime ascending a tower. I alone remain quiet, alas! like one that has not yet received an encouraging omen. I am like unto a babe that does not yet smile.

Forlorn am I, O, so forlorn! It appears that I have no place whither I may return home.

The multitude of men all have plenty and I alone appear empty. Alas! I am a man whose heart is foolish.

Ignorant am I, O, so ignorant! Common people are bright, so bright, I alone am dull.

Common people are smart, so smart, I alone am confused, so confused.

Desolate am I, alas! like the sea. Adrift, alas! like one who has no place where to stay.

The multitude of men all possess usefulness. I alone am awkward and a rustic too. I alone differ from others, but I prize seeking sustenance from our mother.

21. EMPTYING THE HEART.

"Vast virtue's form
Follows Reason's norm.
And Reason's nature
Is vague and eluding.
How eluding and vague
All types including.
How vague and eluding!
All beings including.
How deep, and how obscure.
It harbors the spirit pure,
Whose truth is ever sure,
Whose faith abides for aye
From of yore until to-day.
Its name is without cessation.
It watches the world's formation."

Whereby do I know that it watches the world's formation? By this same Reason!

22. HUMILITY'S INCREASE.

"The deficient will recuperate.
And the crooked shall be straight.
The empty find their fill.
The worn with strength will thrill.
Who have little shall receive.
Who have much will have to grieve."

Therefore the holy man embraces unity and becomes for all the world a model. He is not self-displaying, and thus he shines. He is not self-approving, and thus he is distinguished. He is not self-praising, and thus he acquires merit. He is not self-glorifying and thus he excels. Since he does not quarrel, therefore no one in the world can quarrel with him.

The saying of the ancients: "The deficient will recuperate," is it in any way vainly spoken? Verily, they will recuperate and return home.

23. EMPTINESS AND NON-EXISTENCE.

To be taciturn is the natural way.

A hurricane does not outlast the morning. A cloudburst does not outlast the day. Who causes these events but heaven and earth? If even heaven and earth cannot be unremitting, will not man be much less so?

Therefore one who pursues his business with Reason, the man of Reason, is identified with Reason. The man who pursues his business with virtue is identified with virtue. The man who pursues his business with loss is identified with loss. When identified with Reason, he forsooth joyfully embraces Reason; when identified with virtue, he forsooth joyfully embraces virtue; and when identified with loss, he forsooth joyfully embraces loss.

"He whose faith is insufficient shall not find faith."

24. TROUBLES IN [THE EAGERNESS TO ACQUIRE] MERIT.

A man on tiptoe cannot stand. A man astride cannot walk. A self-displaying man cannot shine. A self-approving man cannot be distinguished. A self-praising man cannot acquire merit. A self-glorying man cannot excel. Before the tribunal of Reason he is like offal of food and like an excrescence in the system which all people are likely to detest. Therefore, one who has Reason does not rely on him.

25. IMAGING THE MYSTERIOUS.

There is Being that is all-containing, which precedes the existence of heaven and earth. How calm it is! How incorporeal! Alone it stands and does not change. Everywhere it goes without running a risk, and can on that account become the world's mother. I know not its name. Its character is defined as Reason. When obliged to give it a name, I call it the Great. The Great I call the Evasive. The Evasive I call the Distant. The Distant I call the Returning.

The saying goes: "Reason is great, Heaven is great, Earth is great, and Royalty also is great. There are four things in the world that are great, and Royalty is one of them."

Man's standard is the Earth. The earth's standard is Heaven. Heaven's standard is Reason. Reason's standard is intrinsic.

26. THE VIRTUE OF DIGNITY.

The heavy is of the light the root, and rest is motion's master.

Therefore the holy man in his daily walk does not depart from dignity. Although he may have magnificent sights, he calmly sits with liberated mind.

But how is it with the master of the ten thousand chariots? In his personal conduct he makes light of the empire. He makes light of it and will lose his vassals. He is passionate and will lose the throne.

27. THE FUNCTION OF SKILL.

"Good travellers leave not trace nor track,
Good speakers, in logic show no lack,
Good counters need no counting rack.

"Good lockers bolting bars need not,
Yet none their locks can loose.
Good binders need not string nor knot,
Yet none unties their noose."

Therefore the holy man is always a good saviour of men, for there are no outcast people. He is always a good saviour of things, for there are no outcast things. This is called concealed enlightenment.

Therefore the good man is the bad man's instructor, while the bad man is the good man's capital. He who does not esteem his instructor, and he who does not love his capital, although he may be prudent, is greatly disconcerted. This I call significant spirituality.

28. RETURNING TO SIMPLICITY.

"Who his manhood shows
And his womanhood knows
Becomes the empire's river.
Is he the empire's river,
He will from virtue never deviate,
And home he turneth to a child's estate.

"Who his brightness shows
And his blackness knows
Becomes the empire's model.
Is he the empire's model,
Of virtue never he'll be destitute,
And home he turneth to the absolute.

"Who knows his fame
And guards his shame
Becomes the empire's valley.
Is he the empire's valley,
For e'er his virtue will sufficient be,
And home he turneth to simplicity."

By scattering about his simplicity he makes [of the people] vessels of usefulness. The holy man employs them as officers; for a great administration does no harm.

29. NON-ASSERTION.

When one desires to take in hand the empire and make it, I see him not succeed. The empire is a divine vessel which cannot be made. One who makes it, mars it. One who takes it, loses it. And it is said of beings:

> "Some are obsequious, others move boldly,
> Some breathe warmly, others coldly,
> Some are strong and others weak,
> Some rise proudly, others sneak."

Therefore the holy man abandons pleasure, he abandons extravagance, he abandons indulgence.

30. BE CHARY OF WAR.

He who with Reason assists the master of mankind will not with arms conquer the empire. His methods [are such as] invite requital.

Where armies are quartered briars and thorns grow. Great wars unfailingly are followed by famines. A good man acts resolutely and then stops. He ventures not to take by force. He is resolute but not boastful; resolute but not haughty; resolute but not arrogant; resolute because he cannot avoid it; resolute but not violent.

Things thrive and then grow old. This is called un-Reason. Un-Reason soon ceases.

31. QUELLING WAR.

Even beautiful arms are unblest among tools, and people had better shun them. Therefore he who has Reason does not rely on them.

The superior man when residing at home honors the left. When using arms, he honors the right. Arms are unblest among tools and not the superior man's tools. Only when it is unavoidable he uses them. Peace and quietude he holds high. He conquers but rejoices not. Rejoicing at a conquest means to enjoy the slaughter of men. He who enjoys the slaughter of men will most assuredly not obtain his will in the empire.

32. THE VIRTUE OF HOLINESS.

Reason, so long as it remains absolute, is unnameable. Although its simplicity seems insignificant, the whole world does not dare to suppress it. If princes and kings could keep it, the ten thousand things would of themselves pay homage. Heaven and earth would unite in dropping sweet dew, and the people with no one to command them would of themselves be righteous.

But as soon as Reason creates order, it becomes nameable. Whenever the nameable in its turn acquires existence, one learns to know when to stop. By knowing when to stop, one avoids danger.

To illustrate Reason's relation to the world we compare it to streamlets and creeks in their course towards great rivers and the ocean.

33. THE VIRTUE OF DISCRIMINATION.

One who knows others is clever, but one who knows himself is enlightened.

One who conquers others is powerful, but one who conquers himself is mighty.

One who knows sufficiency is rich.

One who pushes with vigor has will, one who loses not his place endures. One who may die but will not perish, has life everlasting.

34. TRUST IN ITS PERFECTION.

How all-pervading is the great Reason! It can be on the left and it can be on the right. The ten thousand things depend upon it for their life, and it refuses them not. When its merit is accomplished it assumes not the name. Lovingly it nourishes the ten thousand things and plays not the lord. Ever desireless it can be classed with the small. The ten thousand things return home to it. It plays not the lord. It can be classed with the great.

Therefore, the holy man unto death does not make himself great and can thus accomplish his greatness.

35. THE VIRTUE OF BENEVOLENCE.

"Who holdeth fast to the great Form,
Of him the world will come in quest:

For there they never meet with harm,
But find contentment, comfort, rest."

Music with dainties makes the passing stranger stop. But Reason, when coming from the mouth, how tasteless is it! It has no flavor. When looked at, there is not enough to be seen; when listened to, there is not enough to be heard. However, its use is inexhaustible.

36. THE SECRET'S EXPLANATION.

That which is about to contract has surely been [first] expanded. That which is about to weaken has surely been [first] strengthened. That which is about to fall has surely been [first] raised. That which is about to be despoiled has surely been [first] endowed.

This is an explanation of the secret that the tender and the weak conquer the hard and the strong.

[Therefore beware of hardness and strength:] As the fish should not escape from the deep, so with the country's sharp tools the people should not become acquainted.

37. ADMINISTRATION OF GOVERNMENT.

Reason always practises non-assertion, and there is nothing that remains undone.

If princes and kings could keep Reason, the ten thousand things would of themselves be reformed. While being reformed they would yet be anxious to stir; but I would restrain them by the simplicity of the Ineffable.

"The simplicity of the unexpressed
Will purify the heart of lust.
Where there's no lust there will be rest,
And all the world will thus be blest."

II.

38. DISCOURSING ON VIRTUE.

Superior virtue is un-virtue. Therefore it has virtue. Inferior virtue never loses sight of virtue. Therefore it has no virtue. Superior virtue is non-assertion and without pretension. Inferior virtue asserts and makes pretensions.

Superior benevolence acts but makes no pretensions.

Superior justice acts and makes pretensions. The superior propriety acts and when no one responds to it, it stretches its arm and enforces its rules. Thus one loses Reason and then virtue appears. One loses virtue and then benevolence appears. One loses benevolence and then justice appears. One loses justice and then propriety appears. The rules of propriety are the semblance of loyalty and faith, and the beginning of disorder.

Quick-wittedness is the [mere] flower of Reason, but of ignorance the beginning.

Therefore a great organiser abides by the solid and dwells not in the external. He abides in the fruit and dwells not in the flower. Therefore he discards the latter and chooses the former.

39. THE ROOT OF ORDER.

From of old these things have obtained oneness:

"Heaven through oneness has become pure.
Earth through oneness can endure.
Minds through oneness their souls procure.
Valleys through oneness repletion secure.

"All creatures through oneness to life have been called.
And kings were through oneness as models installed."

Such is the result of oneness.

"Were heaven not pure it might be rent.
Were earth not stable it might be bent.
Were minds not ensouled they'd be impotent.
Were valleys not filled they'd soon be spent.

"When creatures are lifeless who can their death prevent?
Are kings not models, but on highness bent,
Their fall, forsooth, is imminent."

Thus, the noble come from the commoners as their root, and the high rest upon the lowly as their foundation. Therefore, princes and kings call themselves orphans, widowers, and nobodies. Is this not because they [representing the unity of the commoners] take lowliness as their root?

The several parts of a carriage are not a carriage.

Those who have become a unity are neither anxious to be praised with praise like a gem, nor disdained with disdain like a stone.

40. AVOIDING ACTIVITY.

"Homeward is Reason's course,
Weakness is Reason's force."

Heaven and earth and the ten thousand things come from existence, but existence comes from non-existence.

41. SAMENESS IN DIFFERENCE.

When a superior scholar hears of Reason he endeavors to practise it. When an average scholar hears of Reason he will sometimes keep it and sometimes lose it. When an inferior scholar hears of Reason he will greatly ridicule it. Were it not thus ridiculed, it would as Reason be insufficient. Therefore the poet says:

"The reason-enlightened seem dark and black,
The reason-advanced seem going back,
The reason-straight-levelled seem rugged and slack.

"The high in virtue resemble a vale,
The purely white in shame must quail,
The staunchest virtue seems to fail.

"The solidest virtue seems not alert,
The purest chastity seems pervert,
The greatest square will rightness desert.

"The largest vessel is not yet complete,
The loudest sound is not speech replete,
The greatest form has no shape concrete."

Reason so long as it remains hidden is unnameable. Yet Reason alone is good for imparting and completing.

42. REASON'S MODIFICATIONS.

Reason begets unity; unity begets duality; duality begets trinity; and trinity begets the ten thousand things. The ten thousand things are sustained by YIN [the negative principle]; they are encompassed by YANG [the positive principle], and the immaterial CH'I [the breath of life] renders them harmonious.

That which the people find odious, to be an orphan, a widower, or a nobody, kings and princes select as their titles. Thus, on the one hand, loss implies gain, and on the other hand, gain implies loss.

What others have taught I teach also. The strong and aggressive do not die a natural death; but I shall expound the doctrine's foundation.

43. ITS UNIVERSAL APPLICATION.

The world's weakest overcomes the world's hardest. Non-existence enters into the impenetrable. Thereby I comprehend of non-assertion the advantage, and of silence the lesson, There are few in the world who obtain the advantage of non-assertion.

44. SETTING UP PRECEPTS.

"Name or person, which is more near?
Person or fortune, which is more dear?
Gain or loss, which is more sear?

"Extreme dotage leadeth to squandering,
Hoarded wealth inviteth plundering.

"Who is content incurs no humiliation,
Who knows when to stop risks no vitiation,
Forever lasteth his duration."

45. GREATEST VIRTUE.

"The greatest perfection seems imperfect,
But its work undecaying remaineth.
The greatest fulness is emptiness-checked,
But its work 's not exhausted nor waneth."

"The straightest line resembleth a curve;
The greatest sage as apprentice will serve;
Most eloquent speakers will stammer and swerve.'

Motion conquers cold. Quietude conquers heat Purity and clearness are the world's standard.

46. MODERATION OF DESIRE.

When the world possesses Reason, race horses are reserved for hauling dung. When the world is without Reason, war horses are bred in the common.

No greater sin than yielding to desire. No greater misery than discontent. No greater calamity than acquisitiveness.

Therefore, he who knows contentment's contentment is always content.

47. VIEWING THE DISTANT.

"Without passing out of the gate
The world's course I prognosticate.
Without peeping through the window
The heavenly Reason I contemplate.
The further one goes,
The less one knows."

Therefore the holy man does not travel, and yet he has knowledge. He does not see the things, and yet he defines them. He does not labor, and yet he completes.

48. FORGETTING KNOWLEDGE.

He who seeks learnedness will daily increase. He who seeks Reason will daily diminish. He will diminish and continue to diminish until he arrives at non-assertion. With non-assertion there is nothing that he cannot achieve. When he takes the empire, it is always because he uses no diplomacy. He who uses diplomacy is not fit to take the empire.

49. TRUST IN VIRTUE.

The holy man possesses not a fixed heart. The hundred families' hearts he makes his heart.

The good I meet with goodness; the bad I also meet with goodness; for virtue is good [throughout].

The faithful I meet with faith; the faithless I also meet with faith; for virtue is faithful [throughout].

The holy man dwells in the world anxious, very anxious in his dealings with the world. He universalises his heart, and the hundred families fix upon him their ears and eyes. The holy man treats them all as children.

50. THE ESTIMATION OF LIFE.

Going forth is life; coming home is death.

Three in ten are pursuers of life; three in ten are pursuers of death; three in ten of the men that live pass into the realm of death.

Now, what is the reason? It is because they live life's intensity.

Indeed, I understand that one who takes good care of his life, when travelling on land will not fall in with the rhinoceros or the tiger. When coming among soldiers, he need not fear arms and weapons. The rhinoceros finds no place where to insert its horn. The tiger finds no place where to lay his claws. Weapons find no place where to thrust their blades. The reason is that he does not belong to the realm of death.

51. NURSING VIRTUE.

Reason quickens all creatures. Virtue feeds them. Reality shapes them. The forces complete them. Therefore among the ten thousand things there is none that does not esteem Reason and honor virtue. Since the esteem of Reason and the honoring of virtue is by no one commanded, it is forever spontaneous. Therefore it is said that Reason quickens all creatures, while virtue feeds them, raises them, nurtures them, completes them, matures them, rears them, and protects them.

To quicken but not to own, to make but not to claim, to raise but not to rule, this is called profound virtue.

52. RETURNING TO THE ORIGIN.

When the world takes its beginning, Reason becomes the world's mother.

When he who knows his mother, knows in turn that he is her child, and when he who is quickened as a child, in turn keeps to his mother, to the end of life, he is not in danger. When he closes his mouth, and shuts his sense-gates, in the end of life, he will encounter no trouble; but when he opens his mouth and meddles with affairs, in the end of life he cannot be saved.

Who beholds his smallness is called enlightened. Who preserves his tenderness is called strong. Who uses Reason's light and returns home to its enlightenment does not surrender his person to perdition. This is called practising the eternal.

53. GAINING INSIGHT.

If I have ever so little knowledge, I shall walk in the great Reason. It is but assertion that I must fear.

The great Reason is very plain, but people are fond of by-paths.

When the palace is very splendid, the fields are very weedy and granaries very empty.

To wear ornaments and gay clothes, to carry sharp swords, to be excessive in drinking and eating, to have a redundance of costly articles, this is the pride of robbers. Surely, this is un-Reason!

54. THE CULTIVATION OF INTUITION.

"What is well planted is not uprooted;
What's well preserved cannot be looted!"

By sons and grandsons the sacrificial celebrations shall not cease.

Who cultivates Reason in his person, his virtue is genuine. Who cultivates it in his house, his virtue is overflowing. Who cultivates it in his township, his virtue is lasting. Who cultivates it in his country, his virtue is abundant. Who cultivates it in the world, his virtue is universal.

Therefore, by one's person one tests persons. By one's house one tests houses. By one's township one tests townships. By one's country one tests countries. By one's world one tests worlds.

How do I know that the world is such? Through Reason.

55. THE SIGNET OF THE MYSTERIOUS.

He who possesses virtue in all its solidity is like unto a little child. Venomous reptiles do not sting him, fierce beasts do not seize him. Birds of prey do not strike him. His bones are weak, his sinews tender, but his grasp is firm. He does not yet know the relation between male and female, but his virility is strong. Thus his metal grows to perfection. A whole day he might cry and sob without growing hoarse. This shows the perfection of his harmony.

To know the harmonious is called the eternal. To know the eternal is called enlightenment.

To increase life is called a blessing, and heart-directed vitality is called strength, but things vigorous are about to grow old and I call this un-Reason. Un-Reason soon ceases!

56. THE VIRTUE OF THE MYSTERIOUS.

One who knows does not talk. One who talks does not know. Therefore the sage keeps his mouth shut and his sense-gates closed.

> "He will blunt his own sharpness,
> His own tangles adjust;
> He will dim his own radiance,
> And be one with his dust."

This is called profound identification.

Thus he is inaccessible to love and also inaccessible to enmity. He is inaccessible to profit and inaccessible to loss. He is also inaccessible to favor and inaccessible to disgrace. Thus he becomes world-honored.

57. SIMPLICITY IN HABITS.

With rectitude one governs the state; with craftiness one leads the army; with non-diplomacy one takes the empire. How do I know that it is so? Through Reason.

The more restrictions and prohibitions are in the empire, the poorer grow the people. The more weapons the people have, the more troubled is the state. The more there is cunning and skill, the more startling events will happen. The more mandates and laws are enacted, the more there will be thieves and robbers.

Therefore the holy man says: I practise non-assertion, and the people of themselves reform. I love quietude, and the people of themselves become righteous. I use no diplomacy, and the people of themselves become rich. I have no desire, and the people of themselves remain simple.

58. ADAPTATION TO CHANGE.

Whose government is unostentatious, quite unostentatious, his people will be prosperous, quite prosperous. Whose government is prying, quite prying, his people will be needy, quite needy.

Misery, alas! rests upon happiness. Happiness, alas! underlies misery. But who foresees the catastrophe? It will not be prevented!

What is ordinary becomes again extraordinary.

What is good becomes again unpropitions. This bewilders people, which happens constantly since times immemorial.

Therefore the holy man is square but not sharp, strict but not obnoxious, upright but not restraining, bright but not dazzling.

59. HOLD FAST TO REASON.

In governing the people and in attending to heaven there is nothing like moderation. As to moderation, it is said that it must be an early habit. If it is an early habit, it will be richly accumulated virtue. If one has richly accumulated virtue, then there is nothing that cannot be overcome. If there is nothing that cannot be overcome, then no one knows his limits. If no one knows his limits, one can possess the country. If one possesses the mother of the country [viz., moderation], one can thereby last long. This is called having deep roots and a firm stem. To long life and lasting comprehension this is the Way.

60. HOW TO MAINTAIN ONE'S PLACE.

Govern a great country as you would fry small fish: [neither gut nor scale them].

If with Reason the empire is managed, its ghosts will not spook. Not only will its ghosts not spook, but its gods will not harm the people. Not only will its gods not harm the people, but its holy men will also not harm the people. Since neither will do harm, therefore their virtues will be combined.

61. THE VIRTUE OF HUMILITY.

A great state, one that lowly flows, becomes the empire's union, and the empire's wife. The wife always through quietude conquers her husband, and by quietude renders herself lowly. Thus a great state through lowliness toward small states will conquer the small states, and small states through lowliness toward great states will conquer great states.

Therefore some render themselves lowly for the purpose of conquering; others are lowly and therefore conquer.

A great state desires no more than to unite and feed the people; a small state desires no more than to devote itself to the service of the people; but that both may obtain their wishes, the greater one must stoop.

62. PRACTISE REASON.

It is Reason that is the ten thousand things' asylum, the good man's wealth, the bad man's stay.

With beautiful words one can sell. With honest conduct one can do still more with the people.

If a man be bad, why should he be thrown away? Therefore, an emperor was elected and three ministers appointed; but better than holding before one's face the jade table [of the ministry] and riding with four horses, is sitting still and propounding the eternal Reason.

Why do the ancients prize this Reason? Is it not,

say, because when sought it is obtained and the sinner thereby can be saved? Therefore it is world-honored.

63. CONSIDER BEGINNINGS.

Assert non-assertion. Practise non-practice. Taste non-taste. Make great the small. Make much the little.

Requite hatred with goodness.

Contemplate a difficulty when it is easy. Manage a great thing when it is small.

The world's most difficult undertakings necessarily originate while easy, and the world's greatest undertakings necessarily originate while small.

Therefore the holy man to the end does not venture to play the great, and thus he can accomplish his greatness. As one who lightly promises rarely keeps his word, so he to whom many things are easy will necessarily encounter many difficulties. Therefore, the holy man regards everything as difficult, and thus to the end encounters no difficulties.

64. MIND THE INSIGNIFICANT.

What is still at rest is easily kept quiet. What has not as yet appeared is easily prevented. What is still feeble is easily broken. What is still scant is easily dispersed.

Treat things before they exist. Regulate things before disorder begins. The stout tree has originated from a tiny rootlet. A tower of nine stories is raised by heaping up [bricks of] clay. A thousand miles' journey begins with a foot.

He that makes mars. He that grasps loses.

The holy man does not make; therefore he mars not. He does not grasp; therefore he loses not. The people when undertaking an enterprise are always near completion, and yet they fail. Remain careful to the end as in the beginning and you will not fail in your enterprise.

Therefore the holy man desires to be desireless, and does not prize articles difficult to obtain. He learns, not to be learned, and seeks a home where multitudes of the people pass by. He assists the ten thousand things in their natural development, but he does not venture to interfere.

65. THE VIRTUE OF SIMPLICITY.

The ancients who were well versed in Reason did not thereby enlighten the people; they intended thereby to make them simple-hearted.

If people are difficult to govern, it is because they are too smart. To govern the country with smartness is the country's curse. To govern the country without smartness is the country's blessing. He who knows these two things is also a model [like the ancients]. Always to know them is called profound virtue.

Profound virtue, verily, is deep. Verily, it is far-reaching. Verily, it is to everything reverse. But then it will procure great recognition.

66. PUTTING ONESELF BEHIND.

That rivers and oceans can of the hundred valleys be kings is due to their excelling in lowliness. Thus they can of the hundred valleys be the kings.

Therefore the holy man, when anxious to be above the people, must in his words keep underneath them. When anxious to lead the people, he must with his person keep behind them.

Therefore the holy man dwells above, but the people are not burdened. He is ahead, but the people suffer no harm. Therefore the world rejoices in exalting him without tiring. Because he strives not, no one in the world will strive with him.

67. THE THREE TREASURES.

All in the world call me great; but I resemble the unlikely. Now a man is great only because he resembles the unlikely. Did he resemble the likely, how lasting, indeed, would his mediocrity be!

I have three treasures which I preserve and treasure. The first is called compassion. The second is called economy. The third is called not daring to come in the world to the front. The compassionate can be brave; the economical can be generous; those who dare not come to the front in the world can become perfect as chief vessels.

Now, if people discard compassion and are brave;

if they discard economy and are generous; if they discard modesty and are ambitious, they will surely die

Now, the compassionate will in the attack be victorious, and in the defence firm. Heaven when about to save one will with compassion protect him.

68. COMPLYING WITH HEAVEN.

He who excels as a warrior is not warlike. He who excels as a fighter is not wrathful. He who excels in conquering the enemy does not strive. He who excels in employing men is lowly.

This is called the virtue of not-striving. This is called utilising men's ability. This is called complying with heaven—since olden times the highest.

69. THE FUNCTION OF THE MYSTERIOUS.

A military expert used to say: "I dare not act as host [who takes the initiative] but act as guest [with reserve]. I dare not advance an inch, but I withdraw a foot."

This is called marching without marching, threatening without arms, charging without hostility, seizing without weapons.

No greater misfortune than making light of the enemy! When we make light of the enemy, it is almost as though we had lost our treasure—[compassion].

Thus, if matched armies encounter one another, the tenderer one is sure to conquer.

70. DIFFICULT TO UNDERSTAND.

My words are very easy to understand and very easy to practise, but in the world no one can understand, no one can practise them.

Words have an ancestor; Deeds have a master [viz., Reason]. Since he is not understood, therefore I am not understood. Those who understand me are few, and thus I am distinguished.

Therefore the holy man wears wool, and hides in his bosom his jewels.

71. THE DISEASE OF KNOWLEDGE.

To know the unknowable that is elevating. Not to know the knowable that is sickness.

Only by becoming sick of sickness we can be without sickness.

The holy man is not sick. Because he is sick of sickness, therefore he is not sick.

72. HOLDING ONESELF DEAR.

If the people do not fear the dreadful, the great dreadful will come, surely.

Do not render their lives narrow. Do not make their lot wearisome. When it is not made wearisome, then it will not be wearisome.

Therefore, the holy man knows himself but does not display himself. He holds himself dear but does not honor himself. Thus he discards the latter and chooses the former.

73. DARING TO ACT.

Courage, if carried to daring, leads to death; courage, if not carried to daring, leads to life. Either of these two things is sometimes beneficial, sometimes harmful.

> "Why 't is by heaven rejected,
> Who has the reason detected?"

Therefore the holy man also regards it as difficult.

The Heavenly Reason strives not, but it is sure to conquer. It speaks not, but it is sure to respond. It summons not, but it comes of itself. It works patiently but is sure in its designs.

Heaven's net is vast, so vast. It is wide-meshed, but it loses nothing.

74. OVERCOME DELUSION.

If the people do not fear death, how can they be frightened by death?

If we make people fear death, and supposing some would [still] venture to rebel, if we seize them for capital punishment, who will dare?

There is always an executioner who kills. Now to take the place of the executioner who kills is taking the place of the great carpenter who hews. If a man takes the place of the great carpenter who hews, he will rarely, indeed, fail to injure his hand.

75. HARMED THROUGH GREED.

The people hunger because their superiors consume too many taxes; therefore they hunger. The people are difficult to govern because their superiors are too meddlesome; therefore it is difficult to govern. The people make light of death on account of the intensity of their clinging to life; therefore they make light of death.

He who is not bent on life is worthier than he who esteems life.

76. BEWARE OF STRENGTH.

Man during life is tender and delicate. When he dies he is stiff and stark.

The ten thousand things, the grass as well as the trees, are while they live tender and supple. When they die they are rigid and dry. Thus the hard and the strong are the companions of death. The tender and the delicate are the companions of life.

Therefore, he who in arms is strong will not conquer. When a tree has grown strong it is doomed.

The strong and the great stay below. The tender and the delicate stay above.

77. HEAVEN'S REASON.

Is not Heaven's Reason truly like stretching a bow? The high it brings down, the lowly it lifts up. Those who have abundance it depleteth; those who are deficient it augmenteth.

Such is Heaven's Reason. It depleteth those who have abundance but completeth the deficient.

Man's Reason is not so. He depletes the deficient in order to serve those who have abundance. Where is he who would have abundance for serving the world? It is the man of Reason.

Therefore the holy man acts but claims not; merit he accomplishes but he does not linger upon it, and does he ever show any anxiety to display his excellence?

78. TRUST IN FAITH.

In the world nothing is tenderer and more delicate than water. In attacking the hard and the strong nothing will surpass it. There is nothing that herein takes its place. The weak conquer the strong, the tender conquer the rigid. In the world there is no one who does not know it, but no one will practise it. Therefore the holy man says:

> "Him who the country's sin makes his,
> We hail as priest at the great sacrifice.
> Him who the curse bears of the country's failing
> As king of the empire we are hailing."

True words seem paradoxical.

79. KEEP YOUR OBLIGATIONS.

When a great hatred is reconciled, naturally some hatred will remain. How can this be made good?

Therefore the sage keeps the obligations of his contract and exacts not from others. Those who have virtue attend to their obligations; those who have no virtue attend to their claims.

Heaven's Reason shows no preference but always assists the good man.

80. REMAINING IN ISOLATION.

In a small country with few people let there be aldermen and mayors who are possessed of power over men but would not use it. Induce people to grieve at death but do not cause them to move to a distance. Although they had ships and carriages, they should find no occasion to ride in them. Although they had armours and weapons, they should find no occasion to don them.

Induce people to return to [the old custom of] knotted cords and to use them [in the place of writing], to delight in their food, to be proud of their clothes, to be content with their homes, and to rejoice in their customs: then in a neighboring state within sight, the voices of the cocks and dogs would be within hearing, yet the people might grow old and die before they visited one another.

81. PROPOUNDING THE ESSENTIAL.

True words are not pleasant; pleasant words are not true. The good are not contentious; the contentious are not good. The wise are not learned; the learned are not wise.

The holy man hoards not. The more he does for others, the more he owns himself. The more he gives to others, the more he acquires himself.

Heaven's Reason is to benefit but not to injure; the holy man's Reason is to act but not to strive.

TRANSLITERATION OF THE TEXT

SZE-MA-CH'IEN ON LAO-TZE.

司 ₂sz' 835, (ssŭ)

馬 'ma 571,

遷 ₂ts'ien 980, (ch'ien)

史 'shi 760, (shih) Historical

記 ki' 340, (chi) Records

老 lao 508, [of] the old

子 'tsz' 1030, (tzŭ) philosopher

傳 ₂chw'en 119, a tradition

司 ₂sz' 835, (szŭ)

馬 'ma 571,

遷 ₂ts'ien 980, (ch'ien)

曰 yueh 1130, says:

I.

老 'lao 508, The old

子 'tsz' 1030, (tzŭ) philosopher

者 ₂chě 38, [was] one

楚 'ch'u 94, [of] the bramble state,

苦 'k'u 436, [of] the thistle

縣 hien' 201, (hsien) province,

厲 li' 522, [of] grinding

卿 ₂hiang 189, (hsiang) county,

曲 k'üh 458, (ch'ü)

仁 jan 287, (jen) } [of] the good man's bend

里 'li 518, village,

人 jan 286, (jen) a man,

也 ₀'yě 1079, (yeh) indeed.

II.

姓 sing' 810, (hsing) [His] family [was]

李 'li 520, the Plum

氏 shi' 763, gentry.

名 ₂ming 600, His proper name

耳 ₀''rh 720, (erh) [was] Ear.

字 tsz'' 1032, (tzŭ) His appellation [was]

伯 poh' 707, Prince

陽 ₀₂yang 1071, Positive principle

諡 shi' 764, [By his] posthumous title

曰 yueh 1130, [he is] called

聃 ₀₂tan 849, the Long lobed.

周 ₂chěu 47, (chou) In the state of Plenty

守 'sheu 755, (shou) he was in charge of

藏 ₂ts'ang 950, the secret

室 shih, 770, archives

之 ,*chi* 53, (*chih*) as their
史 '*shi* 760, (*shih*) historian,
也 ,*yĕ* 1079, (*yeh*) indeed.

III.

孔 '*k'ung* 465,
子 '*tsz* 1030, (*tzŭ*) } Confucius
適 *shih*, 768, went to
周 ,*chen* 47, (*chou*) the state of Plenty
將 ,*tsiang* 967, (*chiang*) in order to
問 *wăn* 1042, (*wên*) consult
禮 '*li* 520, on ceremonials
於 ,*yü* 1118, with
老 '*lao* 508, the old
子 '*tsz* 1030, (*tzŭ*) philosopher.

IV.

老 '*lao* 508, The old
子 '*tsz* 1030, (*tzŭ*) philosopher
曰 *yueh*, 1130, said;
子 '*tsz* 1030, (*tzŭ*) You, sir,
所 *su'* 817, (*shuo*) of whom
言 ,*yen* 1083, you speak
者 '*chĕ* 38, the ones
其 ,*k'i* 342, (*chi*) these
人 ,*jan* 286, (*jĕn*) men
與 '*yü* 1125, and
骨 *kuh*, 454, (*ku*) their bones
皆 ,*kiai* 358, (*chieh*) altogether
已 '*i* 278, have

朽 '*hiu* 211, (*hsiu*) mouldered.
矣 '*i* 279, [a final particle]
獨 *tuh* 921, (*tu*) Alone
其 ,*k'i* 342, (*chi*) their
言 ,*yen* 1083, words
在 *tsai'* 941, exist
耳 ''*rh* 720, (*err*) only.

V.

且 '*ts'iĕ* 974, (*ch'ich*) Further,
君 ,*kiün*, 418, (*chün*) the superior
子 '*tsz* 1030, (*tzŭ*) sage
得 *tch* 872, when obtaining
其 ,*k'i* 342, (*chi*) his
時 ,*shi* 759, time
則 *tseh*, 956, (*tse*) then
駕 *kia'* 353, (*chia*) he rises;
不 *pu*, 717, [when] not
得 *tch* 872, obtaining
其 ,*k'i* 342, (*chi*) his
時 ,*shi* 759, time,
則 *tseh*, 956, (*tse*) then
蓬 ,*p'ăng* 661, [like] a drifting plant
累 '*lei* 511, he is carried about
而 ,''*rh* 719, (*err*) and
行 ,*hing* 207, (*hsing*) wanders.

VI.

吾 ,*wu* 1060, I
聞 ,*wan* 1041, (*wên*) heard

TRANSLITERATION.

之良賈深藏若虛君子盛德容貌若愚。去子之驕氣多欲態色與淫志是

,chi 53, (chih) it,
,liang 524, a good
'ku 434, merchant
,shan 736, (shen) deeply
,ts'ang 950, conceals [his treasures]
joh, 296, (jo) as if
,hü 227, (hsü) [his house were] empty.
,kiün 418, (chün) The superior
'tsz, 1030, (tsŭ) sage
shing' 772, (sheng) of perfect
tch, 871, (tĕ) virtue
,yung 1146, [in] countenance
mao' 582, [and] outward mien
joh, 296, (jo) resembles
,yü 1120, the stupid.

VII.

'k'ü 445, (ch'ü) Let depart
'tsz' 1030 (tzŭ) } the sir's
,chi 53, (chih) } (viz., your)
,kiao 368, (chiao) haughty
'k'i 348, air,
,to 909, [your] many
yuh, 1139, (yü) wishes,
t'ai' 849, [your] affected
sch, 727, (sĕ) colors,
'yü 1125, and
,yin 1101, [your] exaggerated
chi' 61, (chih) intentions.
shi' 762, (ssu) These

皆無益於子之身吾所以告子若是而已。孔子去謂弟子曰鳥吾知其能

,kiai 358, (chieh) all
,wu 1059, have no
yih, 1092, (yi) use
,yü 1118, to
'tsz' 1030, (tzŭ) } the sir's
,chi 53, (chih) } (viz., your)
,shan 735, (shĕn) person.
,wu 1060, I
su' 817, (shuo) that [rel. pron.]
'i 278, } communicate
kao' 326, }
'tsz' 1030 (tzŭ) to you
joh, 296, (jo) } in this way,
shi' 762, (ssu) }
,rh 719, (erh) and
'i 278, that is all.

VIII.

'k'ung 465, } Confucius
'tsz' 1030' (tzŭ) }
'k'ü 445, (ch'ü) departed.
wei' 1054, He addressed
ti' 879, his younger
'tsz' 1030, (tzŭ) followers
,yuch, 1130, saying:
'niao 632, The birds
,wu 1060, I
chi 53, (chih) know
'k'i 342, (chi) they
,nang 616, (nĕng) can

,fêi 136, fly.
'yü 1119, The fish
,wu 1060, I
,chi 53, (chih) know
,k'i 342, (chi) they
,nang 616, (nêng) can
,yiu 1112, swim.
shêu' 756, The beasts
,wu 1060, I
,chi 53, (chih) know
,k'i 342, (chi) they
,nang 616, (nêng) can
'tseu 961, run.

IX.

'tseu 961, For the running
'chê 38, ones
'k'o 425, } one can
i 278,
,wéi 1047, make
'wang 1044, nooses.
,yiu 1112 For the swimming
,chê 38, ones
'k'o 425, } one can
,i 278,
,wéi 1047, make
,lun 566, nets.
,fêi 136, For the flying
'chê 38, ones

'k'o 425, } one can
,i 278,
,wéi 1047, make
,tsang 951, arrows.

X.

chi' 60, (chih) With reference
,yü 1118, to
,lung 567, the dragon
,wu 1060, I
puh, 717, (pu) not
,nang 616, (nêng) can
,chi 53, (chih) know
,k'i 342, (chi) his
,shing 772, (shêng) bestriding
,fung 155, the wind
,yun 1142, [and] clouds
,rh 719, (erh) and
'shang 741, ascending
t'ien 897, Heaven.
,wu 1060, I
,kin 398, (chin) at the present
ich, 293, (jě) day
kien' 385, (chien) saw
'lao 508, the old
'tsz 1030, (tzŭ) philosopher.
,k'i 342, (chi) [Might] he
,yiu 1112, be like
,lung 567, the dragon?
,yê 1078, [query.]

XI.

老子修道德其學以自隱無名爲務

,lao 508, the old
'tsz' 1030, (tzŭ) philosopher
,siu 811, practised
tao' 867, reason [and]
,teh, 871, virtue.
,k'i 342, (chi) His
hioh, 209, (hsiao) doctrine
'i 278, in
tsz" 1031, (tzŭ) self-
'yin 1103, concealment,
,wu 1059, [and] not having
,ming 600, name
,wéi 1047, consists
wu' 1062, aspiring after.

XII.

居周久之見周之衰乃遂去至關

,kü 437, (chü) He sojourned
,cheu 47, (chou) in the state of Plenty
'kiu 413, (chiu) for a long time
,chi 53, (chih) he [did].
kien' 385, (chien) He saw [presaged]
,cheu 47, (chou) the state of Plenty
,chi 53, (chih) of
,shwai 785, the decay
'nai 612, then
sui' 828, in consequence of it
'k'ü 445, (ch'ü) he departed
chi' 60, (chih) and came to
,kwan 472, the frontier.

XIII.

關令尹喜曰子將隱矣彊爲我著書

,kwan 472, The frontier
ling' 546, officer
'yin 1102,
'h'i 180, (hsi) } Yin-H'i
yueh 1130, said:
'tsz' 1030, (tzŭ) you, sir,
,tsiang 967, (chiang) are going
,yin 1103, to withdraw
'i 279, [a final particle].
,k'iang 366, (chiang) I urge
,wéi 1047, for
'ngo 627, me
chu' 90, to compose
,shu 774, a book.

XIV.

於是老子乃著書上下篇言道德

'yü 1118,
shi' 762, (ssu) } then
lao 508, the old
'tsz' 1030, (tzŭ) philosopher
,nai 612, thereupon
chu' 90, composed
,shu 774, a book
'shang 741, of a former
hia' 183, (hsia) and a latter
,p'ien 690, part
,yen 1083, discussing
tao' 867, Reason
,teh, 871, [and] Virtue

之 ,chi 53, (chih) of
意 i' 282, the concepts
五 'wu 1060, [in] five
千 ,ts'ien 980, (ch'ien) thousand
餘 ,yü 1121, and some
言 ,yen 1083, words;
而 ,rh 719, (erh) and

去 'k'ü 445, (ch'ü) he departed,
莫 moh, 603, (mo) not [one]
知 ,chi 53, (chih) knowing
其 ,k'i 342 (chi) his
所 su' 817 (shuo) [place] where
終 ,chung 106, he died.

THE OLD PHILOSOPHER'S CANON ON REASON AND VIRTUE.

老 ‚*Lao* 508, The Old
子 ‚*tsz*' 1030, (*tzŭ*) Philosopher's
道 *tao*' 867, Reason
德 *teh*, 871, (*tĕ*) [and] Virtue
經 ‚*ching* (404) Canon.

上 '*shang* 741, Former
篇 ‚*p'ien* 690, part.

第 *ti*'' 879,
一 *yih*, 1095, } Chapter 1.
章 ‚*chang* 22,

體 '*t'i* 884, Realising
道 *tao*' 867, Reason.

I.

道 *tao*' 867, The reason
可 '*k'o* 425, that can
道 *tao*' 867, be reasoned
非 ‚*fei* 136, is not

常 ‚*ch'ang* 740, the eternal
道 *tao*' 867, Reason.
名 ‚*ming* 600, The name
可 '*k'o* 425, that can
名 ‚*ming* 600, be named
非 ‚*fei* 136, is not
常 ‚*ch'ang* 740, the eternal
名 ‚*ming* 600, name.

II.

無 ‚*wu* 1059, Not-having
名 ‚*ming* 600, name
天 ‚*t'ien* 897, [is] heaven
地 *ti*'' 879, and earth
之 ‚*chi* 53, (*tzŭ*) of
始 '*shi* 761, (*ssŭ*) the beginning.
有 '*yiu* 1113, Having
名 ‚*ming* 600, name
萬 *wan*' 1040, [is] the ten thousand
物 *wuh*, 1065, things

(Chapter 1.)

之 ,chi 53, (tzŭ) of
母 'mu 605, the mother.

III.

故 ,ku' 434, Therefore
常 ,ch'ang 740, eternally
無 ,wu 1059, not-having
欲 ,yü' 1139, desire
以 'i 278, thereby
觀 ,kwan 474, [one] sees
其 ,ch'i 342, its
妙 miao' 592, spirituality.
常 ,ch'ang 740, Eternally
有 'yiu 1113, having
欲 yü' 1139, desire
以 'i 278, thereby
觀 ,kwan 474, [one] sees
其 ,ch'i 342, its
徼 chiao' 371, limits.

IV.

此 ,ts'z' 1034, (t'zu) These
兩 'liang 526, two
者 'ché 38, things
同 ,t'ung 933, [are] the same
出 ,ch'uh 98, in origin

而 ,'rh 719, (err) but
異 i' 281, different
名 ,ming 600, [in] name.

V.

同 ,t'ung 933, [Their] sameness,
謂 wéi' 1054, called is
之 ,chi 53, (tzŭ) it
玄 ,hüen 231, (hsüen) mystery
玄 ,hüen 231, (hsüen) The mystery
之 ,chi 53, (tzŭ) of
又 yiu' 1114, again
玄 ,hüen 231, (hsüen) a mystery.
衆 ,chung' 108, (tsung) all
妙 miao' 592, spirituality
之 ,chi 53, (tzŭ) of
門 ,mǎn 576, (men) the gate

第 ,ti" 879,
二 'rh' 721, } Chapter 2.
章 ,chang 22,

養 'yang 1072, Nourishing
身 ,shǎn 735, [one's] person

I.

天 ,t'ien 897, } In the
下 hia' 183, (hsia) } world,

TRANSLITERATION.   149

皆 ‚chié 358, [when] all
知 ‚chi 53, know
美 'méi 586, beauty
之 ‚chi 53, (tzŭ) in its
爲 ‚wéi 1047, acting as
美 'méi 586, beauty,
斯 ‚sz' 834, (ssŭ) then [there is]
惡 wu' 1063, ugliness
已 'i 278, only.

II.

皆 ‚chié 358, [When] all
知 ‚chi 53, know
善 shan' 752, goodness
之 ‚chi 53, (tzu) in its
爲 ‚wéi 1047, acting as
善 shan' 752, goodness
斯 ‚sz' 834, (ssu) then [there is]
不 ‚pu' 717, not
善 shan' 752, goodness
已 ‚i 278, only.

III.

故 ku' 434, For

有 ‚yiu 1113, existence
無 ‚wu 1059, [and] non-existence
相 ‚siang 790, (hsiang) mutually
生 shăng 742, (seng) are produced.
難 ‚nan 614, The difficult
易 i', 281 [and] the easy
相 ‚siang 790, (hsiang) mutually
成 ‚ch'ing 77, (ch'eng) are perfected.
長 ‚ch'ang 27, The long
短 'twan 937, [and] the short
相 ‚siang 790, (hsiang) mutually
形 ‚hing 206, (hsing) are shaped.
高 ‚kao 324, The high
下 hia' 183, (hsia) [and] the low
相 ‚siang 790, (hsiang) mutually
傾 ‚ching 408, (ch'ueng) are inclining.
音 ‚yin 1100, Tone [and]
聲 ‚shing 771, (sheng) voice
相 ‚siang 790, (hsiang) mutually
和 ‚hwo 254, (ho) are harmonised.
前 ‚ts'ien 981, (ch'ien) The before [and]
後 heu' 175, (hou) the after
相 ‚siang 790, (hsiang) mutually
隨 ‚sui 826, follow.

(Chapter 2.)

IV.

是 *shi"* 762, (*ssŭ*) ⎫
以 *i*, 278   ⎬ Therefore
聖 *shăng'* 773, (*sheng*) the holy
人 *jăn* 286, (*jen*) man
處 *'ch'u* 94, dwells in
無 *wu* 1059, not-
爲 *wéi* 1047, doing
之 *chi* 53, (*tzŭ*) in his
事 *shi"* 764, (*ssŭ*) business.
行 *hing* 207, (*hsing*) He practises
不 *pu* 717, not-
言 *yen* 1083, saying
之 *chi* 53, (*tzŭ*) in his
敎 *chiao'* 372, education.

V.

萬 *wan'* 1040, The ten thousand
物 *wuh* 1065, things
作 *tsoh* 1005, arise
焉 *yen* 1082, there!
而 *'rh* 719, (*err*) and
不 *pu* 717, not
辭 *ts'z'* 1033, (*tzŭ*) he refuses [them].

VI.

生 *shăng* 742 (*sheng*) He produces
而 *'rh* 719, (*err*) and
不 *pu* 717, not
有 *yiu* 1113, he owns.
爲 *wéi* 1047, He acts
而 *'rh* 719, (*err*) and
不 *pu* 717, not
恃 *shi"* 761, (*ssŭ*) he claims
功 *kung* 460, Merit
成 *ch'ing* 77, (*ch'eng*) he accomplishes
而 *'rh* 719, (*err*) and
弗 *fu* 153, not
居 *chü* 437, he dwells.

VII.

夫 *fu* 142, Forasmuch
惟 *wéi* 1049, just [as]
不 *pu* 717, not
居 *chü* 437, he dwells
是 *shi"* 762, (*ssŭ*) ⎫
以 *i* 278,   ⎬ therefore
弗 *fu* 158, not
去 *ch'ü* 445, he departs.

(Chapter 2.)

TRANSLITERATION. 151

第 ₍ti'' 879,
三 ₍san 723, ⎫ Chapter 3.
章 ₍chang 22, ⎭

安 ₍ngan 620, Keeping at rest
民 ₍min 597, the people.

I.

不 ₍pu 717, Not
尚 shang' 741, (hsang) exalting
賢 ₍hien 197, (hsien) the worthy
使 'shi 761, (ssŭ) causes
民 ₍min 597, people
不 ₍pu 717, not
爭 ₍chăng 29, (tseng) to emulate.

II.

不 ₍pu 717, Not
貴 kwei' 484, prizing
難 ₍nan 614, the difficult
得 teh, 872, (t'ê) to obtain
之 ₍chi 53, (tzŭ) of
貨 hwo' 256, treasures
使 'shi 761, (ssŭ) causes
民 ₍min 597, people
不 ₍pu 717, not
爲 ₍wei 1047, to commit
盜 tao' 868, theft.

III.

不 ₍pu 717, Not
見 chien' 385, seeing
可 'k'o 425, [that which is] able
欲 yŭ' 1138, [to elicit] desire,
使 'shi 761, (ssŭ) causes
心 ₍sin 8c6, (hsin) the heart
不 ₍pu 717, not
亂 lwan' 570, to be disturbed

IV.

是 shi' 762, (ssŭ) ⎫ Therefore
以 'i 278, ⎭
聖 shăng' 773, (sheng) the holy
人 ₍jăn 286, (jen) man
之 ₍chi 53, (tzŭ) of
治 chi' 59, (chih) the government
虛 ₍hŭ 227, (hsŭ) empties
其 ₍ch'i 342, their [the people's]
心 ₍sin 806, (hsin) hearts,
實 shih 769, [and] fills
其 ₍ch'i 342, their
腹 ₍fu 151, stomachs, [the inner; the soul]
弱 joh 295, (jao) he weakens
其 ₍ch'i 342, their

(Chapter 3.)

志 ,chi' 61, (chih) desire [but]
强 ,ch'iang 366, strengthens
其 ,ch'i 342, their
骨 kuh 454, bones.

則 tseh, 956, (tsĕ) then
無 ,wu 1059, there is nothing
不 ,pu 717, not
治 chi' 59, (chih) governed.

V.

常 ,ch'ang 740, Always
使 'shi 761, (ssŭ) he causes
民 ,min 597, people
無 ,wu 1059, not
知 ,chi 53, (chih) to know,
無 ,wu 1059, not
欲 yü' 1138, to be desirous.
使 'shi 761, (ssŭ) He causes
夫 ,fu 142, those
知 ,chi 53, (chih) knowing
者 'chĕ 38, ones
不 ,pu 717 not
敢 'kan 312, to dare
爲 ,wéi 1047, to act,
也 'yĕ 1079, (yeh) indeed.

第 ti' 879, ⎫
四 sz" 836, ⎬ Chapter 4.
章 ,chang 22, ⎭

無 ,wu 1059, Not having
源 ,yuen 1133, source.

I.

道 tao' 867, Reason
冲 ,ch'ung 109, ('t'sung) [is] empty,
而 "rh 719, (err) and
用 yung' 1149, in employing
之 ,chi 53, (tzŭ) it
或 hwo, 259, apparently
不 ,pu 719, [it is] not
盈 ,ying 1106, exhausted.
淵 ,yuen 1131, Profound [it is]
乎 ,hu 224, (hsi) Oh!
似 sz" 837, (ssŭ) it resembles
萬 ,wan, 1040, the ten thousand
物 wuh, 1065, (wu) things

VI.

爲 ,wéi 1047, [When] he does
無 ,wu 1059, not-
爲 ,wéi 1047, doing

TRANSLITERATION. 153

之 ₍chi 53, (tzŭ), of
宗 ₍tsung 1021, (chung) the ancestor.

II.

挫 ts'o' 1004, It blunts
其 ₍ch'i 342, its [own]
銳 jui'' 302, sharpness.
解 ₍chi''e 359, It unravels
其 ₍ch'i 342, its [own]
紛 ₍făn 129, (fen) fetters.
和 ₍hwo 254, It harmonises
其 ₍ch'i 342, its [own]
光 ₍kwang 478, light.
同 ₍t'ung 933, It identifies itself with
其 ₍ch'i 342, its [own]
塵 ₍ch'ăn 20, (chĕn) dust.

III.

湛 tsan' 12, It is tranquil
兮 ₍hi 179, (hsi) Oh!
似 sz'' 837, (ssŭ) it seems
若 joh, 296, (jĕ) like
存 ₍ts'un 1020, to remain.
吾 ₍wu 1060, I
不 ₍pu 717, not
知 ₍chi 53, (chih) know

誰 ₍shui 781,
之 ₍chi 53, (tzŭ), } whose
子 'tsz' 1030 (tzu) son [it is].
象 siang' 792, (hsiang) It seems to be
帝 ti 880,
之 ₍chi 53, (tzŭ). } God's
先 ₍sien 799, (hsien) antecedent.

第 ti' 879,
五 ₍wu 1060, } Chapter 5.
章 ₍chang 22,

虛 ₍hü 227, Emptiness's
用 yung' 1149, function.

I.

天 ₍t'ien 897, Heaven
地 ti'' 879, [and] earth
不 ₍pu 717, are not
仁 ₍jăn 287, (jen) humane.
以 'i 278, They regard
萬 wan' 1040, the ten thousand
物 ₍wuh, 1065, (wu) things
為 ₍wéi 1047, as
芻 ₍ts'u 91, grass-
狗 'keu 329, (kou) dogs.

(Chapters 4-5.)

II.

聖 *shăng*' 773, (*sheng*) The holy
人 ,*jăn* 286, (*jen*) man
不 ,*pu* 717, is not
仁 ,*jăn* 287, (*jen*) humane.
以 '*i* 278, He regards
百 ,*pai* 707, the hundred
姓 *sing*' 810 (*hsing*) families.
爲 ,*wéi* 1047, as
芻 *ts'u* 91, grass-
狗 *keu* 329, (*kou*) dogs.

III.

天 ,*t'ien* 897, Heaven
地 *ti*" 879, [and] earth
之 ,*chi* 53, (*tzŭ*) of [between]
間 ,*chien* 381, the space,
其 ,*ch'i* 342, it
猶 *yiu* 1112, is like unto
橐 ,*t'o* 915,
籥 *yoh*, 1117, (*yo*) } a bellows
乎 ,*hu* 224, indeed.

IV.

虛 ,*hü* 227, (*hsü*) [It is] empty
而 ',*rh* 719, (*err*) and

不 ,*pu* 717, not
屈 ,*ch'ü* 458, it collapses.
動 *tung*' 932, It moves
而 ',*rh* 719, (*err*) and
愈 '*yü* 1126, more and more
出 *ch'uh*, 98 issues.
多 ,*to* 909
言 ,*yen* 1083 } A gossip
數 '*shu* 777, (*su*) frequently
窮 *ch'iúng* 420, is exhausted
不 ,*pu* 717, Not
如 ,*jü* 267, likely
守 '*sheu* 755, (*shou*) will he keep
中 ,*chung* 105, (*tsung*) the middle [path]

第 *ti*" 879,
六 *luh*, 562, } Chapter 6.
章 ,*chang* 22,

成 ,*ch'ung* 77 The completion
象 *siang*' 792 of form.

I.

谷 '*ku* 453, The valley-
神 ,*shăn* 737, (*shen*) spirit
不 ,*pu* 717, not

TRANSLITERATION.

死 ʻsz' 836, (ssŭ) dies.
是 shiʻ 762, (ssŭ) This
謂 wéi' 1054, is called
玄 ‚hüen 231, (hsüen) the mysterious
牝。 ʻp'in 697, woman.

II.

玄 ‚hüen 231, (hsüen) The mysterious
牝 ʻp'in 697, woman
之 ʻchi 53 (tzŭ) of
門。 ‚män 576, (men) the gate,
是 shiʻ 762, (ssŭ) this
謂 wéi' 1054, is called
天 t'ien 897, [of] heaven
地 ti' 879, [and] earth
根 ‚kän 317, (kên) the root.

III.

綿 ‚mien 593, Continually,
々 ‚mien 593, continually
若 joh, 296, (jŏ) it seems
存, ts'un 1020, to remain.
用 yung' 1149, (jung) In using
之 ‚chi 53, (tzŭ) it
不 ,pu 717, [there is] no
勤。 ch'in 402, effort.

第 ti' 879,
七 ts'ih, 987 } Chapter 7.
章 ‚chang 22,

韜 ‚t'ao 869, Dimming
光 ‚kwang 478, radiancy.

I.

天 ‚t'ien 897, Heaven
長 ch'ang 27, is eternal,
地 ti' 879, earth
久 ‚chiu 413, is lasting.
天 ‚t'ien 897, Heaven
地 ti' 879, [and] earth
所 su' 817, (hsuo) } the reason
以 'i 278, } why
能 ‚näng 616, (neng) [they] are able to be
長 ch'ang 27, eternal
且 ts'ié 974, (chieh) and
久 ‚chiu 413, lasting
者 ‚che 38, that
以 ʻi 278, is because
其 ch'i 342, they
不 ,pu 717, [do] not
自 tsz'' 1031, (tzŭ) themselves
生 ‚sh'ang 742, (shêng) live

(Chapters 6-7.)

故 ku' 434, that is the reason.
能 nǎng 616 (neng) [They] can
長 ch'ang 27, eternally
生 shǎng 742, (shēng) live.

無 wu 1059, is not
私 sz' 835, (ssŭ) self-interested?
邪 ye 1078, [Particle of interrogation.]
故 ku' 434, Therefore
能 nǎng 616 (neng) [he] can
成 ch'ing 77, (ch'ēng) accomplish
其 ch'i 342, his
私 sz' 835, (ssŭ) self-interest.

II.

是 shi' 762, (ssŭ) ⎫
以 'i 278, ⎬ Therefore
⎭

聖 shǎng' 773, (sheng) the holy
人 jǎn 286, (jen) man
後 heu' 175, (hou) puts behind
其 ch'i 342, his
身 shǎn 735, (shen) person
而 'rh 719, (err) and
身 shǎn 735, (shen) [his] person
先 sien 799, (hsien) comes to the front.
外 wai' 1037, [He] rejects
其 ch'i 342, his
身 shǎn 735, (shen) person
而 'rh 719, (err) and
身 shǎn 735, (shen) [his] person
存 ts'un 1020, is preserved.
非 fei 136, Is it not
以 'i 278, because
其 ch'i 342, he

第 ti" 879, ⎫
八 pah, 647, ⎬ Chapter 8.
章 chang 22, ⎭

易 yih, 281, Easy by
性 sing' 809, nature.

I.

上 'shang 741, Superior
善 shan' 752, goodness
若 joh, 296 (jĕ) resembles
水 'shui 781, water.
水 'shui 781, Water
善 shan' 752, well (in a good way)
利 li' 521, benefits
萬 wan' 1040, the ten thousand
物 wuh, 1065, things,

而 ‚rh 719, (err) yet
不 ‚pu 717, not
爭。 ‚chăng 29, (tseng) it quarrels.

II.

處 'ch'u 94, It dwells in
衆 chung' 108, (tsung) all
人 ‚jăn 286, (jen) the people
之 ‚chi 53, (tzŭ) their
所 su' 817, (hsuo) place which
惡。 wu' 1063, is loathed.
故 ku' 434, Therefore
幾 ‚chi 333, it approaches
于 ‚yü 1118, to
道 tao' 867, Reason.

III.

居 ‚chü 437, For a dwelling
善 shan' 752, it chooses
地。 ti' 879, the [level] ground.
心 'sin 806, (hsin) For a heart
善 shan' 752, it chooses
淵。 yuen' 1131, the eddies.
與 ‚yü 1125 In generosity
善 shan' 752, it chooses
仁 ‚jăn 287, (jen) humaneness.

言 ‚yen 1083, In words
善 shan' 752, it chooses
信。 sin' 807, (hsin) faith.
政 ching' 76, (chen) In government
善 shan' 752, it chooses
治。 chi`` 59, order.
事 shi`` 764, (ssŭ) In business
善 shan' 752, it chooses
能 ‚năng 616, (neng) ability
動 tung' 932, In its movements
善 shan' 752, it chooses
時 ‚shi 759, (ssŭ) time.
    [rhythm]

IV.

夫 ‚fu 142, Forasmuch
惟 ‚wéi 1049, just as
不 ‚pu 717, not
爭。 ‚chăng 29, (tseng) it quarrels,
故 ku' 434, therefore
無 ‚wu 1059, not
尤。 ‚yiu 1110, it is rebuked.

(Chapter 8.)

第九章 *ti'* 879, *'kiu* 413, *chang* 22, } Chapter 9.

運 *yun'* 1144, An exercise in
夷 *i* 276, placidity.

I.

持 *ch'i,* 64, (*chih*) Holding
而 *'rh* 719, (*err*) and
盈 *ying* 1106, filling
之 *chi* 53, (*tzŭ*) it,
不 *pu* 717, is not
如 *jü* 297, likely
其 *ch'i* 342, its
已 *'i* 278, being stopped?
揣 *'chw'ai* 112, Handling
而 *'rh* 719, (*err*) and
銳 *jui"* 302, sharpening
之 *chi* 53, (*tzŭ*) it,
不 *pu* 717, is not
可 *'k'o* 425, able
長 *ch'ang* 27, long
保 *'pao* 664, to be kept.

II.

金 *chin* 398, [If] gold
玉 *yuh,* 1138, [and] jewel
滿 *'man* 575 fill
堂 *t'ang* 860, the hall,
莫 *moh,* 603, nobody
之 *chi* 53 (*tzŭ*) it
能 *nǎng* 616, (*neng*) can
守 *'shcu* 755, (*hsou*) protect

III.

富 *fu'* 148, [If] wealthy
貴 *kwéi"* 484 [and] exalted
而 *'rh* 719, (*err*) but
驕 *chiao* 368, haughty
自 *tsz"* 1031, (*ssŭ*) they themselves
遺 *i* 277, bring about
其 *ch'i* 342, their
咎 *chiu'* 415, misfortune.
功 *kung* 460, Merit
成 *ch'ing* 77, (*ch'eng*) to accomplish,
名 *ming* 600, fame
遂 *sui"* 828, to complete,
身 *shǎn* 735, (*shen*) [and] his person
退 *t'ui"* 926, to retire,
天 *t'ien* 897, [is] heaven
之 *chi* 53, (*tzŭ*) of,
道 *tao'* 867, the way.

(Chapter 9.)

TRANSLITERATION.

第 ₍ti⁾ 879
十 ₍shih,⟩ 768 } Chapter 10.
章 ₍chang⟩ 22

能 ₍năng⟩ 616, What can
爲 ₍wéi⟩ 1047, be done.

I.

載 ⟨tsai⟩ 941, By sustaining
營 ₍ying⟩ 1107, by disciplining
魄 ₍p'oh,⟩ 711, (t'o) the animal spirit,
抱 ₍pao'⟩ 665, by embracing
一 ₍yi,⟩ 1095, unity
能 ₍năng⟩ 616, (neng) one can be
無 ₍wu⟩ 1059, without
離 ₍li⟩ 517, disintegration.
專 ₍chwen⟩ 116, (chuan) By concentrating
氣 ⟨ch'i"⟩ 348, the vital force,
致 ⟨chi'⟩ 58, by inducing
柔 ₍jeu⟩ 294, (jou) tenderness,
能 ₍năng⟩ 616, (neng) one can be
嬰 ₍ying⟩ 1105, an infant
兒 ⟨'rh⟩ 720, (err) child.

II.

滌 ⟨tih,⟩ 902, By washing,
除 ⟨ch'u⟩ 92, by cleaning,
玄 ₍hüen⟩ 231, (hsüen) by profound

(Chapter 10.)

覽 ⟨'lan⟩ 502, intuition,
能 ₍năng⟩ 616, (neng) one can be
無 ₍wu⟩ 1059, without
疵 ⟨ts'z⟩ 1033, (tzŭ) faults.
愛 ⟨ngai"⟩ 619, In loving
民 ₍min⟩ 597, the people,
治 ⟨ch'ih,⟩ 59, in ruling
國 ⟨kwoh,⟩ 491, the country,
能 ₍năng⟩ 616, (neng) one can practise
無 ₍wu⟩ 1059, non-
爲 ₍wéi⟩ 1047, action.

III.

天 ⟨t'ien⟩ 897, The Heaven's
門 ₍măn⟩ 576, (men) gate
開 ⟨k'ai⟩ 308, opening
闔 ⟨hoh,⟩ 218, [and] closing
能 ₍năng⟩ 616, (neng) one can
爲 ₍wéi⟩ 1047, act
雌 ⟨ts'z'⟩ 1033, (t'zu) [like] a mother-bird
明 ₍ming⟩ 599, Bright,
白 ⟨poh,⟩ 706, (pai) white,
四 ⟨sz"⟩ 836, (ssŭ) the four [quarters].
達 ⟨tah,⟩ 840, penetrating
能 ₍năng⟩ 616, (neng) one can be

無 ‚wu 1059, not-
知 ‚chi 53, knowing.

IV.

生 ‚shăng 742, (sheng) Quickening
之 ‚chi 53, (tzŭ) them,
畜 ch'uh 98, (hsü) feeding
之 ‚chi 53, (tzŭ) them,
生 ‚shăng 742, (seng) he produces
而 ‚rh 719, (err) and
不 ‚pu 717, not
有 ‚yiu 1113, owns.
爲 ‚wei 1047, He acts
而 ‚rh 719, (err) and
不 ‚pu 717, not
恃 shi' 761 (ssŭ) claims.
長 ‚ch'ang 27, He raises
而 ‚rh 719, (err) and
不 ‚pu 717, not
宰 'tsai 941, rules.
是 shi' 762, (ssŭ) This
謂 ‚wei 1054, is called
玄 ‚hüen 231 (hsüen) profound
德 teh, 871, (tê) virtue.

第 ti' 879,
十 shih, 768,
一 yih, 1095,
章 ‚chang 22,
} Chapter 11.

無 ‚wu 1059, Of non-existence
用 yung' 1149, the use.

I.

三 ‚san 723, Three
十 shi, 768, [times] ten
輻 ‚fu 151, spokes
共 kung' 464, unite
一 yi' 1095, in one
轂 ‚ku 454, nave.
當 ‚tang 857, Through
其 ‚ch'i 342, its
無 ‚wu 1059, void,
有 'yiu 1113, there is
車 ‚ch'ê 39, (chü)
之 ‚chi 53, (tzŭ)
} the wheel's
用 yung' 1149, utility.

II.

埏 ‚yen 1085, By kneading
埴 ch'i' 66, clay

TRANSLITERATION.

以 ,'i 278, thereby
爲 ,wéi 1047, is made
器 ch'i' 349, the vessel.
當 ,tang 857, Through
其 ,ch'i 342, its
無 ,wu 1059, void,
有 'yiu 1113, there is
器 ch'i' 349 ⎫
之 ,chi 53, (tzŭ) ⎬ the vessel's
用 yung' 1149, utility.

III.

鑿 tso, 1006, (tsao) By cutting out
戶 hu' 225, doors
牖 'yiu 1114, [and] windows,
以 'i 278, thereby
爲 ,wéi 1059, is made
室 shih, 770, a room.
當 ,tang 857, Through
其 ,ch'i 342, its
無 ,wu 1059, void
有 'yiu 1113, there is
室 shih, 770, ⎫
之 ,chi 53, (tzŭ) ⎬ the room's
用 yung' 1149, utility.

IV.

故 ku' 434, Therefore,
有 'yiu 1113, ⎫
之 ,chi 53, (tzŭ) ⎬ existence's
以 'i 278, thus
爲 ,wéi 1047, being
利 li' 521, profitable
無 ,wu 1059, ⎫ [is] non-
之 ,chi 53, (tzŭ) ⎬ existence's
以 'i 278 thus
爲 ,wéi 1047, being
用 yung' 1149, useful.

第 ti' 879, ⎫
十 shih, 768,
二 'rh' 721, ⎬ Chapter 12
章 ,chang 22, ⎭

檢 'kien 385, Abstaining
欲 yuh, 1139, from desire.

I.

五 ,wu 1060, The five
色 seh, 727, colors
令 ling' 546, make
人 ,jăn 286, (jen) the human

(Chapter 11-12.)

目 ₁*muh*, 607, eye
盲 ₁*mang* 609, blind.
五 ₁*wu* 1060, The five
音 ₁*yin* 1100, notes
令 *ling'* 546, make
人 ₁*jăn* 286, (*jen*) the human
耳 ʰ*rh* 720, (*err*) ear
聾 ₁*lung* 568, deaf.
五 ₁*wu* 1060, The five
味 *wéi"* 1053, tastes
令 *ling'* 546, make
人 ₁*jăn* 286, (*jen*) the human
口 *'k'eu* 331, (*k'ou*) mouth
爽 ʰ*shwang* 787, blunt.

II.

馳 ₁*ch'i* 64, Horse-racing,
騁 ʰ*chăng* 80, (*cheng*) over-
riding,
田 ₁*t'ien* 898, [and] field-
獵 *lieh*, 532 hunting
令 *ling'* 546, make
人 ₁*jăn* 286, (*jen*) the human
心 ₁*sin* 806, (*hsin*) heart
發 *fah*, 121, turn
狂 ₁*kw'ang* 479, mad.

難 ₁*nan* 614, The difficulty
得 *teh*, 872, (*té*) in the obtaining
之 ₁*chi* 53, (*tzŭ*) of
貨 *hwo'* 256, treasures
令 *ling'* 546, makes
人 ₁*jăn* 286, (*jen*) the human
行 ₁*hing* 207, (*hsing*) conduct
妨 ₁*fang* 133, checked.

III.

是 *shi"* 762, (*ssŭ*)
以 *'i* 278, } Therefore
聖 *shăng'* 773, (*sheng*) the
holy
人 ₁*jăn* 286, (*jen*), man
為 ₁*wéi* 1047, attends to
腹 *fuh*, 151, the inner [the
soul]
不 ₁*pu* 717, not
為 ₁*wéi* 1047, he attends
目 *muh*, 607, to the eye [the
visible, the outer].
故 *ku'* 434, Therefore
去 *'ch'ü* 445, he dismisses
彼 *'pi* 674, the latter,
取 *'ts'ü* 1010, (*ch'ü*) he takes
此 *'ts'z'* 1034 (*tzŭ*) the former

(Chapter 12.)

TRANSLITERATION.

第 *tǐ* 879,
十 *shih*, 768,
三 *san* 723,
章 *chang* 22,
} Chapter 13.

厭 *yen'* 1089, Loathing
恥 *'ch'i* 65, shame.

I.

寵 *ch'ung* 110, (*ts'ung*) Favor
辱 *juh*, 299, [and] disgrace
若 *joh*, 296, (*jĕ*) are like
驚 *ching* 403, fear.
貴 *kwéi'* 484, Esteem
大 *ta'* 839, great
患 *hwan'* 248, anxiety
若 *joh*, 296 (*jĕ*) like,
身 *shăn* 735, (*shen*) the body.

II.

何 *ho* 215, What
謂 *wéi'* 1054, is meant by
寵 *ch'ung* 110, (*ts'ung*) favor
辱 *juh*, 229, [and] disgrace
若 *joh*, 296, (*jĕ*) are like
驚 *ching* 403, fear?

寵 *'ch'ung* 110, (*tsung*) Favor
為 *wéi* 1047, renders
下 *hia'* 183, (*hsia*) lowly.
得 *teh*, 872 (*tĕ*) The obtaining
之 *chi* 53, (*tzŭ*) of it
若 *joh*, 296 (*jĕ*) is like
驚 *ching* 403, fear.
失 *shih*, 769, The losing
之 *chi* 53, (*tzŭ*) of it
若 *joh*, 296, (*jĕ*) is like
驚 *ching* 403, fear.
是 *shi"* 762, (*ssŭ*) This
謂 *wéi'* 1054, means
寵 *'ch'ung* 110, (*tsung*) [that] favor
辱 *juh*, 299, [and] disgrace
若 *joh*, 296, (*jĕ*) are like
驚 *ching* 403, fear.

III.

何 *ho* 215, What
謂 *wéi'* 1054, is meant by
貴 *kwéi'* 484, esteeming
大 *ta'* 839, great
患 *hwan'* 248, anxiety
若 *joh*, 296 (*jĕ*) as like

(Chapter 13.)

身 ,shăn 735, (shen) one's person?
吾 ,wu 1060, I
所 su' 817, (shuo) } the reason
以 'i 278,   } why
有 'yiu 113, have
大 ta' 839, great
患 hwan' 248, anxiety
者 'che 38, that
爲 ,wéi 1047, is that
吾 ,wu 1060, I
有 'yin 1113, have
身 ,shăn 735, (shen) a body.
及 chih, 394, When
吾 ,wu 1060, I
無 ,wu 1059, have no
身 ,shăn 735, (shen) body,
吾 ,wu 1060, I
有 'yiu 1113, have
何 ,ho 215, what
患 hwan' 248, anxiety? [Answer: None!]

IV.

故 ku' 434, Therefore:
貴 kwéi" 384, Who esteems
以 'i 278, as

身 ,shăn 735, (shen) [his own] body
爲 ,wéi 1047, when administrating,
天 t'ien 897,   } the
下 hia' 183, (hsia) } empire
者 'ché 38, the one,
則 tseh, 956, then
可 'k'o 425, [he] is able
以 'i 278, thereby
寄 chi" 339, to be trusted
天 t'ien 897,   } with the
下 hia' 183, (hsia) } empire.

V.

愛 ngai" 619, Who lovingly
以 'i 278, as
身 ,shăn 735, (shen) [his own] body
爲 ,wéi 1047, administers
天 t'ien 897,   } the
下 hia' 183, (hsia) } empire
者 'ché 38, the one,
則 tseh, 956, then
可 'k'o 425, [he] is able
以 'i 278, thereby
託 t'oh, 915, to be entrusted

(Chapter 13.)

天 t'ien 897, } with the
下 hia' 183, (hsia) } empire.

第 ti" 879,
十 shih, 768,
四 sz" 836,   } Chapter 14.
章 chang 22,

贊 tsan' 945, Praising
玄 hüen 231, the profound.

I.

視 shi' 763, (ssŭ) [When] looking
之 chi 53, (tsŭ) at it
不 pu 717, not
見 chien' 385, it is seen.
名 ming 600, } It is called
曰 yueh, 1130,
夷 i 276, colorless.
聽 t'ing 906, [When] listening
之 chi 53, (tsŭ) to it
不 pu 717, not
聞 wăn 1041, (wen) it is heard.
名 ming 600, } It is called
曰 yueh, 1130,
希 hi 176, (hsi) soundless.

搏 poh, 706, (p'uan) [When] grasping
之 chi 53, (tzŭ) it
不 pu 717, not
得 tch, 872, (tê) it is seized.
名 ming 600, } It is called
曰 yueh, 1130,
微 wéi 1050, incorporeal.

II.

此 ts'z' 1034, (ssŭ) These
三 san 723, three
者 ché 38, things
不 pu 717, not
可 k'o 425, can be
致 chi" 58, subjected
詰 ch'ih, 396, to scrutiny.
故 ku' 434, Therefore
混 'hwun 269, (hun) they are mingled together
而 'rh 719, (err) and
為 wéi 1047, form
一 yih, 1095, a unity.

III.

其 ch'i 342, Its
上 'shang 741, surface
不 pu 717, is not
皦 'chiao 369, clear;

(Chapters 13-14.)

其 ‚ch'i 342, its
下 ‚hia' 183, (hsia) bottom
不 ‚pu 717, is not
昧 mêi" 586, obscure.

IV.

繩 ‚shăng 772, (sheng) Continuously
々 ‚shăng 772, (sheng) [and] continuously
兮 ‚hi 179, (hsi) Oh!
不 ‚pu 717, not
可 'k'o 425, it can be
名 ‚ming 600, named.
復 fuh, 151, It reverts
歸 kwéi, 480, [and] returns
于 ‚yü 1118, to
無 ‚wu 1059, non-
物 wuh, 1065, existence.
是 shi' 762, (ssŭ) This
謂 wéi' 1054, is called
無 ‚wu 1059,
狀 chwang' 114, } of non-form
之 ‚chi 53, (tzŭ)
狀 chwang' 114, the form,
無 ‚wu 1059,
象 ‚siang' 792, (hsiang) } of non-image
之 ‚chi 53, (tzŭ)

(Chapter 22.)

象 siang' 792, (hsiang) the image.

V.

是 shi' 762, (ssŭ) This
謂 ‚wéi 1047, is called
惚 ‚hu 267, abstrusely
恍 'hwang 253, abstruse.
迎 ‚ying 1108, In the front
之 ‚chi 53, (tzŭ) of it
不 ‚pu 717, not
見 chien' 385, is seen
其 ‚ch'i 342, its
首 ‚sheu 756, (shou) head.
隨 ‚sui 826, In the rear
之 ‚chi 53, (tzu) of it
不 ‚pu 717, not
見 chien' 385, is seen
其 ‚ch'i 342, its
後 heu' 175, (hou) back.

VI.

執 chih, 67, By holding fast to
古 'ku 432 the ancients
之 ‚chi 53, (tzŭ) of,
道 tao' 867, the Reason,
以 ‚i 278, thereby

御 yü' 1127, [the sage] governs
今 ‚chin 398, the present day
之 ‚chi 53, (tzŭ) of,
有 'yiu 1113, existence,
以 'i 278, [and] thus
知 ‚chi 53, (chih) [he] knows
古 'ku 432, of the olden time
始 'shi 761, (ssŭ) the beginning.
是 shi' 762, (ssŭ) This
謂 wéi' 1054, is called
道 tao' 867, Reason's
紀 'chi 337, thread.

第 ti' 879, ⎫
十 shih 768, ⎬ Chapter 15.
五 ‚wu 1060, ⎪
章 ‚chang 22, ⎭

顯 chien 199, (hsien) Revealers
德 teh, 871, of virtue.

I.

古 'ku 432, ⎫ In olden
之 ‚chi 53, (tzŭ) ⎭ time
善 shan' 752, [who] well
為 ‚wéi 1047, [were entitled] to be
士 shi' 762, (ssŭ) masters

者 ‚chĕ 38, the ones
微 ‚wéi 1050, [were] subtle,
妙 miao' 592, spiritual,
玄 ‚hüen 231, (hsüen) profound
通 ‚t'ung 932, [and] penetrating.
深 ‚shĕn 736, (shen) Their profundity
不 ‚pu 717, not
可 'k'o 425, could be
識 shih, 770, understood.

II.

夫 ‚fu 142, ⎫ Since
惟 ‚wéi 1049, ⎭
不 ‚pu 717, not
可 'k'o 425, they can be
識 shih, 770, understood,
故 ku' 434, therefore
強 ‚ch'iang 366, I try
為 ‚wéi 1047, to make
之 ‚chi 53, (tzŭ) them
容 ‚yung 1146, intelligible.
與 'yü 1125, Cautious!
兮 ‚hi 179, (hsi) Oh!
若 joh, 296, (jŏ) [they were] like
冬 ‚tung 931, in winter

(Chapters 14-15.)

涉 *sheh*, 750, (*shê*) wading
川 ,*chw'en* 119, (*ch'uan*) a river.
猶 ,*yiu* 1112, Reluctant!
兮 ,*hi* 179, *hsi*) Oh!
若 *joh*, 296, (*jê*) like
畏 *wéi"* 1054, fearing
四 *sz"* 836, (*ssŭ*) in the four [quarters]
隣 ,*lin* 541, neighbors.
儼 '*yen* 1088, (*nien*) Reserved
兮 ,*hi* 179, (*hsi*) oh!
其 ,*ch'i* 342, they were
若 *joh*, 296, (*jê*) like
客 *k'oh*, 429, guests.
渙 *hwan'* 249, Elusive!
兮 ,*hi* 179, (*hsi*) Oh!
若 *joh*, 296, (*jê*) like
冰 ,*ping* 698, ice
之 ,*chi* 53, (*tzŭ*) which
將 ,*tsiang* 967, (*chiang*) is going
釋 *shih*, 767, to melt.
敦 ,*tun* 927, Simple!
兮 ,*hi* 179, (*hsi*) Oh!
其 ,*ch'i* 342, they were
若 *joh*, 296, (*jê*) like

樸 *p'oh*, 710, (*p'u*) unseasoned wood.
曠 *kwang'* 480, Empty!
兮 ,*hi* 179, (*hsi*) Oh!
其 ,*ch'i* 342, they were
若 *joh*, 296, (*jê*) like
谷 *kuh*, 453, a valley.
渾 ,*hwun* 268, Obscure!
兮 ,*hi* 179, (*hsi*) Oh!
其 ,*ch'i* 342, they were
若 *joh*, 296, (*jê*) like
濁 *choh*, 83, (*tso*) disturbed water.

III.

孰 *shuh*, 780, (*su*) Who
能 ,*năng* 616, (*neng*) can
濁 *choh*, 83, (*tso*) the disturbed
以 '*i* 278, by
靜 *tsing'* 994, (*ching*) quieting
之 ,*chi* 53, (*tzŭ*) it
徐 ,*sü* 819, (*hsü*) gradually
清 ,*ts'ing* 995, (*ch'ing*) purify?
孰 *shuh*, 780, (*su*) Who
能 ,*năng* 616, (*neng*) can
安 ,*ngan* 620, the quiet
以 '*i* 278, by

(Chapter 15.)

TRANSLITERATION.

動 *tung'* 932, moving
之 *chi* 53, (*tzŭ*) them
徐 *sü* 819, (*hsü*) gradually
生 *shăng* 742, (*sheng*) bring to life..

IV.

保 '*pao* 664, Who keeps
此 *ts'z'* 1034 (*tzŭ*) this
道 *tao'* 867, Reason
不 *pu* 717, does not
欲 *yuh*, 1139, (*yü*) wish
盈 *ying* 1106, to be filled.
夫 *fu* 142, ⎫
惟 *wei* 1049, ⎬ Since
         ⎭
不 *pu* 717, not
盈 *ying* 1106, filled
故 *ku'* 434, therefore
能 *năng* 616, (*neng*) he is able
弊 *pi'* 676, to grow old
不 *pu* 717, [and need] not
新 *sin* 806, (*hsin*) newly
成 *ch'ing* 77, (*cheng*) be fashioned.

第 '*ti* 879, ⎫
十 *shih*, 768, ⎪
六 *luh*, 562, ⎬ Chapter 16
章 *chang* 52, ⎭

歸 *kwei*, 480, Returning
根 *kăn* 317, to the root.

I.

致 *chi'* 58, Attain to
虛 *hü* 227, (*hsü*) vacuity's
極 *chih*, 393, summit.
守 '*sheu* 755, (*shou*) Keep
靜 *tsing'* 994, (*ching*) tranquility's
篤 *tuh*, 921, essence.
萬 *wan'* 1040, The ten thousand
物 *wuh*, 1065, things
并 *ping'* 700, altogether
作 *tsoh*, 1005, arise.
吾 ,*wu* 1060, I
以 '*i* 278, thereby
觀 ,*kwan* 474, recognise
其 *ch'i* 342, their
復 ,*fu*, 151, returning.
夫 ,*fu* 142, Now
物 *wu*, 1065, (*wu*) things

(Chapters 15-16.)

芸 ͵yun 1142, bloom
芸 ͵yun 1142, in bloom
各 koh, 426, each one
復 ͵fu 151, reverts
歸 kwéi, 480, [and] returns
其 ͵ch'i 342, to its
根 ͵kăn 317, (ken) root.

II.

歸 kwéi, 480, The returning
根 ͵kăn 317, (ken) to the root
曰 yueh, 1130, is called
靜 tsing' 994, (ching) tranquillity.
是 shi' 762, This
謂 wéi' 1054, is called
復 ͵fu 151, the returning
命 ming' 601, to destiny.
復 ͵fuh, 151, The returning
命 ming' 601, to destiny
曰 yueh, 1130, is called
常 ͵ch'ang 740, the eternal.
知 ͵chi 53, (chih) To know
常 ͵ch'ang 740, the eternal
曰 yuch, 1130, is called
明 ͵ming 599, enlightenment.

不 ͵pu 717, [When] not
知 ͵chi 53, (chih) one knows
常 ͵ch'ang 740, the eternal,
妄 wang 1045, disorder
作 tsoh, 1005, arises,
凶 ͵hiung 213, (shiung) [which is] evil!

III.

知 ͵chi 53, Knowing
常 ͵ch'ang 740, the eternal
容 ͵yung 1146, [makes] comprehensive
容 ͵yung 1146, Comprehensive
乃 'nai 612, means
公 ͵kung 459, catholic (broad)
公 ͵kung 459, Catholic
乃 'nai 612, means
王 ͵wang 1043, royal.
王 ͵wang 1043, Royal
乃 'nai 612, means
天 ͵t'ien 897, heavenly.
天 ͵t'ien 897, Heavenly
乃 'nai 612, means
道 tao' 867, rational.
道 tao' 867, Rational
乃 'nai 612, means

(Chapter 16.)

久 'chiu 413, everlasting.
沒 muh, 606, (mo) The end
身 ‚shăn 735, (shen) of the body
不 ‚pu 717, it is not
殆 tai' 846, dangerous.

第 ti' 879,
十 shih, 768,
七 ts'ih 987, } Chapter 17.
章 ‚chang 22,

淳 ‚shun 783, Simplicity
風 fung 155, of habit.

I.

太 t'ai' 848, [Under] the great
上 'shang 741, superiors
下 hia' 183, (hsia) the inferiors
不 ‚pu 717, not
知 ‚chi 53, (chih) know
有 'yiu 1113, the existence
之 ‚chi 53 (tzŭ) of them.
其 ch'i 342, [Where] their
次 ts'z'' 1034,(t'zŭ) next [rule]
親 ts'in 991, (chin) [the people] are attached
之 ‚chi 53, (tzu) to them,

譽 ‚yü 1122, they praise
之 ‚chi 53, (tzu) them.
其 ch'i 342, [Where] their
次 ts'z'' 1034,(t'zŭ) next [rule]
畏 wéi' 1054, [the people] fear
之 ‚chi 53, (tzŭ) them.
其 ch'i 342, [Where] their
次 ts'z'' 1034, (t'zŭ) next[rule]
侮 'wu 1061, [the people] despise
之 ‚chi 53, (tzŭ) them.

II.

故 ku' 434, Therefore
信 sin' 807, (shin) [when] faith
不 ‚pu 717, is not
足 tsuh, 1014, sufficient
焉 ‚yen 1082, [particle of affirmation]
有 'yiu 1113, one finds
不 ‚pu 717, not
信 sin' 807, (shin) faith.

III.

猶 ‚yiu 1112, [How] reluctantly!
兮 ‚hi 179, (hsi) Oh!
其 ‚ch'i 342, they
貴 kwéi' 484, esteem
言 ‚yen 1083, [their] words.

(Chapters 16-17.)

功 ,kung 460, Merits
成 ,ch'ing 77, (cheng) [they] perform,
事 shi' 764, (ssŭ) deeds
遂 sui' 828, [they] accomplish;
百 ,pai 707, [and] the hundred
姓 sing 810, (shing) families
皆 ,chiĕ 358, all
謂 wéi' 1054, say
我 'ngo 627, we [are]
自 tsz'' 1031, (tzŭ) self-
然 ,jan 285, like.

第 ti' 879,
十 shih, 768
八 pah, 647, } Chapter 18.
章 ,chang 22,

1.

俗 suh, 822, Vulgarity's
薄 poh' 705, palliation.

大 ta' 839, [When] the great
道 tao' 867, Reason
廢 féi' 138, degenerates,
有 'yiu 1113, we have
仁 jăn 287, (jen) benevolence

義 i' 280, [and] righteousness.
智 chi' 58, [When] prudence
慧 hwui' 265, [and] wisdom
出 ch'uh, 98, appear,
有 'yiu 1113, we have
大 ta' 839, great
偽 wéi' 1055, hypocrisy.
六 luh, 562, (lia) [When] the six
親 ts'in 991, (chin) family relations
不 ,pu 717, are not
和 ,hwo 254, friendly,
有 'yiu 1113, we have [the preaching of]
孝 hiao' 193, (hsiao) filial piety
慈 ts'z' 1033, (tzŭ) [and] paternal affection.
國 ,kwo 491, [When] the state
家 ,chia 351, with its families
昏 ,hwun 267, is confused
亂 lwan' 570, [and] out of order,
有 'yiu 1113, there are
忠 ,chung 106, (tsung) loyalty
信 sin' 807, (hsin) [and] faithfulness.

(Chapters 17-18.)

第十九章 *li*' 879, *shih*, 768, *kiu* 413, *chang* 22, } Chapter 19.

還 *hwan* 244, Returning
淳 *shun* 783, to purity.

I.

絕 *tsüeh*, 1011, (*chüeh*) Abandon
聖 *shăng*' 773, (*shêng*) saintliness,
棄 *ch'i*' 349, relinquish
智 *chi*' 58, prudence;
民 *min* 597, the people
利 *li*' 521, will benefit [increase]
百 *poh*, 707, hundred
倍 *pei*' 670, times.
絕 *tsüeh*, 1011, (*chüeh*) Abandon
仁 *jăn* 287, (*jen*) benevolence,
棄 *ch'i*' 349, relinquish
義 *i*' 280, righteousness;
民 *min* 597, the people
復 *fuh*, 151, will return to
孝 *hiao*' 193, (*hsiao*) filial piety
慈 *ts'z*' 1033, (*tzŭ*) [and] parental affection.

(Chapter 19.)

絕 *tsüeh*, 1011, (*chüeh*) Abandon
巧 '*ch'iao* 374, cleverness,
棄 *ch'i*' 349, relinquish
利 *li*' 521, gain;
盜 *tao*' 868, thieves
賊 *tsch*, 957, [and] robbers
無 *wu* 1059, will not
有 '*yiu* 1113, appear.

II.

此 *ts'z*' 1034, (*ssŭ*) These are
三 *san* 723, three
者 '*ché* 38, things
以 '*i* 278, wherein
爲 *wéi* 1047, to have
文 *wan* 1041, (*wen*) culture
不 *pu* 717, is not
足 *tsuh*, 1014, sufficient.
故 *ku*' 434, Therefore
令 *ling*' 546, let them
有 *yiu* 1113, hold
所 *su*' 817, (*shuo*) that which
屬 *shuh*, 780, (*su*) is reliable
見 *chien*' 385, Recognise
素 *su*' 816, simplicity,

抱 ,pao' 665, embrace
樸 ,p'u 716, purity,
少 'shao 746, lessen
私 ,sz' 835, (ssŭ) the own [self-ishness],
寡 'kwa 467, diminish
欲 yuh, 1139, (yü) desires.

第二十章 } ti' 879, 'rh 721, shih, 768, chang 22, } Chapter 20.

異 î' 281, Different from
俗 suh, 822, the vulgar.

I.

絕 tsüeh, 1011, (chüeh) Abandon
學 hioh, 209, (hsüeh) learnedness
無 ,wu 1059, [and] you have no
憂 ,yiu 1109, anxiety.
唯 'wéi 1052, The yes
之 ,chi 53, (tzŭ) in its
與 'yü 1125, addition to [contrast to]
阿 'o 643, the yea
相 ,siang 790, (hsiang) mutually
去 'ch'ü 445, differ

幾 ,chi 333, } how little?
何 ,ho 215,
善 shan' 752, The good
之 ,chi 53, (tzŭ) in its
與 'yü 1125, addition to [contrast to]
惡 wu' 1063, the bad
相 ,siang 790, (hsiang) mutually
去 'ch'ü 445, differ
何 ,ho 215, } how much?
若 joh, 296, (je)

II.

人 ,jăn 286, (jĕn) } By the people
之 ,chi 53, (tzŭ)
所 su' 817, (shuo) that which
畏 wéi' 1054, is feared
不 ,pu 717, not
可 'k'o 425, can
不 ,pu 717, not
畏 wéi' 1054, be feared.
荒 ,hwang 250, Desolation!
兮 ,hi 179, (hsi) Oh!
其 ,ch'i 342, It
未 wéi' 1052, has not yet
央 ,yang 1070, reached the limit,
哉 ,tsai 940, indeed!

(Chapters 19-20.)

TRANSLITERATION. 175

III.

衆 ,chung' 108, (tsung) All
人 ,jăn 286, (jen) people
熙 ,hi 177, (hsi) [are] joyful,
熙 ,hi 177, (hsi) joyful.
如 ,jü 297, They are like
享 'hiang 189, (hsiang) celebrating
大 ta' 839, (t'ai) a great
牢 ,lao 507, feast.
如 ,jü 297, They are like
春 ,ch'un 104, (ts'ëng) in springtime
登 ,tăng 862, (chun) ascending
臺 ,t'ai 847, a tower.
我 'ngo 627, I
獨 tuh, 921, alone
泊 poh, 707, am calm,
兮 ,hi 179, (hsi) Oh!
其 ,ch'i 342, as he
未 wéi' 1052, [who has] not yet
兆 chao' 34, an omen.
如 ,jü 297, (jĕ) I am like
嬰 ,ying 1105, } an infant child
兒 ,'rh 720, (err)
之 ,chi 53, (tzŭ) who

未 wéi' 1052, does not yet
孩 ,hai 160, smile.

IV.

乘 ,shing 772, (ch'eng) Forlorn
乘 ,shing 772, (ch'eng) [so] forlorn
兮 ,hi 179, (hsi) Oh!
若 joh, 296, (jĕ) like
無 ,wu 1059, not having
所 su' 817, (shuo) any place whereto
歸 kwéi' 480, to return.
衆 ,chung' 108, (tsung) The multitude of
人 ,jăn 286, (jen) people
皆 ,chi'ĕ 358, all
有 'yiu 1113, have
餘 ,yü 1121, plenty.
而 ,'rh 719, (err) But
我 'ngo 627, I
獨 tuh, 921, alone
若 joh, 296, (jĕ) [am] like
遺 ,i 277, wanting.
我 'ngo 627, I [am]
愚 ,yü 1120, a foolish
人 ,jăn 286, (jen) man
之 ,chi 53 (tzŭ) in

(Chapter 20.)

心 ₍sin 806, (hsin) the heart,
也 'yé 1079,
哉 ₍tsai 940 } indeed!

v.

沌 tun' 928, Ignorant
々 tun' 928, [so] ignorant,
兮 ₍hi 179, (hsi) Oh!
俗 ₍su 822, Common
人 ₍jăn 286, (jen) people [are]
昭 ₍chao 31, bright
々。 ₍chao 31, [so] bright.
我 ₍ngo 627, I
獨 tuh, 921, alone
若 joh, 296, (jê) resemble
昏。 ₍hwun 267, the dull.
俗 ₍su 822, Common
人 ₍jăn 286, (jen) people
察 ch'ah, 9, (ts'a) [are] smart
々。 ch'ah, 9, (ts'a) [so] smart.
我 'ngo 627, I [am]
獨 tuh, 921, alone
悶 măn' 577, (men) confused,
々。 măn' 577, (men) [so] confused.
忽 hwuh, 267, (hu) Desolate!

兮 ₍hi 179, (hsi) Oh!
若 joh, 396, (jê) like
海。 'hai 160, the ocean.
漂 ₍p'iao 683, Adrift!
兮 ₍hi 179, (hsi) Oh!
若 joh, 296, (jê) like
無 ₍wu 1059, not having
所 su' 817, (shuo) any place
止 ʼchi 56, (tzŭ) for anchorage

vi.

眾 chung' 108, (tsung) The multitude
人 ₍jăn 286, (jen) of people
皆 ₍chi'e 358, all
有 'yiu 1113, have
以 ʼi 278, usefulness.
而 ʼrh 719, (err) But
我 'ngo 627, I
獨 tuh, 921, alone
頑 ₍wan 1038, am awkward
且 ts'ié 974, (ch'ich) and also
鄙 'pi 674, a rustic.
我 'ngo 627, I
獨 tuh, 921, alone
異 i' 281, differ

(Chapter 20.)

TRANSLITERATION. 177

于 ₍yü 1118, from
人 ₍jăn 286, (jen) the people,
而 ₍'rh 719, (err) but
貴 kwéi' 484, [I] prize
求 ₍ch'iu 416, the seeking
食 shih, 766, food
於 ₍yü 1118, from
母 'mu 605, [our] mother [viz. the Tao].

第 ti" 879,
二 'rh' 721,
十 shih, 768,   } Chapter 21.
一 yih, 1095,
章 ₍chang 22,

虛 hü 227, (hsü) Emptiness
心 sin, 806, (hsin) of heart.

I.

孔 'k'ung 465, Vast
德 teh, 871, (tĕ)
之 ₍chi 53, (tzŭ) } virtue's
容 ₍yung, 1146, manner [attitude]
惟 ₍wéi 1049, will exactly
道 tao' 867, Reason
是 shi' 762, (ssŭ) thus

從 ₍ts'ung 1024, follow.
道 tao' 867,
之 ₍chi 53, (tzŭ) } Reason's
爲 ₍wéi 1047, active
物 wuh, 1065, nature
惟 ₍wéi 1049, is exactly
恍 'hwang 253, abstruse [not settled],
惟 ₍wéi 1049, is exactly
惚 hu, 267, elusive [indeterminable].
惚 hu, 267, Elusive
兮 ₍hi 179, (hsi) Oh!
恍 'hwang 253, [and] abstruse!
其 ₍ch'i 342, [Within] its
中 ₍chung 105, (tsung) inside [middle]
有 'yiu 1113, [it] contains
象 siang' 792, (hsiang) forms [images, types].
恍 'hwang 253, Abstruse!
兮 ₍hi 179, (hsi) Oh!
惚 hu, 267, [and] indeterminable.
其 ₍ch'i 342, [Within] its
中 ₍chung 105, (tsung) inside
有 'yiu 1113, it contains
物 wuh, 1065, the beings.
窈 'yao 1077, Deep!

(Chapters 20–21.)

兮 ,hi 179, (hsi) Oh!
冥 ,ming 600, [and] obscure!
兮 ,hi 179, (hsi) Oh!
其 ,ch'i 342, [Within] its
中 ,chung 105, (tsung) inside
有 'yiu 1113, it contains
精 ,tsing 992, (ching) spirit [essence].
其 ,c'hi 342, Its
精 ,tsing 992, (ching) spirit [essence].
甚 shăn' 738, (shen) [is] very
眞 ,chan 15, (chen) real [sure].
其 ,ch'i 342, [Within] its
中 ,chung 105, (tsung) inside
有 'yiu 1113, it contains
信 sin' 807, (shin) faith.
自 tsz" 1031, (tzŭ) From
古 'ku 432, of yore
及 chih, 394, until
今 ,chin 398, now,
其 ,ch'i 342, its
名 ,ming 600, name
不 ,pu 717, not
去 'ch'ü 445, departs.
以 ,i 278, Thereby

閱 yueh, 1131, it watches
眾 chung' 108, (tsung) [of] all
甫 'fu 146, the beginning.

II.

吾 ,wu 1060, I
何 ,ho 215, what-
以 ,'i 278, by
知 ,chi 53, [can] know [that]
眾 chung' 108, (tsung) all
甫 'fu 146, the beginning
之 ,chi 53, (tzŭ) of it
然 ,jan 285, is such
哉 ,tsai 940, indeed?
以 ,'i 278, [It is] by
此 'ts'z' 1034, (t'zŭ) this [viz. Reason].

第 ti' 879,
二 'rh' 721,
十 shih, 768, } Chapter 22
二 'rh' 721,
章 ,chang 22,

益 yih, 1092, Increase
謙 k'ien 389, through humility

I.

曲 'ch'ü 458, The crooked

TRANSLITERATION. 179

則 ‚tseh, 956. then will be
全 ‚ch'üen 1013, perfect.
枉 ‚wang 1044, The distorted
則 ‚tseh, 956, then will be
直 chih, 70, straightened.
窪 ‚wa 1036, The empty
則 ‚tseh, 956, then will be
盈 ‚ying 1106, filled.
弊 p'i" 676, The worn out
則 ‚tseh, 956, then will be
新 ‚sin 806, (shin) renewed.
少 'shao 746, The having little
則 ‚tseh, 956, then will
得 teh, 872, (tê) obtain.
多 ‚to 909, The having much
則 ‚tseh, 956, then will be
惑 hwo, 259, (ho) bewildered.

II.

是 shi' 762, (ssŭ) ⎫
以 'i 278,   ⎬ Therefore
              ⎭
聖 shăng' 773, (sheng) the holy
人 ‚jăn 286, (jen) man
抱 p'ao' 665, embraces
一 yi, 1095, unity.

爲 ‚wéi 1047, [and] becomes
天 t'ien 897, ⎫
下 hia' 183, (hsia) ⎬ the world's
式 shih, 767, model.   ⎭
不 ‚pu 717, Not
自 tsz" 1031, (tzŭ) himself
見 chien' 385, he makes seen
故 ku' 434. Therefore
明 ‚ming 599, he is enlightened.

III.

不 ‚pu 717, Not
自 tsz" 1031, (tzŭ) himself
是 shi' 762, (ssŭ) he asserts,
故 ku' 434, therefore
彰 ‚chang 23, he is distinguished.
不 ‚pu 717, Not
自 tsz" 1031, (tzŭ) himself
伐 ‚fa, 122, he boasts,
故 ku' 434, therefore
有 ‚yiu 1113, he has
功 ‚kung 460, merit.
不 ‚pu 717, Not
自 tsz" 1031, (tzŭ) himself
矜 ‚ching 405, he approves,

(Chapter 22.)

故 ₍ku' 434, therefore
長 ₍ch'ang 27, he lasts.
夫 ₍fu 142, Forasmuch
惟 ₍wéi 1049, as he will
不 ₍pu 717, not
爭 ₍chăng 29, (tseng) quarrel
故 ₍ku' 434, therefore
天 ₍t'ien 897,⎫
下 hia' 183, (hsia)⎬ the world
莫 moh, 603, not
能 ₍năng 616, (neng) can
與 'yü 1125, with
之 ₍chi 53, (tzŭ) him
爭 ₍chăng 29, (tseng) quarrel.

IV.

古 'ku 432,⎫
之 ₍chi 53, (tzŭ)⎬ Of yore
所 su' 817, (shuo) that which
謂 wéi' 1054, was said:
曲 ₍ch'ü 458, The crooked
則 tseh, 956, then will be
全 ₍ch'üen 1013, perfect,
者 'ché 38, that
豈 ₍ch'i 346, by any means
虛 hü 227, (hsü) [is it] a false

(Chapters 22-23.)

言 ₍yen 1083, saying,
哉 ₍tsai 940, indeed?
誠 ₍ch'ăng 78, (cheng) Truly
全 ₍ch'üen 1013, perfected [they will be]
而 ₍rh 719, (err) and
歸 kwéi, 480, return
之 ₍chi 53, (tzŭ) they [will].

第 ti' 879,⎫
二 'rh' 721,⎪
十 shih, 768,⎬ Chapter 23
三 ₍san 723,⎪
章 ₍chang 22,⎭

虛 hü 227, Emptiness [and]
無 ₍wu 1059, Non-existence.

I.

希 hi 176, (hsi) Seldom
言 ₍yen 1083, to speak
自 tsz" 1031, (tzŭ)⎫ is
然 jan 285,⎬ natural.
飄 ₍p'iao 683, A whirl-
風 ₍fung 155, (feng) wind
不 ₍pu 717, not
終 ₍chung 106, (tsung) outlasts

TRANSLITERATION.   181

朝 ｡chao 32, the morning.
驟 tseu' 962, (tsou) A violent
雨 'yü 1124, rain
不 ｡pu 717, not
終 ｡chung 106, (tsung) outlasts
日｡ jih, 293, the day.
孰 ｡shu 780, Who
爲 ｡wei 1047, causes [them]
此 'ts'z' 1034, (tzŭ) then,
者｡ 'ché 38, [who is] the one?
天 ｡t'ien 897, [It is] heaven
地｡ ti' 879, [and] earth.
天 ｡t'ien 897, Heaven
地 ti' 879, [and] earth
尚 shang' 741, even
不 ｡pu 717, not
能 ｡năng 616, (neng) can be
久｡ 'chiu 413, persistent.
而 ｡'rh 719, (err) And
況 hwang' 254, much less
于 ｡yü 1118, for
人 ｡jăn 286, (jen) man,
乎｡ ｡hu 224, indeed! [Used as a query.]

II.

故 ku' 434, Therefore

從 ｡ts'ung 1024, [who] pursues
事 shi'' 764, (ssŭ) business
于 ｡yü 1118, with
道 tao' 867, reason,
者 ｡ché 38, the one,
道 tao' 867, a rational
者｡ ｡ché 38, one
同 ｡t'ung 933, identifies himself
于 ｡yü 1118, with
道 tao' 867, reason.
從 ｡ts'ung 1024, [Who] pursues
事 shi'' 764, (ssŭ) business
于 ｡yü 1118, with
德 teh, 87, (tê), virtue,
者 ｡ché 38, the one
同 ｡t'ung 938, identifies himself
于 ｡yü 1118, with
德｡ teh, 871, (tê) virtue.
從 ｡ts'ung 1024, [Who] pursues
事 shi'' 764, (ssŭ) business
于 ｡yü 1118, with
失 shih, 769, loss,
者 ｡ché 38, the one
同 ｡t'ung 938, identifies himself

(Chapter 23.)

于 ,yü 1118, with
失 shih, 769, loss.

III.

同 ,t'ung 938, [Who] identifies himself
于 ,yü 1118, with
道 tao' 867, reason,
者 ,ché 38, the one,
道 tao' 867, reason
亦 yih, 1093, also
樂 loh, 554, he enjoys
得 teh, 872, (tê) to obtain
之 ,chi 53, (tzŭ) he [does].
同 ,t'ung 938, [Who] identifies himself
于 ,yü 1118, with
德 teh, 871, (tê) virtue,
者 ,ché 38, the one,
德 teh, 871, (tê) virtue
亦 yih, 1093, also
樂 loh, 554, he enjoys
得 teh, 872, (tê) to obtain
之 ,chi 53, (tzŭ) he [does].
同 ,t'ung 938, [Who] identifies himself
于 ,yü 1118, with
失 shih, 769, loss,
者 ,ché 38, the one

失 shih, 769, loss
亦 yih, 1093, also
樂 loh, 554, he enjoys
得 teh, 872, (tê) to obtain
之 ,chi 53, (tzŭ) he [does].
信 sin' 807, (hsin) [When]
   faith
不 ,pu 717, is not
足 ,tsu 1014, sufficient,
焉 'yen 1082, indeed,
有 ,yiu 1113, he will receive
不 ,pu 717, not
信 sin' 807, (hsin) faith.

第 ti' 879, ⎫
二 'rh' 721, ⎪
十 shih, 708, ⎬ Chapter 24
四 sz" 836, ⎪
章 ,chang 22, ⎭

苦 'k'u 436, Troubles
恩 ,ngan 623, in merit.

I.

跂 ,ch'i 345, On tiptoe
者 ,ché 38, one
不 ,pu 717, not

(Chapters 23–24.)

TRANSLITERATION.

立 ₍lih, 538, stands.
跨 ₍kw'a' 468, Being astride
者 ₍ché 38, one
不 ₍pu 717, not
行 ₍hing 207, (hsing) walks.
自 tsz" 1031, (tzŭ) A self-
見 chien' 385, displaying
者 ₍ché 38, one
不 ₍pu 717, not
明 ₍ming 599, is bright.
自 tsz" 1031, (tzŭ) A self-
是 shi' 762, (ssŭ) asserting
者 ₍ché 38, one
不 ₍pu 717, not
彰 ₍chang 23, can shine.
自 tsz" 1031, (tzŭ) A self-
伐 fa, 122. approving
者 ₍ché 38, one
無 ₍wu 1059, has not
功 ₍kung 460, merit.
自 tsz" 1031, A self-
矜 ₍ching 405, praising
者 ₍ché 38, one
不 ₍pu 717, not

長 ₍ch'ang 27, grows.

II.

其 ₍ch'i 342. Their [relation]
于 ₍yü 1118, with
道 tao' 867, Reason,
也 'yé 1079, indeed,
曰 yueh, 1130, is called
餘 ₍yü 1121, offal
食 shih, 766, of food,
贅 chui' 101, (tsui') an excrescence
行 ₍hing 207, (hsing) in the system:
物 wuh, 1065, beings
或 hwoh, 259, (ho) are likely
惡 wu' 1063, to detest
之 ₍chi 53, (tzŭ) them.
故 ku' 434, Therefore
有 'yiu 1113, [who] has
道 tao' 867, reason
者 ₍ché 38, the one
不 ₍pu 717, does not
處 'ch'u 94, dwell [rely on him],
也 'yé 1079, indeed.

(Chapter 24.)

第 ti' 879
二 'rh' 721,
十 shih, 768,   ⎫
五 'wu 1060,   ⎬ Chapter 25.
章 ,chang 22,   ⎭

I.

象 siang' 792, Imaging
玄 ,hüen 231, the mysterious.

I.

有 ,yiu 1113, There is
物 wuh, 1065, being
混 'hwun 269, containing everything
成 ,ch'äng 77, (cheng) completely.
先 ,sien 799, (hsien) Before
天 ,t'ien 897, heaven
地 ti' 879, and earth
生 ,shäng 742, (sheng) it exists.
寂 tsih, 985, (ch'i) Calm!
兮 ,hi 179, (hsi) Oh!
寥 ,liao 528, Incorporeal!
兮 ,hi 179, (hsi) Oh!
獨 tuh, 921, Alone
立 lih, 538, it stands
而 ,'rh 719, (err) and

不 ,pu 717 not
改 'kai 307, changes.

II.

周 ,cheu 47, (chou) Everywhere
行 ,hing 207, (hsing) it goes
而 ,'rh 719, (err) and
不 ,pu 717, not
殆 tai" 846, [it is] hindered.
可 'k'o 425, It can
以 'i 278, thereby
為 ,wéi 1047, become
天 ,t'ien 897,   ⎫
下 hia' 183(hsia) ⎬ the world's
母 'mu 605, mother.
吾 ,wu 1060, I
不 ,pu 719, not
知 ,chi 53, know
其 ,ch'i 342, its
名 ,ming 600, name.
字 tsz" 1032, (tzŭ) I characterise
之 ,chi 53, (tzŭ) it
曰 yueh, 1130, [and] call [it]
道 tao' 767, Reason.

III.

強 ,ch'iang 366, Constrained

(Chapter 25.)

為 ˌwéi 1047, to make
名 ˌming 600, a name
之 ˌchi 53, (tzŭ) for it
曰 yueh, 1130 [I] call [it]
大 ta' 839, the great.
大 ta' 839, The great
曰 yueh, 1130, I call
逝 shi' 764, the evasive.
逝 shi' 764, The evasive
曰 yueh, 1130, I call
遠 'yuen 1137, the far.
遠 'yuen 1137, The far
曰 yueh, 1130, I call
反 ˌfan 126, the reverting.

IV.

故 ku' 434, For [it is said]
道 tao' 867, Reason
大 ta' 839, [is] great.
天 ˌt'ien 897, Heaven
大 ta' 839, [is] great.
地 ti'' 879, Earth
大 ta' 839, [is] great.
王 ˌwang 1043, Royalty
亦 yih, 1093, (yeh) [is] also

大 ta' 839, great.
域 yuh, 1141, (yü) ⎫
中 ˌchung 105, (tsung) ⎬ In the world
有 'yiu 1113, there are
四 shih, 708, (ssü) four
大 ta' 839, greatnesses,
而 ˌ'rh 719, (err) and
王 ˌwang 1043, royalty
居 ˌchü 437, dwells
其 ch'i 342, among them
一 yih, 1095, as one
焉 ˌyen 1082, there.

v.

人 ˌjăn 286, (jen) Man
法 ˌfa 123, follows
地 ti'' 879, earth.
地 ti'' 879, Earth
法 ˌfa 123, follows
天 ˌt'ien 897, heaven.
天 ˌt'ien 897, Heaven
法 ˌfa 123, follows
道 tao' 867, reason.
道 tao' 867, Reason
法 ˌfa 123, follows

(Chapter 25.)

自 *tsz"* 1031, (*tzŭ*) the self
然 *jan* 285, like.

第 '*ti* 879,
二 '*rh*' 721,
十 *shih*, 768, } Chapter 26.
六 *luh*, 562,
章 *chang* 22,

重 *chung'* 108, Dignity's
德 *teh*, 871, virtue.

I.

重 *chung'* 108, (*tsung*) The
爲 heavy
　 wéi 1047, is
輕 *ch'ing* 407, of the light
根 *kăn* 317, (*ken*) the root.
靜 *tsing'* 994, (*ching*) The
爲 quiet
　 wéi 1047, is
躁 *tsao'* 954, of the moving
君 *chiün* 418, the master.

II.

是 *shi* 762, (*ssŭ*) } Therefore
以 '*i* 278,
聖 *shăng'* 773, (*sheng*) the
　 holy
人 *jăn* 286, (*jen*) man

終 *chung* 106, [in his] all
日 *jeh*, 293, (*jih*) day
行 *hing* 207, (*hsing*) walks
不 *pu* 717, not
離 *li* 515, departs from
輜 *tsz'* 1030, (*tzŭ*) the baggage
　 waggon,
重 *chung'* 108, (*tsung*) the
　 weighty.

III.

雖 *sui* 826, Though
有 *yiu* 1113, he have
榮 *yung* 1146, magnificent
觀 *kwan* 474, sights,
燕 *yen'* 1090, he calmly
處 '*ch'u* 94, sits
超 '*ch'ao* 36, [in an] unconcerned
然 *jăn* 285, manner.

IV.

奈 *nai"* 613, } How [is it that]
何 *ho* 215,
萬 *wan'* 1040, the ten thousand
乘 *shăng* 772, (*cheng*) chariots
之 *chi* 53, (*tsŭ*) of,
主 '*chu* 87, the master
而 '*rh* 719, (*err*) yet

TRANSLITERATION.

以 ,'i 278, as to
身 ,shăn 735, (shen) his person
輕 ,ch'ing 407, is too light for
天 ,t'ien 897, } the
下 hia' 183, (hsia) } empire,
輕 ,ch'ing 407, being too light,
則 tsch, 956, then will
失 shih, 769, he lose
臣 ,ch'ăn 20, (chen) his vassals;
躁 tsao' 954, being too restless,
則 tsch, 956, then will
失 shih, 769, he lose
君 ,chiün 418, mastership [the throne].

第 ti" 879,
二 ,'rh' 721,
十 shih, 768,   } Chapter 27.
七 ts'ih, 987,
章 ,chang 22,

巧 'k'iao 374, Skill's
用 yung' 1149, function.

I.

善 shan' 752, Good
行 ,hing 207, (hsing) walkers

無 ,wu 1059, have no
轍 ch'eh 42, rut [and]
迹 tsih, 985 (chi') track.
善 shan' 752, Good
言 ,yen 1083, speakers
無 ,wu 1059, have no
瑕 ,hia 183, (hsia) blemish
謫 tsch, 959, [and] error.
善 shan' 752, Good
計 chi' 338, counters
無 ,wu 1059, have no
籌 ,ch'eu 51, (chou) counting
策 ts'ch, 960, bamboo slips.
善 shan' 752, Good
閉 pi' 676, lockers
無 ,wu 1059, have no
關 ,kwan 472, bolts [and]
鍵 chien' 386, keys,
而 ',rh 719, (erh) and
不 ,pu 717, not
可 ,k'o 425, one can
開 ,k'ai 308, open [their locks].
善 shan' 752, Good
結 chieh, 376, binders

(Chapters 26–27.)

無 *wu* 1059, have no
繩 *shăng* 772, (*sheng*) rope [and]
約 *yoh*, 1117, (*yüeh*) string,
而 *'rh* 719, (*crr*) and
不 *pu* 1059, not
可 *'k'o* 425, one can
解 *'chie* 359, loosen [their knots].

II.

是 *shi'* 762, (*ssŭ*)
以 *'i* 278, } Therefore
聖 *shăng'* 773, (*sheng*) the holy
人 *jăn* 286, (*jen*) man
常 *chang* 740, always
善 *shan'* 752, in goodness
救 *chiu'* 415, saves
人 *jăn* 286 (*jen*) men;
故 *ku'* 434, for
無 *wu* 1059, there is no
棄 *ch'i'* 349, outcast
人 *jăn* 286 (*jen*) man.
常 *chang* 740, Always
善 *shan'* 752, in goodness
救 *chiu'* 415, he saves
物 *wuh*, 1065, things,

故 *ku'* 434, for
無 *wu* 1059, there is no
棄 *ch'i'* 349, outcast
物 *wuh*, 1065, thing.
是 *shi'* 762, (*ssŭ*) This
謂 *wéi'* 1054, is called
襲 *sih*, 805, (*hsi*) concealed
明 *ming* 599, enlightenment.

III.

故 *ku'* 434, Therefore
善 *shan'* 752, the good
人 *jăn* 286, (*jen*) man,
者 *'ché* 38, the one,
不 *pu* 717, the not-
善 *shan'* 752, good
人 *jăn* 286, (*jen*) man
之 *chi* 53, (*tzŭ*) of,
師 *shi* 758, (*ssŭ*) is the instructor.
不 *pu* 717, The not-
善 *shan'* 752, good
人 *jăn* 286, (*jen*) man,
者 *'ché* 38, the one,
善 *shan'* 752, the good
人 *jăn* 286, (*jen*) man

(Chapter 27.)

TRANSLITERATION.

之 ,chi 53, (tzŭ) of,
資 ,tsz' 1027 (t'zŭ) is the capital.
不 ,pu 717, [Who] not
貴 kwéi' 484, esteems
其 ,ch'i 342, his
師 ,shi 758, (ssŭ) instructor.
不 ,pu 717 [Who] not
愛 ngai' 619, loves
其 ,ch'i 342, his
資 ,tsz' 1027, (t'zŭ) capital,
雖 ,sui 826, though
智 chi' 58, intelligent,
大 ta' 839, greatly
迷 ,mi 589, is bewildered.
是 shi' 762, (ssŭ) This
謂 wéi' 1054, is called
要 yao' 1077, significant
妙 miao' 592, spirituality.

第 ti" 879,
二 'rh' 721,
十 shih, 768   } Chapter 28.
八 pah, 647,
章 ,chang 22,

反 ,fan 126, Returning to
樸 p'oh 710, simplicity.

I.

知 ,chi 53 [Who] knows
其 ,chi 342, his
雄 ,hiung 214, (hsiung) manhood,
守 'sheu 775, (shou) [and] keeps
其 ,ch'i 342, his
雌 ,ts'z' 1033, (tzŭ) womanhood,
爲 ,wéi 1047, becomes
天 ,t'ien 897,   } the
下 hia' 183, (hsia) } world's
谿 ,k'i 341, (hsi) valley.
爲 ,wéi 1047, Being
天 ,t'ien 897,   } the
下 hia' 183, (hsia) } world's
谿 ,k'i 341, (hsi) valley,
常 ,chang 740, the eternal
德 teh, 871, (tê) virtue
不 ,pu 717, not
離 ,li 515, departs.
復 ,fu 151, He reverts
歸 kwéi, 480, [and] returns
于 ,yü 1118, to [the state of]

(Chapters 27-28.)

嬰 ‚ying 1105 } an infant
兒 ‚'rh 720, (err) } child.

無 ‚wu 1059, The un-
極 ‚chi 393, limited.

II.

知 ‚chi 53, [Who] knows
其 ‚ch'i 342, his
白 ‚pai 706, whiteness,
守 'sheu 755, (shou) [and] keeps
其 ‚ch'i 342, his
黑 ‚hei 218, blackness,
爲 ‚wéi 1047, becomes
天 ‚t'ien 897, } the world's
下 hia' 183, (hsia) }
式 shih, 767, model.
爲 ‚wéi 1047, Being
天 ‚t'ien 897, } the world's
下 hia' 183, (hsia) }
式 shih, 767, model,
常 ‚chang 740, the eternal
德 teh, 871, (tê) virtue
不 ‚fu 717, not
忒 t'ch, 872, (tê) is faulty.
復 ‚fu 151, He reverts
歸 kwéi, 480, [and] returns
于 ‚yü 1118, to

III.

知 ‚chi 53, [Who] knows
其 ‚ch'i 342, his
榮 ‚yung 1146, glory,
守 'sheu 755, (shou) [and] keeps
其 ‚ch'i 342, his
辱 ju' 299, shame,
爲 ‚wéi 1047, becomes
天 ‚t'ien 897, } the world's
下 hia' 183, (hsia) }
谷 'ku 453, vale.
爲 ‚wéi 1047, Being
天 ‚t'ien 897, } the world's
下 hia' 183, (hsia) }
谷 'hu 453, vale,
常 ‚chang 740 the eternal
德 teh, 871, (tê) virtue
乃 'nai 612, then
足 ‚tsu 1014, suffices.
復 ‚fu 151, He reverts
歸 kwéi, 480, [and] returns
于 ‚yü 1118, to

(Chapter 28.)

TRANSLITERATION.

朴 ,*t'u* 710, simplicity.

IV.

朴 ,*t'u* 710, Simplicity
散 '*san* 724, being scattered,
則 *tsch*, 956, (*tsê*) he then will
爲 ,*wéi* 1047, make
器 *ch'i'* 349, vessels [of usefulness].
聖 *shăng'* 773, (*sheng*) The holy
人 ,*jăn* 286, (*jen*) man
用 *yung'* 1149, utilising
之 ,*chi* 53, (*tzŭ*) them,
則 *tsch*, 956, (*tsê*) then will
爲 ,*wéi* 1047, make [them]
官 ,*kwan* 472, officers
長 ,*ch'ang* 27, [and] chiefs.
故 *ku'* 434, Therefore
大 *ta'* 839, a great
制 *chi'* 59, (*chih*) administration
不 *pu* 717, does not
割 ,*ko* 428, injure [cut, hurt].

第 *ti"* 879,
二 ,*'rh'* 721
十 *shih*, 768, } Chapter 29
九 ,*'kiu* 413,
章 ,*chang* 22,

無 ,*wu* 1059, Not-
爲 ,*wéi* 1047, doing.

I.

將 ,*tsiang* 967, (*chiang*) [One who] is going to
欲 *yü'* 1139, desire
取 ,*'ts'ü* 1010, (*chü*) to take
天 *t'ien* 897, } the empire
下 *hia'* 183, (*hsia*)
而 ,*'rh* 719, (*err*) and
爲 ,*wéi* 1047, to make
之 ,*chi* 53, (*tzŭ*) it.
吾 ,*wu* 1060, I
見 *chien'* 385, see
其 ,*ch'i* 342, him
不 ,*pu* 717, not.
得 *teh*, 872, (*tê*) obtain it;
已 '*i* 278, that is all.
天 ,*t'ien* 897, } The empire
下 *hia'* 183, (*hsia*)

(Chapters 28–29.)

神 ,shăn 737, (shen) [is] a divine
器 ch'i' 349, vessel.
不 ,pu 717, Not
可 'k'o 425, can it be
爲 ,wéi 1047, made,
也 'yĕ 1079, indeed.
爲 ,wéi 1047, [Who] makes it,
者 'chĕ 38, the one,
敗 pai' 648, mars
之 ,chi 53, (tzŭ) it.

II.

執 chih, 67, [Who] takes hold of it,
者 'chĕ 38, the one
失 shih, 769, loses
之 ,chi 53, (tzŭ) it.
故 hu' 434, Therefore
物 wuh, 1065, of beings
或 hwo' 259, some
行 ,hing 207, (hsing) go on,
或 hwo' 1065, others
隨 ,sui 826, follow,
或 hwo' 1065, some
呴 hü' 229, (hsü) breathe warmly,
或 hwo' 1065, others

吹 ,ch'ui 101, (tsui) breathe coldly,
或 hwo' 1065, some
強 ,ch'iang 366, [are] strong
或 hwo' 1065, others
羸 ,léi 511, [are] weak,
或 hwo' 1065, some
載 'tsai 941, succeed [are filled with a cargo]
或 hwo' 1065, others
隳 ,hwui 261, succumb [come out vanquished].

III.

是 shi" 762, (ssŭ) ⎫
以 'i 278,   ⎬ Therefore
                  ⎭
聖 shăng' 773, (sheng) the holy
人 ,jăn 286, (jen) man
去 ch'ü 445, abandons
甚 shăn 738, (shĕn) pleasures
去 'ch'ü 445, abandons
奢 shăn' 73, (shen) extravagance,
去 'ch'ü 445, abandons
泰 t'ai' 848, indulgence.

第 ti' 879, ⎫
三 ,săn 723, ⎬ Chapter 30.
十 shih 768, ⎪
章 ,chang 22, ⎭

(Chapters 29-30.)

TRANSLITERATION. 193

儉 ‚kien' 387, Be stingy
武 'wu 1061, with wars.

I.

以 ‚'i 278, [Who] with
道 tao' 867, reason
佐 tso' 1002, assists
人 ‚jăn 286, (jen) the people's
主 'chu 87, master,
者 'ché 94, the one,
不 ‚pu 717, not
以 ‚'i 278, with
兵 ‚ping 698, arms
強 ‚ch'iang 366, strengthens
天 ‚t'ien 897, } the
下 hia' 183, (hsia) } empire.
其 ‚ch'i 342, His
事 shi'' 764, (ssŭ) business methods
好 'hao 171, render good [make welcome]
還 ‚hwan 244, repayment [requital].

II.

師 ‚shi 758, (ssŭ) }
之 ‚chi 53, (tzu) } An army's
所 su' 817, (shuo) place [which]
處 'ch'u 94, it occupies,
荊 ‚ching 403, briars

棘 ‚chi 392, [and] thorns
生 ‚shăng 742, (sheng) grow
焉 ‚yen 1082, there.
大 ta' 839, A great
軍 ‚chiün 419, }
之 ‚chi 53, (tzŭ) } war's
後 heu' 175, (hou) sequence [after]
必 pi' 692, surely
有 'yiu 1113, are
凶 ‚hiung 213 (hsiung) bad
年 ‚nien 634, harvests.
善 shen' 752, (shan) The good
者 'ché 38, one
果 'kwo 489, [is] resolute
而 ‚'rh 719, (err) and
已 ‚'i 278, that is all [then he stops].
不 ‚pu 717, Not
敢 'kan 312, dares he
以 ‚'i 278, thereby
取 ts'ü 1010, (ch'ü) to take
強 ‚ch'iang 366, by force.
果 'kwo 489, One should be resolute,
而 ‚'rh 719, (err) and
勿 wuh, 1065, (wu) not

(Chapter 30.)

矜 ,ching 405, boasting;
果 'kwo 489, resolute,
而 ,'rh 719, (err) and
勿 wuh, 1065, (wu) not
伐 fa, 122, haughty [bragging]
果 'kwo 489, resolute,
而 ,'rh 719, (err) but
無 wuh, 1665, (wu) not
驕 ,chiao 368, arrogant;
果 'kwo 489, resolute,
而 ,'rh 719, (err) but [only when]
不 ,pu 717, not
得 teh, 872, (tĕ) he can
已 'i 278, avoid [it];
果 'kwo 489, resolute,
而 ,'rh 719 (err) but
勿 wuh, 1065, not
強 ,ch'iang 366, violent.

III.

物 wuh, 1065, (wu) Things
壯 chwang' 114, flourish
則 tsch, 956, [and] then
老 'lao 508, they decay.
是 shi' 762, (ssŭ) This

謂 wei' 1054, is called
不 ,pu 717, un-
道 tao' 867, reason.
不 ,pu 717, Un-
道 tao' 867, reason
早 'tsao 953, soon
已 'i 278, ends.

第 ti' 879,
三 ,san 723,
十 shih, 768, } Chapter 31
一 yih, 1095,
章 ,chang 22,

偃 'yen 1086, Quelling
武 'wu 1061, war.

I.

夫 ,fu 142, Even
佳 ,chia 351, excellent
兵 ,ping 698, arms [are]
不 ,pu 717, an un-
祥 ,siang 792, (hsiang) bliss
之 ,chi 53, (tzŭ) among
器 ch'i' 349, tools.

物 ,wuh, 1065, (wu) [all] beings
或 ,hwo, 259, [are] likely
惡 ,wu' 1063, to detest
之 ,chi 53, (tzŭ) them.
故 ,ku' 434, Therefore
有 'yiu 1113, [who] has
道 ,tao' 867, reason,
者 'ché 38, the one,
不 ,pu 717, not
處 'chu 94, dwells there [re-
lies on them].

II.

君 ,chiün 418, The masterly
子 'tsz' 1030, (tzŭ) philosopher
居 ,chü 437, while at home,
則 ,tseh, 956, then
貴 ,kwéi 484, he esteems
左 'tso 1002, the left.
用 ,yung' 1149, While using
兵 ,ping 698, arms
則 ,tseh, 956, then
貴 ,kwéi' 484, he esteems
右 ,yiu' 1115, the right.
兵 ,ping 698, ⎫
者 'ché 38,   ⎬ Arms [are]
            ⎭

不 ,pu 717, an un-
祥 ,siang 792, (hsiang) bliss
之 ,chi 53, (tzŭ) among
器 ,ch'i' 349, tools,
非 ,féi 136, [and] not
君 ,chiün 418, a masterly
子 'tsz' 1030, (tzŭ) man
之 ,chi 53, (tzŭ) his
器 ,ch'i' 349, tools.
不 ,pu 717, [When] not
得 ,teh, 872, (té) he obtains
已 'i 278, avoiding [it]
而 ',rh 719, (erh) and [then
only]
用 ,yung' 1149, he uses
之 ,chi 53, (tzŭ) them.

III.

恬 ,t'ien 899, Peace
淡 ,tan' 853, [and] quietude
為 ,wéi 1047, he makes
[holds]
上 'shang 741, high.
勝 ,shing 771, (sheng) Victorious [he is]
而 ',rh 719, (erh) but
不 ,pu 717, not
美 'méi 586, enjoys [it];
而 ',rh 719, (erh) and

(Chapter 31.)

美 'méi 586, [who] enjoys
之 ‚chi̱ 53, (tzŭ) it [a victory]
者 chê 38, the one
是 shi' 762, (ssŭ) this [means]
樂 lö' 554, [he] likes
殺 shah, 731, (sah) to kill
人 jăn 286, (jen) people.
夫 fu 142, Now
樂 lö' 554, [when] one likes
殺 shah, 731, (sah) to kill
人 jăn 286, (jen) people,
者 'chê 38, the one,
則 tsch, 956, then he will
不 ‚pu 717, not
可 'k'o 425, be able
以 'i 278, thereby
得 teh, 872, (tĕ) to obtain
志 chi' 61, his wishes
于 ‚yü 1118, in
天 t'ien 897, } the
下 hia' 183, (hsia) } empire
矣 'i 279, [a final particle]

IV.

吉 ‚chi 391, In propitious
事 shi' 764, (ssŭ) affairs
尚 shang' 741, we honor
左 'tso 1002, the left.
凶 ‚hiung 213, (hsiung) In unpropitious
事 shi' 764, (ssŭ) affairs
尚 shang' 741, we honor
右 yiu' 1115, the right.
偏 ‚p'ien 689, The assistant
將 ‚tsiang 967, (chiang) army
軍 ‚chiün 419, leader
居 ‚chü 437, sits
左 'tso 1002, to the left.
上 'shang 741, The superior
將 ‚tsiang 967, (chiang) } army
軍 ‚chiün 419, } leader
居 ‚chü 437, sits
右 yiu' 1115, to the right.
言 ‚yen 1083, [This] means [that]
居 ‚chü 437, occupying
上 'shang 741, a superior
勢 shi' 765, position
則 tsch, 956, then
以 'i 278, according to
喪 ‚sang 725, the funeral

(Chapter 31.)

TRANSLITERATION. 197

禮 ‚'li 520, ceremony
處 ‚'ch'u 94, is managed
之 ‚chi 53, (tzŭ) it.
殺 shah, 731, (sah) The killing
人 ‚jăn 286, (jen) of people
衆 chung, 108, (tsung) multitudes,
多 ‚'to 909, many
以 ‚'i 278, with
悲 ‚pei 668, sorrow
哀 ‚ngai 619, [and] lamentations
泣 ch'i' 396, [we ought to] weep
之 ‚chi 53 (tzŭ) for them.
戰 chan' 45, [When] In war
勝 ‚shăng 771, (sheng) a victor
以 'i 278, according to
喪 ‚sang 725, the funeral
禮 ‚'li 520, ceremony
處 ‚ch'u 94, must be treated
之 ‚chi 53, (tzŭ) he.

第 ti" 879, ⎫
三 ‚san 723   ⎪
十 shih, 768, ⎬ Chapter 32.
二 ‚'rh 721   ⎪
章 ‚chang 22, ⎭

聖 shing' 773, Of holiness
德 teh, 871, the virtue.

1.

道 tao' 867, Reason,
常 ‚chang 740, in its eternal aspect,
無 ‚wu 1057, is un-
名 ‚ming 600, nameable.
朴 ‚p'u 710, Simplicity
雖 ‚sui 826, (shui) though
小 'siao 795, (shiao) insignificant,
天 ‚t'ien 897, ⎫
下 hia' 183, (hsia) ⎬ the world
不 ‚pu 717, not
敢 'kan 312, dares to
臣 ‚ch'ăn 20, (ch'en) subject [it].
侯 ‚heu 174, (hou) Princes
王 ‚wang 1043, [and] kings
若 ioh, 296, (jŏ) if
能 ‚năng 616, (neng) they can
守 'sheu 755, (shou) keep it,
萬 wăn' 1040, the ten thousand
物 wuh, 1065, (wu) things
將 ‚tsiang 967, (chiang) are going
自 tsz" 1031, (tzŭ) of themselves
賓 ‚pin 695, to pay homage.

(Chapter 31-32.)

天 ｢t'ien 897, Heaven
地 ti' 879, [and] earth
相 ｢siang 790, (hsiang) mutually
合 ｢hö 217, combined,
以 ｢i 278, thereby
降 chiang' 364, drop
甘 ｢kan 310, sweet
露 lu' 557, dew.
民 ⁻min 597, The people
莫 mo' 603, will have none
之 ｢chi 53, (tzŭ) as their
令 ling' 546, commanders,
而 ｢'rh 719 (err) but
自 tsz" 1031, (tzŭ) of themselves
均 ｢chün 418, they will be righteous.

II.

始 'shi 761, (ssŭ) [When] at first
制 chi' 59, creating order
有 'yiu 1113, } [it becomes] the
名 ｢ming 600, } nameable.
名 ｢ming 600, [When] the nameable
亦 yi' 1093, also
既 chi' 339, already
有 'yiu 1113, exists

夫 ｢fu 142, then
亦 yi' 1093, in turn
將 ｢tsiang 967, (chiang) one is going
知 ｢chi 53, (tzŭ) to know
止 'chi 56, where to stop.
知 ｢chi 53, (tzŭ) Knowing
止 'chi 56, where to stop
所 su' 817, (shuo) } is the reason why
以 ｢i 278,
不 ｢pu 717, there is no
殆 tai' 846, danger.

III.

譬 p'i' 681, To illustrate:
道 tao' 867,
之 ｢chi 53, (tzŭ) } Reason's
在 tsai' 941, being
天 ｢t'ien 897, } in the
下 hia' 183, (hsia) } universe
猶 ｢yiu 1112, resembles
川 ｢chw'an 119, rivers
谷 ｢ku, 453, [and] streams
之 ｢chi 53, (tzŭ) [in their relation]
於 ｢yü 1118, to
江 ｢chiang 362, great rivers

(Chapter 32.)

TRANSLITERATION.

海 ʻ*hai* 160, [and] the oceans,
也 ʻ*yé* 1079, indeed.

第 *ti*ʼ 879,
三 ₍*san* 723,
十 *shih*, 768, } Chapter 33.
三 ₍*san* 723,
章 ₍*chang* 22,

辨 *pien*ʼ 688, To discriminate
德 *teh*, 871, virtue.

I.

知 ₍*chi* 53, [Who] knows
人 ₍*jăn* 286, (*jen*) others
者 ʻ*ché* 38, the one,
智 *chi*ʼ 58, is intelligent.
自 *tsz*ʼʼ 1031, (*tzŭ*) Himself
知 ₍*chi* 53, [who] knows
者 ʻ*ché* 38, the one
明 ₍*ming* 599, is enlightened.
勝 ₍*shăng* 771, (*sheng*) [Who] conquers
人 ₍*jăn* 286, (*jen*) others
者 ʻ*ché* 38, the one.
有 ʼ*yiu* 1113, has
力 *li*ʼʼ 536, force

自 *tsz*ʼʼ 1031, (*tzŭ*) Himself
勝 ₍*shăng* 771, (*sheng*) [who] conquers
者 ʻ*ché* 38, the one
強 ₍*chʻiang* 366, is mighty.
知 ₍*chi* 53, [Who] knows
足 ₍*tsu* 1014, contentment
者 ʻ*ché* 38, the one
富 *fu*ʼ 148, is rich.

II.

強 ₍*chʻiang* 366, [Who] dares
行 ₍*hing* 207, (*hsing*) to act [move]
者 ʻ*ché* 38, the one
有 ʼ*yiu* 1113, has
志 *chi*ʼ 61, will.
不 ₍*pu* 717, Not
失 *shih*, 769, [who] loses
其 ₍*chʻi* 342, his
所 *su*ʼ 817, (*shuo*) position
者 ʻ*ché* 38, the one,
久 ʼ*chiu* 413, lasts.

III.

死 ʼ*sz*ʼ 836, (*ssu*) [Who] dies
而 ₍*rh* 719 (*err*) yet
不 ₍*pu* 717, not
亡 ₍*wang* 1044, perishes

者 'ché 38, the one
壽 sheu' 757, (shou) is long lived [immortal].

第 ti" 879,
三 ,san 723,
十 shih, 768, } Chapter 34.
四 sz" 836,
章 ,chang 22,

任 jăn 289, Trust
成 ,ch'ing 77, in its perfection.

I.

大 ta' 839, The great
道 tao' 867 reason
汎 fan' 128, is all-pervading
兮 ,hi 179, (hsi) Oh!
其 ,ch'i 342, It
可 'k'o 425, can [be]
左 ,tso 1002, on the left
右 yiu' 1115, [and] on the right
萬 wán' 1040, the ten thousand
物 wuh, 1065, (wu) things
恃 shi" 761, (ssŭ) relying on
之 ,chi 53, (tzŭ) it,
以 'i 278, thereby

生 ,shăng 742, (sheng) living,
而 ,'rh 719, (err) yet
不 ,pu 717, not
辭 ,ts'z' 1033, (tzŭ) it refuses [them].

II.

功 ,kung 460, Merit
成 ,ch'ăng 77, (cheng) it acquires,
不 ,pu 717, [but] not
名 ,ming 600, the name
有 'yiu 1113, [it] takes.
愛 ngai" 619, It loves
養 'yang 1072, [and] nourishes
萬 wán' 1040, the ten thousand
物 wuh, 1065, (wu) things,
而 ,'rh 719, (err) yet
不 ,pu 717, not
爲 ,wei 1047, act as
主 'chu 87, [their] owner.
常 ,chang 740, Always
無 ,wu 1059, it has no
欲 yü, 1139, desires.
可 'k'o 425, It can be
名 ,ming 600, named
于 ,yü 1118, with

小 'siao 795, (hsiao) the small.
萬 wán' 1040, The ten thousand
物 wuh, 1065, (wu) things
歸 kwéi, 480, return
焉 ,yen 1082, thereto.
而 ,rh 719, (err) Yet
不 ,pu 717, not
爲 ,wéi 1047, it acts as
主 'chu 87, [their] owner
可 'k'o 425, It can be
名 ,ming 600, named
爲 ,wéi 1047, as
大 ta' 839, the great.

III.

是 shï 762, (ssŭ) ⎫ Therefore
以 'i 278,   ⎭
聖 shăng' 773, (sheng) the holy
人 ,jăn 286, (jen) man
終 ,chung 106, (tsung) to the end
不 ,pu 717, not
爲 ,wéi 1047, acts as
大 ta' 839, the great.
故 ku' 434, Therefore
能 ,năng 616, (neng) he can

成 chăng 77, (cheng) accomplish
其 ,chi 342, his
大 ta' 839. greatness.

第 ti'' 879,
三 ,san 723,
十 shih, 768, ⎫ Chapter 35
五 'wu 1060, ⎭
章 ,chang 22,

仁 ,jăn 287. Benevolence
德 teh, 871, virtue.

I.

執 chih, 67, [Who] takes hold of
大 ta' 839, the great
象 siang' 792, (hsiang) form
天 ,t'ien 897, ⎫ the world
下 hia' 183, (hsia) ⎭
往 'wang 1044, goes [to him].
往 'waag 1044, [It] goes
而 ',rh 719, (err) and
不 ,pu 717, not
害 hai' 161, is injured.
安 ,ngan 620, Contentment
平 ,p'ing 701, peace,

(Chapters 34-35.)

II.

泰 t'ai' 848, rest [is there].

樂 lö' 554, Music
與 ,yü 1125, and
餌 "rh 720, (err) dainties
過 ,k'wo 490, the passing
客 k'ö' 429, people
止 'chi 56, (tzŭ) make stop.
道 tao' 867, ⎫
之 ,chi 53, (tzŭ) ⎬ Reason's
出 ch'u 98, going out of
口 k'eu 331, (kou), the mouth
淡 tan' 853, [how] is insipid.
乎 ,hu 224, Oh!
其 ,ch'i 342, it
無 ,wu 1059, has no
味 wéi 1053, taste.
視 shi' 763, (ssŭ) [When] looked at
之 ,chi 53, (tzŭ) it
不 ,pu 717, not
足 ,tsu 1014, is enough
見 chien' 385, to be precious.
聽 ,t'ing 906, [When] listened
之 ,chi 53, (tzŭ) to it,
不 ,pu 717, not
足 ,tsu 1014, is enough to
聞 ,wăn 1041, (wen) be heard
用 yung' 1149, The use
之 ,chi 53, (tzŭ) of it
不 ,pu 717, not
可 'k'o 425, can be
既 chi' 339, exhausted

第 ti" 879, ⎫
三 ,san 723, ⎪
十 shih, 768, ⎬ Chapter 36
六 luh, 562, ⎪
章 ,chang 22, ⎭

微 ,wéi 1050, The secret's
明 ,ming 599, explanation.

I.

將 ,tsiang 967, (chiang) [That which] is going
欲 yü' 1137, to desire [viz., to have the tendency]
噏 hih, 203, (hsi) to contract
之 ,chi 53, (tzŭ) itself,
必 pi' 692, surely
固 ku' 435, assuredly
張 ,chang 22, has extended

(Chapters 35–36.)

TRANSLITERATION. 203

之 ‚chi 53, (tzŭ) itself.
將 ‚tsiang 967, (chiang) [That which] is going
欲 yü' 1137, to desire
弱 joh, 295, (jŏ) to weaken
之 ‚chi 53 (tzŭ) itself,
必 pi' 692, surely
固 ku' 435, assuredly
強 ‚ch'iang 366, [has] strengthened
之 ‚chi 53, (tzŭ) itself.
將 ‚tsiang 967, (chiang) [That which] is going
欲 yü' 1137, to desire
廢 fei' 138, to ruin
之 ‚chi 53, (tzŭ) itself,
必 pi' 692, surely
固 ku' 435, assuredly
興 hing' 205, (hsing) has raised
之 ‚chi 53, (tzŭ) itself.
將 ‚tsiang 967, (chiang) [That which] is going
欲 yü' 1137, to intend
奪 to 913, to deprive
之 ‚chi 53, (tzŭ) itself.
必 pi' 692, surely
固 ku' 435, assuredly
與 'yü 1125, [it has] endowed

(Chapter 36.)

之 ‚chi 53, (tzŭ) itself.

II.

是 shi' 762, (ssŭ) This
謂 wéi' 1054, is called
微 ‚wéi 1050, the secret's
明 ‚ming 599, explanation.
柔 ‚jeu 294, (jou) The tender
弱 joh, 295, (jŏ) [and] the weak
勝 ‚shăng 771, (sheng) conquer
剛 ‚kang 318, the stiff
強 ‚ch'iang 366, [and] the strong.

III.

魚 ‚yü 1119, [As] the fish
不 ‚pu 717, not
可 'k'o 425, should
脫 t'o 914, escape
于 ‚yü 1118, from
淵 ‚yuen, 1131 the deep,
國 kwo 491, [so] the empire's
之 ‚chi 53, (tzŭ)
利 li' 521, sharp
器 ch'i' 349, tools
不 ‚pu 717, not
可 k'o' 425, should

以 ,i 278, thereby
示 'shi' 763, (ssŭ) be shown
人。 ,jŭn 286, (jen) to the people.

第 ,ti' 879,
三 ,san 723,
十 shih, 768,   } Chapter 37.
七 ts'ih, 987,
章 chang 22,

爲 ,wéi 1047, Administering
政 ching' 76, the government.

I

道 tao' 867, Reason
常 ,chang 740, is always
無 ,wu 1059, non-
爲 ,wéi 1047, action,
而 ',rh 719, (err) and
無 ,wu 1059, nothing
不 ,pu 717, [remains] un-
爲。 ,wéi 1047, done.
侯 ,heu 174, (hou) Princes
王 ,wang 1043, [and] kings
若 ,joh, 296, (jŏ) if
能 ,năng 616, (neng) they can

守 'sheu 755, (shou) keep [it]
萬 wăn' 1040, the ten thousand
物 wuh, 1065, (wu) things
將 ,tsiang 967, (chiang) will
自 tsz" 1031, (tzŭ) of themselves
化。 hwa' 240, reform.
化 hwa' 240, [If] reformed.
而 ',rh 719, (err) yet
欲 yü 1137, they may desire
作 tso' 1005, to stir.
吾 ,wu 1060, I
將 ,tsiang 967, (chiang) will
鎭 chăn' 17, pacify
之 ,chi 53, (tzŭ) them
以 ,i 278, by
無 ,wu 1059, the un-
名 ,ming 600, nameable
之 ,chi 53, (tzŭ) its
朴 ,p'u 710, simplicity.

II.

無 ,wu 1059, The un-
名 ,ming 600, nameable
之 ,chi 53, its
朴 ,p'u 710, simplicity

(Chapters 36–37.)

亦 *yi*, 1093, in turn
將 ₍tsiang 967, (*chiang*) will [afford]
不 ₍pu 717, not
欲 *yü*' 1137, to desire [to lust].
不 ₍pu 717, [There being] no
欲 *yü*' 1137, desire,
以 *i* 278, thereby
靜 *tsing*' 994, (*ching*) there is rest.
天 ₍t'ien 897, [Then] the
下 *hia*' 183, (*hsia*) world
將 ₍tsiang 967, (*chiang*) will
自 *tsz*'' 1031, (*tzŭ*) be self-
定 *ting*' 905, (*cheng*) enraptured.

下 *hia* 183' (*hsia*) the latter
篇 *p'ien* 690, part.

第 *ti*' 879,
三 ₍san 723,
十 *shih*, 768, } Chapter 38.
八 *pah*, 647,
章 ₍chang 22,

論 *lun*' 566, a discussion
德 *teh*, 871, of virtue.

I.

上 'shang 741, Superior
德 *teh*, 871, (*tê*) virtue
不 ₍pu 717, is un-
德 *teh*, 871, (*tê*) virtue.
是 *shi*' 762 (*ssŭ*) ⎫
以 '*i* 278, ⎭ Therefore
有 'yiu 1113, it has
德 *teh*, 871 (*tê*) virtue.
下 *hia*' 183, (*hsia*) Inferior
德 *teh*, 871 (*tê*) virtue
不 ₍pu 717, not
失 *shih*, 769, loses
德 *teh*, 871, (*tê*) virtue,
是 *shi*' 762 (*ssŭ*) ⎫
以 '*i* 278, ⎭ therefore
無 'wu 1059, it has no
德 *teh*, 871 (*tê*) virtue.
上 'shang 741, Superior
德 *teh*, 871, (*tê*) virtue
無 ₍wu 1059, is non-
爲 ₍wéi 1047, action.
而 '*rh* 719, (*err*) And
無 ₍wu 1059, it has not
以 '*i* 278, thereby

(Chapters 37-38.)

爲 ,wéi 1047, pretensions.
下 hia' 183, (hsia) Inferior
德 teh, 871, (tê) virtue
爲 ,wéi 1047, is acting
之 ,chi 53, (tzŭ) itself,
而 ',rh 719, (err) and
有 'yiu 1113, has
以 'i 278, thereby
爲 ,wéi 1047, pretensions.
上 'shang 741, Superior
仁 ,jăn 287, (jen) benevolence
爲 ,wéi 1047, is acting
之 ,chi 53, (tzŭ) itself
而 ',rh 719, (err) but
無 ,wu 1059, not
以 'i 278, thereby
爲 ,wéi 1047, pretends.

II.

上 'shang 741, Superior
義 ,i' 280, righteousness [justice]
爲 ,wéi 1047, is acting
之 ,chi 53, (tzŭ) itself
而 ',rh 719, (err) but
有 'yiu 1113, has
以 'i 278, thereby

爲 ,wéi 1047, pretensions.
上 'shang 741, Superior
禮 ,li 520, propriety
爲 ,wéi 1047, is acting
之 ,chi 53, (tzŭ) itself
而 ',rh 719, (err) but
莫 ,mo' 603, when no one
之 ,chi 53, (tzŭ) to it
應 ,ying 1106, responds.
則 ,tseh, 956, (tsê) Then
攘 ,jang 290, it stretches
臂 ,pi' 678, (pei) its arm
而 ',rh 719, (err) and
仍 ,jăng 291, (jeng) enforces
之 ,chi 53, (tzŭ) it.

III

故 ,ku' 434, Therefore
失 ,shih, 769, when one loses
道 ,tao' 867, reason
而 ',rh 719, (err) and
后 ,heu' 175 (hou) then [there is]
德 ,teh, 871, (tê) virtue.
失 ,shih, 769, One loses
德 ,teh, 871, (tê) virtue,
而 ',rh 719, (err) and

(Chapter 38.)

后 *heu'* 175, (*hou*) then [there is]
仁 ,*jăn* 287, (*jen*) benevolence.
失 *shih,* 769, One loses
仁 ,*jăn* 287, (*jen*) benevolence
而 ',*rh* 719, (*err*) and
后 *heu'* 175, (*hou*) then [there is]
義 *i'* 280, righteousness.
失 *shih,* 769, One loses
義 *i'* 280, righteousness
而 ',*rh* 719, (*err*) and
后 *heu'* 175, (*hou*) then [there is]
禮 '*li* 520, propriety.

IV.

夫 '*fu* 142, Now
禮 '*li* 520, propriety's
者 '*ché* 38, things [are]
忠 ,*chung* 106, (*tsung*) loyalty
信 *sin'* 807, (*hsin*) [and] faith
之 ,*chi* 53, (*tzŭ*) in their
薄 *po'* 705, attenuation
而 ',*rh* 719, (*err*) and
亂 *lwan'* 570, disorder
之 ,*chi* 53, (*tzŭ*) in its
首 '*sheu* 756, (*shou*) beginning;
前 ,*ts'ien* 981(*chien*) premature

(Chapter 38.)

識 *shih,* 770, knowledge
者 '*ché* 38, that [is]
道 *tao'* 867, reason
之 ,*chi* 53, (*tzŭ*) in its
華 ,*hwa* 239, [mere] flower,
而 ',*rh* 719, (*err*) and
愚 ,*yü* 1120, ignorance
之 ,*chi* 53, (*tzŭ*) in its
始 '*shi* 761, (*ssŭ*) beginning.

V.

是 *shi'* 762, (*ssŭ*) ⎫
以 '*i* 278, ⎬ Therefore
　　　　　　　　⎭
大 *ta'* 839, a great
丈 *chang'* 25, large
夫 ,*fu* 142, organiser [man of affairs]
處 '*ch'u* 94, dwells
其 ,*ch'i* 342, in its
厚 *heu'* 176 (*hou*) solidity
不 ,*pu* 717, [and] not
居 ,*chü* 437, abides
其 ,*ch'i* 342, in its
薄 *po'* 705, externality.
處 '*ch'u* 94, He dwells
其 ,*ch'i* 342, in its
實 *shih,* 769, fruit,

不 *pu* 717, not
居 *chŭ* 437, abides
其 *ch'i* 342, in its
華 *hwa* 239, flower.
故 *ku'* 434, Therefore
去 *'ch'ü* 445, he avoids
彼 *'pi* 674, the latter,
取 *'ts'ü* 1010, (*ch'ü*) and choses
此 *'ts'z'* 1034, (*tzŭ*) the former.

第 *ti'* 879,
三 *san* 723,
十 *shih*, 768,   } Chapter 39.
九 *'kiu* 413,
章 *chang* 22,

法 *fah*, 123, Law's
本 *'pĕn* 655, root.

I.

昔 *sih*, 802, (*hsi*) } Of old
之 *chi* 53, (*tzŭ*)
得 *tch*, 872, (*tĕ*) those who attained
一 *yi'* 1095, unity
者 *'chĕ* 38, the ones [are]:

II.

天 *t'ien* 897, Heaven
得 *tch*, 872, (*tĕ*) attained
一 *yi*, 1095, unity,
以 *'i* 278, thereby
清 *ts'ing* 995, (*ching*) it is clear.
地 *ti'* 879, Earth
得 *tch*, 872, (*tĕ*) attained
一 *yi*, 1095, unity,
以 *'i* 278, thereby
寧 *ning* 637, it is peaceful.
神 *shăn* 737, (*shen*) Spirit
得 *tch*, 872, (*tĕ*) attained
一 *yi*, 1095, unity,
以 *'i* 278, thereby
靈 *ling* 543, it is mental.
谷 *'ku* 453, Valleys
得 *tch*, 872, (*tĕ*) attained
一 *yi*, 1095, unity,
以 *'i* 278, thereby
盈 *ying* 1106, they are filled
萬 *wăn'* 1040, The ten thousand
物 *wuh*, 1065, (*wu*) things
得 *tch*, 872, (*tĕ*) attained
一 *yi*, 1095, unity,

(Chapters 38–39.)

以 ,'i 278, thereby
生 ,shăng 742, (sheng) they have life,
侯 ,heu 174, (hou) Princes
王 ,wang 1043, [and] kings
得 teh, 872, (tê) attained
一 yi, 1095, unity,
以 'i 278, thereby
爲 ,wéi 1047, they become
天 ,t'ien 897, } the world's
下 hia' 183, (hsia)
正 chăng' 75, (cheng) standard.
其 ,ch'i 342, That which
致 chi'' 58. produces
之 ,chi 53, (tzŭ) it
一 yi, 1095, [is] unity,
也 'yĕ 1079, indeed.

III.

天 ,t'ien 897, Heaven,
無 ,wu 1059, were it not
以 'i 278, thereby
淸 ,ts'ing 995, (ching) clear,
將 ,tsiang 967, (chiang) it would
恐 'k'ŭng 422, presumably
裂 lieh, 531, crack.

地 ti'' 879, Earth,
無 ,wu 1059, were it not
以 'i 278, thereby
寧 ,ning 637, steady,
將 ,tsiang 967, (chiang) it would
恐 'k'ŭng 422, presumably
發 ,fa 121, break down.
神 ,shăn 737, (shen) Spirits
無 ,wu 1059, are they not
以 'i 278, thereby
靈 ,ling 543, mental,
將 ,tsiang 967, (chiang) they would
恐 'k'ŭng 422, presumably
歇 hieh, 195, (hsieh) give out
谷 'ku 453, Valleys,
無 ,wu 1059, were they not
以 'i 278, thereby
盈 ,ying 1106, filled,
將 ,tsiang 967, (chiang) they would
恐 'k'ŭng 422, presumably
竭 chieh, 378, be exhausted.
萬 wăn' 1040, The ten thousand
物 wuh, 1065, (wu) things
無 ,wu 1059, were they not

(Chapter 39.)

以 'i 278, thereby
生 ˏshăng 742, (sheng) having life,
將 ˏtsiang 967, (chiang) they would
恐 'k'ŭng 422, presumably
滅 mieh˴ 593, be exterminated [as by fire].
侯 ˏheu 174, (hou) Princes
王 ˏwang 1043, [and] kings
無 ˏwu 1059, were they not
以 'i 278, thereby
正 chăng' 75, (cheng) the standard,
而 'rh 719, (err) but
貴 kwéi' 484, esteemed themselves
高 ˏkao 324, [their] high,
將 ˏtsiang 967, (chiang) they would
恐 'k'ŭng 422, presumably
蹶 ˏchŭé 446, fall.

IV.

故 ku' 434, Therefore
貴 kwéi' 484, the noble
以 'i 278, from
賤 tsien' 979, (chien) the commoners
爲 ˏwéi 1047, take
本 'păn 655, (pen) [their] root.
高 ˏkao 324, The high

(Chapter 39.)

以 'i 278, upon
下 hia' 183, (hsia) the low
爲 ˏwéi 1047, have
基 ˏchi 336, [their] foundation.
是 shi" 762, (ssŭ) ⎫
以 'i 278, ⎬ Therefore
侯 ˏheu 174, (hou) Princes ⎭
王 ˏwang 1043, [and] kings
自 tsz" 1031, (t'zŭ) themselves
謂 wéi' 1054, call
孤 ˏku 431, orphans,
寡 'kwa 467, widowers,
不 ˏpu 717, [and] un-
穀 'ku 453, worthies.
此 'ts'z' 1034, (tzŭ) [Is] this [because]
其 ˏch'i 342, they
以 'i 278, from
賤 tsien' 979, (chien) the commoners
爲 ˏwéi 1047, take
本 'păn 655, (pen) their root?
耶 ˏyé 1078, (yeh) [query]
非 féi 136, [Is it] not so?
乎 ˏhu 224, [query]

V.

故 ku' 434, Therefore

致 ,chi' 58, (chih) let
數 'shu 777, (su) go to pieces
車 ,ch'ê 39, a carriage [wheel],
無 ,wu 1059, it is no [longer]
車 ,ch'ê 39, a carriage [wheel].
不 ,pu 717, [Unities] do not
欲 yü' 1137, desire
瑑 lu' 563, to be respected,
瑑 lu' 563, [and] respected
如 ,jü 297, like
玉 yü' 1138, a gem
落 lo' 553, to be let down
落 lo 553, [and] let down
如 ,jü 297, like
石 shih, 766, a stone.

第 ti' 879,
四 sz" 836, } Chapter 40.
十 shih, 768,
章 ,chang 22,

去 'k'ü 445, Avoiding
用 yung' 1149, function.

I.

反 'fan 126, Returning
者 'chê 38, that [is]

道 tao' 867,
之 ,chi 53, (tzŭ) } reason's
動 tung' 932, motion.
弱 joh, 295, (jê') Weakness
者 'chê 38, that [is]
道 tao' 867,
之 ,chi 53, (tzŭ) } reason's
用 yung' 1149, function.

II.

天 ,t'ien 897, Heaven,
地 ti' 879, [and] earth
萬 wân' 1040, [and] the ten thousand
物 wuh, 1065, (wu) things
生 ,shăng 742, (sheng) are produced
于 ,yü 1118, from
有 'yiu 1113, existence,
有 'yiu 1113, existence
生 ,shăng 742, (sheng) is produced
于 ,yü 1118, from
無 ,wu 1059, non-existence.

LAO-TZE'S TAO-TEH-KING.

第 ,*ti'* 879,
四 ,*sz"* 836,
十 ,*shih*, 768, } Chapter 41.
一 ,*yih*, 1095,
章 ,*chang* 22,

同 ,*t'ung* 933, Identity
異 ,*i'* 281, and non-identity.

I.

上 'shang* 741, A superior
士 ,*shi'* 762, (*ssŭ*) scholar
聞 ,*wăn* 1041, (*wen*) listening to [or, hearing of]
道 ,*tao'* 867, reason.
勤 ,*ch'in* 402, he is strenuous
而 ,*rh* 719, (*err*) and
行 ,*hing* 207, (*hsing*) practises
之 ,*chi* 53, (*tzŭ*) it.
中 ,*chung* 105, (*tsung*) An average
士 ,*shi'* 762, (*ssŭ*) scholar
聞 ,*wăn* 1041, (*wen*) listening to
道 ,*tao'* 867, reason,
若 ,*joh*, 296, (*jê*) sometimes
存 ,*ts'un* 1020, keeps,
若 ,*joh*, 296, (*jê*) sometimes
亡 ,*wang* 1044, loses [it].

下 ,*hia'* 183, (*hsia*) An inferior
士 ,*shi'* 762, (*ssŭ*) scholar
聞 ,*wăn* 1041, (*wen*) listening to
道 ,*tao'* 869, reason
大 ,*ta'* 839, greatly
笑 ,*siao'* 795, (*hsiao*) ridicules
之 ,*chi* 53, (*tzŭ*) it.
不 ,*pu* 717, [If] not
笑 ,*siao'* 795, (*hsiao*) he ridiculed [it],
不 ,*pu* 717, [it will] not
足 ,*tsu* 1014, could
以 ,*'i* 278, thus
為 ,*wéi* 1047, to be regarded as
道 ,*tao'* 869, reason.

II.

故 ,*ku'* 434, Therefore
建 ,*chien'* 386, who builds
言 ,*yen* 1083, words
者 ,*'ché* 38, the one
有 ,*'yiu* 1113, says
之 ,*chi* 53, (*tzŭ*) that:
明 ,*ming* 599, Those enlightened
道 ,*tao'* 869, by reason
若 ,*joh*, 296, (*je*) resemble
昧 ,*méi'* 587, the dark.

(Chapter 41.)

進 *tsin'* 990, (*chin*) Those advanced
道 *tao'* 869, in reason
若 *joh,* 296, (*ye*) resemble
退 *t'ui'* 926, the retreating.
夷 *i* 276, The straight
道 *tao'* 869, in reason
若 *joh,* 296, (*je*) resemble
類 *léi'* 512, the rugged.
上 *'shang* 741, The high
德 *teh,* 871, (*tê*) in virtue
若 *joh,* 296, (*je*) resemble
谷 *'ku* 453, a valley.
大 *ta'* 839, The perfect
白 *po'* 706, in whiteness
若 *joh,* 296, (*je*) are likely
辱 *ju'* 299, to be put to shame.
廣 *'kwang* 478, The broadest
德 *teh,* 871, (*tê*) in virtue
若 *joh,* 296, (*je*) resemble
不 *,pu* 717, the not-
足 *,tsu* 1014, sufficient.
建 *chien'* 386, Firmly established
德 *teh,* 871, (*tê*) virtue
若 *joh,* 296, (*je*) resembles

偷 *,t'eu* 875, (*t'ou*) the remiss
質 *chih,* 68, Simple
貞 *,ching* 73, chastity
若 *joh,* 296, (*je*) resembles
渝 *,yü* 1123, the changing [the fickle].
大 *ta'* 839, The greatest
方 *,fang* 132, square
無 *,wu* 1059, has no
隅 *,yü* 1119, corner.
大 *ta'* 839 The greatest
器 *ch'i'* 349, vessel
晚 *'wan* 1038, not yet is
成 *,ch'ăng* 77, (*ch'eng*) completed.
大 *ta'* 839, The greatest
音 *,yin* 1100, sound
希 *,hi* 176, (*hsi*) is void
聲 *,shing* 771, (*sheng*) of speech [voice, harmony].
大 *ta'* 839, The greatest
象 *siang'* 792, (*hsiang*) form
無 *,wu* 1059, has no
形 *,hing* 206, (*hsing*) shape.

III.

道 *tao'* 867, Reason
隱 *'yin* 1103, when hidden,
無 *,wu* 1059, [is] not having

(Chapter 41.)

名 ,*ming* 600, name.
夫 ,*fu* 142, However
唯 ,'*wéi* 1052, it is exactly
道 ,*tao*' 867, reason [that]
善 ,*shan*' 752, can
貸 ,*tai*' 845, give
且 ,'*ts'ié* 974 (*ch'ieh*) and
成 ,*ch'ing* 77, (*cheng*) complete.

第 ,*ti*' 879,
四 ,*sz*" 836,
十 ,*shih*, 708, } Chapter 42.
二 ,'*rh*' 721,
章 ,*chang* 22,

道 ,*tao*' 867, Reason's
化 ,*hwa*' 240, transformation.

I.

道 ,*tao*' 867, Reason
生 ,*shăng* 742, (*sheng*) produces
一 ,*yi*' 1095, unity.
一 ,*yi*' 1095, Unity
生 ,*shăng* 742, (*sheng*) produces
二 ,'*rh*' 721, (*err*) duality.
二 ,'*rh*' 721, (*err*) Duality

生 ,*shăng* 742, (*sheng*) produces
三 ,*san* 723, trinity.
三 ,*san* 723, Trinity
生 ,*shăng* 742, (*sheng*) produces
萬 ,*wăn*' 1040, the ten thousand
物 ,*wuh*, 1065, (*wu*) things.
萬 ,*wăn*' 1040, The ten thousand
物 ,*wuh*, 1065, (*wu*) things
負 ,*fu*' 149, bear
陰 ,*yin* 1099, the negative principle,
而 ,'*rh* 719, (*err*) and
抱 ,*pao*' 665, embrace
陽 ,*yang* 1071, the positive principle.
冲 ,*ch'ung* 109, (*tsung*) The immaterial
氣 ,*ch'i*' 348, vitality
以 ,'*i* 278, thereby
為 ,*wéi* 1047, makes [them]
和 ,*hwo* 254, (*ho*) harmonious

II.

人 ,*jăn* 286, (*jĕn*) } The people's
之 ,*chi* 53, (*tzŭ*)
所 ,*su*' 817, (*shuo*) that which
惡 ,*wu*' 1063, is detested,
唯 ,*wéi* 1052, exactly is
孤 ,*ku* 431, [to be] orphans,

TRANSLITERATION.   215

寡 ῾*kwa* 467, widowers
不 ῾*pu* 717, [and] un-
穀 *k'u* 453, worthies.
而 ῾*rh* 719, (*err*) Yet
王 ῾*wang* 1043, kings
公 ῾*kung* 459, [and] lords
以 ῾*i* 278, thereby
爲 ῾*wéi* 1047, take [it]
稱 ῾*ch'ing* 76, (*cheng*) [for their] titles.
故 *ku'* 434, Therefore
或 *kwo'* 259, sometimes
損 ῾*sun* 829, you lose
之 ῾*chi* 53, (*tzŭ*) it
而 ῾*rh* 719, (*err*) but
益 *yi'* 1092, [there is] gain.
或 *hwo'* 259, Sometimes
益 *yi'* 1092, you gain
之 ῾*chi* 53, (*tzŭ*) it
而 ῾*rh* 719, (*err*) but
損 ῾*sun* 829, [there is] loss.

III.

人 ῾*jăn* 286, (*jen*) ⎱
之 ῾*chi* 53, (*tzŭ*)   ⎰ Of others
所 *su'* 817, (*shuo*) that which
教 *chiao'* 372, is taught.

我 ῾*ngo* 627, I
亦 *yi'* 1093, also
敎 *chiao'* 372, teach
之 ῾*chi* 53, (*tzŭ*) it.
強 ῾*ch'iang* 366, The strong
梁 ῾*liang* 525, [and] aggressive
者 ῾*ché* 38, ones
不 ῾*pu* 717, do not
得 *teh*, 872, (*tê*) obtain
其 ῾*ch'i* 342, their
死 ῾*sz'* 836, (*ssŭ*) [natural] death.
吾 ῾*wu* 1060, [But] I
將 ῾*tsiang* 967, (*chiang*) shall
以 ῾*i* 278, thereby
爲 ῾*wéi* 1047, make [viz., expound]
敎 *chiao'* 372, the doctrine's
父 *fu'* 147, father [foundation].

第 ῾*ti* 879, ⎫
四 *sz"* 836, ⎬
十 *shih*, 708, ⎬ Chapter 43
三 ῾*san* 723, ⎬
章 ῾*chang* 22, ⎭

偏 *pien'* 689, The universal
用 ῾*yung'* 1149, function.

(Chapters 42-43.)

I.

天 *t'ien* 897,
下 *hia'* 183, (*hsia*)
之 *chi* 53, (*tzŭ*) } the world's
至 *chi'* 60, (*chih*) most
柔 *jeu* 294, (*jou*) tender,
馳 *ch'i* 64, (*chih*) gallops
騁 *'ch'ing* 80, (*p'ing*) and courses over
天 *t'ien* 897,
下 *hia'* 183, (*hsia*) } the world's
之 *chi* 53, (*tzŭ*)
至 *chi'* 60, (*chih*) most
堅 *chien*, 380, hard.

II.

無 *wu* 1059, The not having [material]
有 *'yiu* 1113, existence
入 *ju'* 299, enters
無 *wu* 1059, the im-
間 *chien* 381, penetrable.

III.

吾 *wu* 1060, I
是 *shi* 762, (*ssŭ*)
以 *'i* 278, } therefore
知 *chi* 53, (*chih*) know
無 *wu* 1059, the not-

為 *wéi* 1047,
之 *chi* 53, (*tzŭ*) } doing's
有 *'yiu* 1113, having
益 *yi*, 1092, advantage,
不 *pu* 717, the not-
言 *yen* 1083,
之 *chi* 53, (*tzŭ*) } speaking's [gen.]
教 *chiao'* 372, doctrine,
無 *wu* 1059, the not-
為 *wéi* 1047,
之 *chi* 53, (*tzŭ*) } doing's [gen.]
益 *yi*, 1092, advantage
天 *t'ien* 897,
下 *hia'* 183, (*hsia*) } in the world
希 *hi* 176, (*hsi*) [there are] few
及 *chi'* 394, [that can] obtain
之 *chi* 53, (*tzŭ*) them.

第 *ti'* 879,
四 *sz"* 836,
十 *shih*, 768, } Chapter 44
四 *sz"* 836,
章 *chang* 22,
立 *lih*, 538, Setting up
戒 *kiai'* 360, precepts.

(Chapter 43-44.)

I.

名 ₁*ming* 600, Name
與 'yü 1125, and
身 ₁*shan* 735, (*shen*) person
孰 ₁*shu* 780, which [is]
親 ₁*ts'in* 991, (*chin*) nearer?
身 ₁*shan* 735, (*shen*) Person
與 'yü 1125, and
貨 *hwo*' 256, treasure,
孰 ₁*shu* 780, which [is]
多 ₁*to* 909, more?
得 *teh*, 872, (*té*) Gain
與 'yü 1125, and
亡 ₁*wang* 1044, loss,
孰 ₁*shu* 780, which is more
病 *ping*' 700, painful?

II.

甚 *shăn*' 738, (*shen*) Extreme
愛 *ngai*' 619, fondness
必 *pi*'' 692, surely
大 *ta*' 839, greatly
費 *féi*' 139, wastes.
多 ₁*to* 909, Much
藏 ₁*ts'ang* 950, hoarding
必 *pi*'' 692, surely [brings]

厚 *heu*' 176, (*hou*) intense
亡 ₁*wang* 1044, loss.

III.

知 ₁*chi* 53, (*chih*) [One who] knows
足 *tsu* 1014, contentment
不 ₁*pu* 717, not
辱 *ju*' 299, is despised.
知 ₁*chi* 53, (*chih*) [One who] knows
止 '*chi* 56, (*tzŭ*) when to stop
不 ₁*pu* 717, is not
殆 *tai*' 846, endangered.
可 '*k'o* 425, He will be able
以 '*i* 278, thereby
長 ₁*ch'ang* 27, to last
久 '*chiu* 413, [and] to continue.

第 *ti*' 879,
四 *sz*'' 836,
十 ₂*shih*, 768, } Chapter 45
五 '*wu* 1060,
章 ₁*chang* 22,

洪 ₁*hung* 236, Grand
德 *teh*, 871, virtue.

I.

大 *ta*' 839, Great

(Chapters 44-45.)

成 ,ch'ing 77, (cheng) perfection
若 joh, 296, (jê) seems
缺 ch'üeh, 448, imperfect.
其 ,ch'i 342, [But] its
用 yung' 1149, function [use,
utility]
不 ,pu 717, not
弊 pi' 676, is worn out.
大 ta' 839, Great
盈 ,ying 1106, fulness
若 joh, 296, (jê) seems
冲 ,ch'ung 109, (tsung) empty.
其 ,ch'i 342, [But] its
用 yung' 1149, function
不 ',pu 342, is not
窮 ,ch'iung 420, exercised.

II.

大 ta' 839, Great
直 chih, 70, straightness
若 joh, 296, (jê) seems
屈 ,ch'ü, 458, crooked.
大 ta' 839, Great
巧 'ch'iao 374, skill
若 joh, 296, (jê) seems
拙 ,cho 83, clumsy.

大 ta' 839, Great
辯 pien' 688, eloquence
若 joh, 296, (jê) seems
訥 no' 640, stammering.

III.

躁 tsao' 954, Motion
勝 ,shing 771, (sheng) conquers
寒 ,han 163, cold.
靜 tsing' 994, (ching) Quietude
勝 ,shing 771, (sheng) conquers
熱 jeh, 293, (jê) heat.
清 ,ts'ing 995, (ch'ing) Purity
淨 tsing' 994, (ching) [and]
clearness
爲 ,wéi 1047, are
天 ,t'ien 897,⎫
下 hia' 183, (hsia) ⎬ the world's
正 ching' 75, (cheng) standard.

第 ti' 879,⎫
四 sz" 836, ⎪
十 shih, 708 ⎬ Chapter 46.
六 luh, 562, ⎪
章 ,chang 22, ⎭

儉 'kien 385, To moderate
欲 yuh, 1137, desires.

I.

天 ‚t'ien 897, } [When]
下 hia' 183, (hsia) } the world
有 ‚yiu 1113, has
道 tao' 867, reason,
却 ch'ioh, 411, [people] curb
走 ‚tseu 961, (tsou) race
馬 ‚ma 571, horses
以 ‚i 278, for
糞 făn' 132, (fen) hauling dung.
天 ‚t'ien 897, } [When]
下 hia' 183, (hsia) } the world
無 ‚wu 1059, has no
道 tao' 867, reason,
戎 ‚jung 303, war
馬 ‚ma 571, horses
生 ‚shăng 742, (sheng) are raised
于 ‚yü 1118, in
郊 ‚chiao 367, the common.

II.

罪 tsui' 1016, Sin
莫 mo' 603, there is none
大 ta' 839, greater
于 ‚yü 1118, than
可 ‚k'o 425, to
欲 yü' 1137, desire.
禍 hwo' 256, Misfortune
莫 mo' 603, there is none
大 ta' 839, greater
于 ‚yü 425, than
不 ‚pu 717, not
知 ‚chi 53, (chih) to know
足 ‚tsu 1014, contentment
咎 chiu' 415, Calamity
莫 mo' 603, there is none
大 ta' 839, greater
于 ‚yü 425, than
欲 yü' 1137, desire
得 tch. 872, (tê) for gaining

III.

故 ku' 434, Therefore
知 ‚chi 53, (chih) [who] knows
足 ‚tsu 1014, } content-
之 ‚chi 53, (tzŭ) } ment's
足 ‚tsu 1014, contentment
常 ‚chang 740, is always
足 ‚tsu 1014, contented.

(Chapter 46.)

第 *ti'* 879,
四 *sz"* 836,
十 *shih* 768,   } Chapter 47.
七 *ts'ih* 987,
章 *chang* 22,

鑒 *kien'* 387, Seeing
遠 *yuen* 1137, the distant.

I.

不 *pu* 717, Not
出 *ch'u* 98, going out of
戶 *hu'* 225, the door
知 *chi* 53, (*chih*) I know
天 *t'ien* 897,   } the
下 *hia'* 183, (*hsia*) } world.
不 *pu* 717, not
窺 *kwéi* 487, peeping through
牖 *yiu* 1114, the window
見 *chien'* 385, I see
天 *t'ien* 897, heaven's
道 *tao'* 867, reason.
其 *ch'i* 342, [When] one
出 *ch'u* 98, goes out
彌 *mi* 589, more and more
遠 *yuen* 1137, to the distance,
其 *ch'i* 342, one's

知 *chi* 53, (*chih*) knowledge
彌 *mi* 589, more and more
少 *shao* 746, grows little.

II.

是 *shi'* 762, (*ssŭ*)   } Therefore
以 *'i* 278,
聖 *shăng'* 773, (*sheng*) the holy man
人 *jăn* 286, (*jen*) man
不 *pu* 717, not
行 *hing* 207, (*hsing*) goes about
而 *rh* 719, (*err*) but
知 *chi* 53, (*chih*) he knows.
不 *pu* 717, Not
見 *chien'* 385, he sees
而 *rh* 719, (*err*) but
名 *ming* 600, he defines [determines by names]
不 *pu* 717, Not
為 *wéi* 1047, he labors
而 *rh* 719, (*err*) but
成 *ch'ing* 77, (*cheng*) he completes.

(Chapter 47.)

TRANSLITERATION. 221

第 ｡ti'' 879,
四 ｡sz'' 836,
十 ｡shih, 768, } Chapter 48.
八 ｡pah, 647,
章 ｡chang 22,

忘 ｡wang 1044, To forget
知 ｡chi 53, knowledge.

I.

爲 ｡wéi 1047, [Who] attends to
學 ｡hioh, 209, (hsüeh) learning
日 ｡jih 293, daily
益 ｡yi' 1092, he gains.
爲 ｡wéi 1047, [Who] practises
道 ｡tao' 867, reason
日 ｡jih 293, daily
損 'sun 829, he diminishes.
損 'sun 829. He diminishes
之 ｡chi 53, (tzŭ) himself
又 ｡yiu' 1114, and again
損 'sun 829, he diminishes.
以 '。i 278, Thus
至 chi'' 60, (chih) [he] attains
于 ｡yü 425, unto
無 ｡wu 1059, non-
爲 ｡wéi 1047, doing.

無 ｡wu 1059, He does non-
爲 ｡wéi 1047, doing,
而 '。rh 719, (err) yet
無 ｡wu 1059, there is nothing
不 ｡pu 717, un-
爲 ｡wéi 1047, done.

II.

取 'ts'ü 1010, (chü) To take
天 ｡t'ien 897, } the empire
下 hia' 183, (hsia)
常 ｡chang 740, always
以 '。i 278, he uses
無 ｡wu 1059, non-
事 shi'' 764, (ssŭ) diplomacy [business]
及 chi'' 394' When
有 '。yiu 1113, using
事 shi'' 764, (ssŭ) diplomacy
不 ｡pu 717, not
足 ｡tsu 1014, is he fit
以 '。i 278, thereby
取 'tsü 1010, (chü) to take
天 ｡t'ien 897, } the empire
下 hia' 183, (hsia)

(Chapter 48.)

第 ,ti' 879,
四 ,sz'' 836,
十 ,shih, 768, } Chapter 49.
九 ,'kiu 413,
章 ,chang 22,

任 jăn' 289, Trust in
德 teh, 871, virtue.

I.

聖 ,shăng 773, (sheng) The holy
人 ,jăn 286, (jen) man
無 ,wu 1059, has no
常 ,chang 740, fixed
心 ,sin 806, (hsin) heart.
以 ,'i 278, In
百 poh, 707, (po) the hundred
姓 sing' 810, (hsing) families
之 ,chi' 53, (tzŭ) their
心 ,sin 806, (hsin) heart
爲 ,wéi 1047, he finds
心。 ,sin 806, (hsin) his own heart.

II.

善 shan' 752, Good
者 'ché 38, ones
吾 ,wu 1060, I

善 shan' 752, treat with goodness
之 ,chi 53, (tzŭ) them.
不 ,pu 717, Not
善 shan' 752, good
者 'ché 38, ones
吾 ,wu 1060, I
亦 yi' 1093, also
善 shan' 752, treat with goodness
之。 ,chi 53, (tzŭ) them.
德 teh, 871, (tê) [For] virtue
善。 shan' 752, is good.
信 sin' 807, (hsin) The faithful
者 'ché 38, ones,
吾 ,wu 1060, I
信 sin' 807, (hsin) treat faithfully
之。 ,chi 53, (tzŭ) them.
不 ,pu 717, The un-
信 sin' 807, (hsin) faithful
者 'ché 38, ones
吾 ,wu 1060, I
亦 yi' 1093, also
信 sin' 807, (hsin) treat faithfully
之。 ,chi 53, (tzŭ) them.
德 teh, 871, (tê) [For] virtue

(Chapter 49.)

信 sin' 807, (hsin) is faithful.

III.

聖 shăng' 773, (sheng) The holy
人 jăn 286, (jen) man
在 tsai' 941, lives
天 t'ien 897, } in the
下 hia' 183, (hsia) } world,
慄 tieh, 890, cautiously,
慄 tieh, 890, so cautiously
爲 wéi 1047, dealing
天 t'ien 897, } with the
下 hia' 183, (hsia) } world.
渾 hwun 268, He universalises
其 ch'i 342, his
心 sin 806, (hsin) heart.
百 poh, 707, (po) The hundred
姓 sing' 810, (hsing) families
皆 chié 358, all
注 chu' 89, fix upon [him]
其 ch'i 342, their
耳 'rh 720, (err) ears
目 mu' 607, [and] eyes.
聖 shăng' 773, (sheng) The holy
人 jăn 286, (jen) man

皆 chié 358, all
孩 hai 160, treats as children
之。chi 53, (tzŭ) them.

第 ti' 879,
五 'wu 1060,
十 shih 768, } Chapter 50
章 chang 22,

貴 kwéi' 484, Esteem
生 shăng 742, life.

I.

出 ch'u 98, Going forth
生 shăng 742, (sheng) is life
入 ju' 299, coming home
死。sz' 836, (ssŭ) is death.
生 shăng 742, (sheng) } Life's
之 chi 53, (tzŭ) }
徒 tu 919, pursuers
十 shih, 768, [in] ten
有 'yiu 1113, you have
三。san 723, three.
死 'sz' 836, (ssŭ) } Death's
之 chi 53, (tzŭ) }
徒 tu 919, pursuers

(Chapters 49-50.)

十 *shih*, 768, [in] ten
有 *'yiu* 1113, you have
三 *san* 723, three.
人 *jăn* 286, (*jen*) Of the people
之 *chi* 53, (*tzŭ*) who from their
生 *shang* 742, (*sheng*) life
動 *tung'* 932, are moving
之 *chi* 53, (*tzŭ*) to their
死 *'sz'* 836, (*ssŭ*) death
地 *ti'* 879, place,
亦 *yi'* 1093, also
十 *shih*, 768, in ten
有 *'yiu* 1113, you have
三 *san* 723, three.
夫 *fu*, 142, Now
何 *ho* 213, what
故 *ku'* 434, is the reason?
以 *'i* 278, Because
其 *ch'i* 342, they
生 *shang* 742, (*sheng*) live
生 *shang* 742, (*sheng*) } life's
之 *chi* 53, (*tzŭ*)
厚 *heu'* 176, (*hou*) intensity

II.

蓋 *kai'* 307, Indeed

聞 *wăn* 1041, (*wen*) I hear:
善 *shan'* 752, [Who] ably
攝 *sheh*, 750, (*shê*) manages
生 *shang* 742, (*sheng*) his life,
者 *'chě* 38, the one,
陸 *luh*, 562, (*lu*) [when] on land
行 *h'ing* 207, (*hsing*) he travels,
不 *pu* 717, not
遇 *yü'* 1128, he meets
兕 *sz"* 837, (*ssŭ*) the rhinoceros,
虎 *'hu* 224, [and] the tiger,
入 *ju'* 299, [when] coming among
軍 *chün* 419, soldiers,
不 *pu* 717, not
避 *pi'* 675, [need he] shun
甲 *'chia*, 355, arms
兵 *ping* 698, [and] weapons.
兕 *sz"* 837, [*ssŭ*] The rhinoceros
無 *wu* 1059, has no
所 *su'* 817, [*shuo*] place where
投 *t'eu* 876, (*tou*) to insert
其 *ch'i* 342, its
角 *chüě* 409, horn.
虎 *'hu* 224, The tiger

(Chapter 50.)

TRANSLITERATION. 225

無 ˏwu 1059, has no
所 su' 817, (shuo) place where
措 ts'u' 1008, (ts'o) to put
其 ˏch'i 342, his
爪 'chao 34, (tsao) claws.
兵 ˏping 698, Soldiers
無 ˏwu 1059, have no
所 su' 817, (shuo) place where
容 ˏyung 1146, to let enter
其 ˏch'i 342, their
双 jăn' 288, (jen) blades.
夫 ˏfu 142, Now
何 ˏho 213, what
故 ku' 434, is the reason?
以 'i 278, Because
其 ˏch'i 342, he
無 ˏwu 1059, has no [does not belong to]
死 'sz' 836, (ssu) death's
地 ti' 879, place.

第 ti' 879,
五 'wu 1060,
十 shih, 768,   } Chapter 51.
一 yih, 1095,
章 ˏchang 22,

簑 ˏyang 1072, To nurse
德 tch, 871, virtue.

I.

道 tao' 867, Reason
生 ˏshăng 743, (sheng) gives life to
之 ˏchi 53, (tzŭ) them [living creatures]
德 tch, 871, (té), Virtue
畜 ch'uh, 98, (hsü) nurses
之 ˏchi 53, (tzŭ) them.
物 wuh, 1065, (wu) Concrete things [reality]
形 ˏhing 206, (hsing) shape
之 ˏchi 53, (tzŭ) them.
勢 shi' 765, (shih) Energy
成 ˏch'ing 77, (cheng) completes
之 ˏchi 53, (tzŭ), them.
是 shi' 762, (ssŭ) }
以 'i 278,   } Therefore
萬 wan' 1040, [among] the ten thousand
物 wuh, 1065, (wu) things
莫 mo' 603, no one
不 ˏpu 717, not
尊 ˏtsun 1019, honors
道 tao' 867, reason
而 ˏrh 719, (erh) and
貴 kwei' 484, esteems

(Chapters 50-51.)

德 *teh*, 871, (*tê*) virtue.

II.

道 *tao'* 867,
之 ,*chi* 53, (*tzŭ*) } Reason's
尊 ,*tsun* 1019, honorableness
德 *teh*, 871, (*tê*)
之 ,*chi* 53, (*tzŭ*) } virtue's
貴 *kwéi'* 484, esteemableness,
夫 ,*fu* 142, however,
莫 *mo'* 603, no one
之 ,*chi* 53, (*tzŭ*) it
命 *ming'* 601, commands,
而 ',*rh* 719, (*err*) but
常 ,*chang* 740, always
自 *tsz"* 1031, (*tzŭ*) self
然 ,*jan* 285, so } they are spontaneous.
故 *ku'* 434, Therefore
道 *tao'* 867, reason
生 ,*shăng* 743, (*sheng*) gives life to
之 ,*chi* 53, (*tzŭ*) them,
德 *teh*, 871, (*tê*) [but] virtue
畜 *ch'uh*, 98, (*hsü*) nurses
之 ,*chi* 53, (*tzŭ*) them,
長 ,*ch'ang* 27, raises
之 ,*chi* 53, (*tzŭ*) them,

育 *yü*, 1140, nurtures
之 ,*chi* 53, (*tzŭ*) them,
成 ,*ch'ing* 77, (*cheng*) completes
之 ,*chi* 53, (*tzŭ*), them,
熟 *shuh*, 780, (*su*) matures
之 ,*chi* 53, (*tzŭ*) them
養 '*yang* 1072, rears
之 ,*chi* 53, (*tzŭ*) them
覆 ,*fu* 151, protects
之 ,*chi* 53, (*tzŭ*) them,

III.

生 ,*shang* 742, (*sheng*) to give life to [them]
而 ',*rh* 719, (*err*) but
不 ,*pu* 717, not
有 '*yiu* 1113, to own,
為 ,*wéi* 1047, to make [them]
而 ',*rh* 719, (*err*) but
不 ,*pu* 717, not
恃 *shi'* 761, (*ssŭ*) to claim;
長 ,*ch'ang* 27, to raise [them]
而 ',*rh* 719, (*err*) but
不 ,*pu* 717, not
宰 '*tsai* 941, to rule;
是 *shi'* 762, (*ssŭ*) this
謂 *wéi'* 1054, is called

(Chapter 51.)

TRANSLITERATION.

玄 ‚hüen 231, (hsüen) profound
德 teh, 871, (tê) virtue.

第 ‚ti' 879,
五 wu' 1060,
十 shih, 768, } Chapter 52.
二 'rh' 721,
章 ‚chang 22,

歸 kwéi, 480, Return
元 ‚yuen 1134, to the origin.

I.

天 ‚t'ien 897, } [When]
下 hia' 183, (hsia) } the world
有 ‚yiu 1113, takes
始 'shi 761, (ssŭ) its beginning,
以 'i 278, thereby
為 ‚wéi 1047, [the Tao] becomes
天 ‚t'ien 897, } the
下 hia' 183, (hsia) } world's
母 'mu 605, mother.
既 chi' 339, When
知 ‚chi 53 (chih) one knows
其 ‚ch'i 342, one's
母 'mu 605, mother,

復 ‚fu 151, in turn
知 ‚chi 53, (chih) it knows
其 ‚ch'i 342, its
子 'tsz' 1030, (tzŭ) son.
既 chi' 339, When
生 ‚chi 53, (chih) it knows
其 ‚ch'i 342, its
子 'tsz' 1030, (tzŭ) son,
復 ‚fu 151, in turn
守 'sheu 755, (shou) he keeps
其 ‚ch'i 342, to his
母 'mu 605, mother.
沒 mo' 606, To the end
身 ‚shăn 735, (shen) of life [the body, the person]
不 ‚pu 717, he is not
殆 tai' 846, in danger.

II.

塞 seh' 728, (sê) [Who] closes
其 ‚ch'i 342, his
兌 tui' 925, mouth
閉 pi' 676, [and] shuts
其 ‚ch'i 342, his
門 ‚măn 576, (mên) sense-gates,
終 ‚chung 106, (tsung) to the end
身 ‚shăn 735, (shen) of life

(Chapters 51-52.)

不 ₁*fu* 717, not
勤 ₁*chin* 402, is troubled.
開 ₁*k'ai* 308, [Who] opens
其 ₁*ch'i* 342, his
兌 *tui'* 925, mouth,
濟 *tsi'* 964, (*chi*) [and] meddles
其 ₁*ch'i* 342, with
事 *shi'* 764, (*ssŭ*) affairs,
終 ₁*chung* 106, (*tsung*) in the end
身 ₁*shăn* 735, (*shen*) of life
不 ₁*fu* 717, not
救 *chiu'* 415, can he be saved.

III.

見 *chien'* 385, To see
小 ₁*siao* 795, (*hsiao*) [one's] smallness
曰 *yueh*, 1130, is called
明 ₁*ming* 599, enlightenment.
守 *sheu* 755, (*shou*) To keep
柔 ₁*jeu* 294, (*jou*) one's tenderness
曰 *yueh*, 1130, is called
強 ₁*ch'iang* 366, strength.
用 *yung'* 1149, [Who] employ
其 ₁*ch'i* 342, its [i.e., reason's]
光 ₁*kwang* 478, light,
復 ₁*fu* 151, [and] reverts

歸 ₁*kwéi* 480, [and] goes home to
其 ₁*ch'i* 342, its
明 ₁*ming* 599, enlightenment
無 ₁*wu* 1059, does not
遺 ₁*i* 277, surrender
身 ₁*shăn* 735, (*shen*) his person
殃 ₁*yang* 1070, to perdition.
是 *shi'* 762. (*ssŭ*) This
謂 *wéi'* 1053, is called
習 ₁*sih*, 805, (*hsi*) practising
常 ₁*chang* 740, the eternal.

第 *ti'* 879,
五 '*wu* 1060,
十 ₁*shih*, 768, } Chapter 53
三 ₁*san* 723,
章 ₁*chang* 22,

益 *yih*, 1092, To gain
證 *ching'* 76, insight.

I.

使 '*shi* 761, (*ssŭ*) If
我 '*ngo* 627, I
介 *chié'* 360, in an insignificant
然 ₁*jan* 285, manner
有 '*yiu* 1113, have

知 ‚chi 53, (chih) knowledge,
行 ‚hing 207, (hsing) I walk
于 ‚yü 1118, in
大 ta' 839, the great
道 tao' 867, reason;
唯 'wéi 1052, it is only
施 ‚shi 758, (ssŭ) assertion;
是 shi'' 762, (ssŭ) this
畏 wéi'' 1054, I fear.

II.

大 ta' 839, The great
道 tao' 867, reason
甚 shăn' 738, (shen) is very
夷 ‚i 276, plain,
而 ‚'rh 719, (err) but
民 ‚min 597, the people
好 'hao 171, like
徑 ching' 407, by-paths.
朝 ‚chao 32, [When] the palace, [seat of government]
甚 shăn' 738, (shen) is very
除 ‚ch'u 92, splendid,
田 ‚t'ien 898, the fields
甚 shăn 738, (shen) [are] very
蕪 ‚wu 1059, weedy

倉 ‚ts'ang 949, [and] granaries
甚 shăn' 738, (shen) very
虛 ‚hü 227, (hsü) empty.
服 ‚fu 152, To wear
文 ‚wăn 1041, (wen) ornaments
綵 'ts'ai 944, [and] gaudy colors
帶 tai'' 846, to carry
利 li'' 521, sharp
劍 chien' 388, swords,
厭 yen' 1089, to be excessive
飲 'yin 1102, in drinking
食 shih‚ 766, [and] eating,
財 ‚ts'ai 943, wealth
貨 hwo' 256, [and] treasure
有 'yiu 1113, to have
餘 ‚yü 1121, in abundance,
是 shi'' 762, (ssŭ) this
謂 wéi'' 1054, is called
盜 tao' 868, robbers'
夸 ‚kw'a 468, pride.
非 ‚féi 136, [It is] anti-
道 tao' 867, reason,
哉 ‚tsai 940, indeed.

(Chapter 53.)

第 ｢ti｣' 879,
五 ｢'wu 1060,
十 ｢shih, 768, } Chapter 54.
四 ｢sz" 836,
章 ｢chang 22,

修 ｢siu 811, To cultivate
觀 ｢kwan 474, intuition,

I.

善 shăn 752, [What is] well
建 chien' 386, planted
者 'chĕ 38, the thing
不 ｢pu 717, not
拔 ｢pa 647, is uprooted.
善 shan 752, [What is] well
抱 pao' 665, is preserved
者 'chĕ 38, the thing
不 ｢pu 717, not
脫 t'o 914, is taken away.

II.

子 'tsz' 1030, (tzŭ) Sons',
孫 ｢sun 829, [and] grandsons'
祭 tsi' 965, (chi) offerings
祀 sz' 838, (ssŭ) and ancestor worship
不 ｢pu 717, not
輟 ch'oh' 81, (ch'o) will cease.

修 ｢siu 811, (hsiu) Who practises
之 ｢chi 53, (tzŭ) it [i. e., Tao]
于 ｢yü 1118, in
身 ｢shăn 735, (shen) person
其 ｢ch'i 342, his
德 teh, 871, (tĕ) virtue
乃 'nai 612, then
眞 ｢chăn 15, (chen) is real.
修 ｢siu 811, (hsiu) [Who] practise
之 ｢chi 53 (tzŭ) it
于 'yü 1118, in
家 ｢chia 351, his family,
其 ｢ch'i 342, his
德 teh, 871, (tĕ) virtue
有 'yiu 1113, is
餘 ｢yü 1120, overflowing.
修 ｢siu 811, (hsiu) [Who] practises
之 ｢chi 53, (tzŭ) it
于 ｢yü 1118, in
鄉 ｢hiang 189, (hsiang) his township,
其 ｢ch'i 342, his
德 teh, 871, (tĕ) virtue
乃 'nai 612, then
長 ｢ch'ang 27, is lasting.

(Chapter 54.)

修 ,siu 811, (hsiu) [Who] practises
之 ,chi 53, (tzŭ) it
于 ,yü 1118, in
國 ,kwo 491, his country,
其 ,ch'i 342, his
德 teh, 871, (tê) virtue
乃 'nai 612, then
豐 ,făng 157, (fêng) is abundant [prolific].
修 ,siu 811, (hsiu) [Who] practises
之 ,chi 53, (tzŭ) this
于 ,yü 1118, in
天 ,t'ien 897,
下 hia' 183, (hsia) } the world,
其 ,ch'i 342, his
德 teh, 871, (tê) virtue
乃 'nai 612, then
普 'p'u 716, is universal.

III.

故 ku' 434, Therefore
以 ,'i 278, by
身 ,shăn 735, (shen) one's person
觀 ,kwan 474, one tests
身 ,shăn 735, (shen) persons.
以 ,'i 278, By
家 ,chia 351, one's family

觀 ,kwan 474, one tests
家 ,chia 351, families.
以 ,'i 278, By
鄉 ,hiang 189, (hsiang) one's township
觀 ,kwan 474, one tests
鄉 ,hiang 189, (hsiang) townships.
以 ,'i 278, By
國 ,kwo 491, one's country
觀 ,kwan 474, one tests
國 ,kwo 491, countries.
以 ,'i 278, By
天 ,t'ien 897,
下 hia' 183, (hsia) } one's world
觀 ,kwan 474, one tests
天 ,t'ien 897,
下 hia 183, (hsia) } worlds
吾 ,wu 1060, I
何 ,ho 215, what-
以 ,'i 278, by
知 ,chi 53, (chih) know
天 ,t'ien 897,
下 hia' 183, (hsia) } the world's
之 ,chi 53, (tzŭ)
然 ,jan 285, being such ?
哉 ,tsai 940, [Query.]

(Chapter 54.)

以 ,'i 278, [It is] by
此。 ts'z' 1034, (tzŭ) this [viz., reason].

第 ti' 879,
五 'wu 1060,
十 shih, 768, } Chapter 55.
五 'wu 1060,
章 ,chang 22,

玄 ,hüen 231, Of the Mysteri-
符。 ,fu 144, the seal.   [ous
                                                    1.
含 ,han 162, [Who] embodies
德 teh, 871. (tĕ) virtue
之 ,chi 53, (chih) [in] its
厚。 heu' 176, (hou) fulness [so-
                                            lidity]
比 'pi 674, is comparable
于 ,yü 1118, to
赤 ch'ih, 72, } an infant
子。 'tsz' 1030, (tzŭ)   child.
毒 ,tu 922, Poisonous
蟲 ,ch'ung 110, (tsung) in-
                                            sects
不 ,pu 717, not
螫。 shih, 769, sting [him].
猛 ,măng 610, (mĕng) Wild
獸 sheu' 756, (hsou) beasts

不 ,pu 717, not
據 chü' 442, seize [him].
攫 ,chüĕ 411, Carnivorous
鳥 'niao 632, birds
不 ,pu 717, not
搏 poh' 706, (po) strike [him]
骨 ,ku 454, The bones
弱 joh, 296, are weak,
筋 ,chin 396, the muscles
柔 ,jĕu 294, (jou) are tender
而 ',rh 719, (err) yet
握 wo' 1064, the grasp
固。 ku' 435, is firm.
未 wĕi' 1052, He does not yet
知 ,chi 53, (chih) know
牝 'p'in 697, the female
牡 'mu 588, [and] the male
之 ,chi 53, (tzŭ) [in] their
合 ,hŏ 217, relation.
而 ',rh 719, (err) yet
峻 ,tsui* [K., vol, 31, p. 1]
                the child's virility
作。 tso' 1005, is erect.

*This character is missing in Williams, but a similar form of the same word, which like the above means "the privates of a child," is referred to on page 821.

(Chapters 54-55.)

精 ,tsing 992, (ching) His spirit [semen]
之 ,chi 53, (tzŭ) [grows to] its
至 chi' 60, (chih) perfection,
也 'ye' 1079, (yeh) indeed.
終 ,chung 106, (tsung) All
日 jih, 293, the day
號 hao' 173, he cries
而 ',rh 719, (err) and
嗌 yi' 1092, sobs
不 ,pu 719, [yet] not
嗄 sha' 731, becomes hoarse.
和 ,ho 254, His harmony
之 ,chi 53, (tsŭ) [is shown in] its
至 chi' 60, perfection,
也 'ye' 1079, (yeh) indeed.

II.

知 ,chi 53, (chih) To know
和 ,ho 254, the harmonious
曰 yueh, 1130, is called
常 ,chang 740, eternal.
知 ,chi 53, (chih) To know
常 ,chang 740, the eternal
曰 yueh, 1130, is called
明 ,ming 599, enlightened.

益 yi' 1092, To increase
生 ,shăng 743, (sheng) life
曰 yueh, 1130, is called
祥 ,siang 792, (hsiang) a blessing
心 ,sin 806, (hsin) The heart
使 'shi 761, (ssŭ) directing
氣 ch'i' 348, spirit
曰 yueh, 1130, is called
強 ,ch'iang 366, strength.
物 wuh, 1065, (wu) Things
壯 chwang' 114, fully grown
將 ,tsiang 967, (chiang) are about
老 'lao 508, to decay.
謂 wei' 1054, We call
之 ,chi 53, (tzŭ) it
不 ,pu 717, un-
道 tao' 867, reason.
不 ,pu 717, Un-
道 tao' 867, reason
早 'tsao 953, soon
已 'i 278, ceases.

(Chapter 55)

第 *ti'* 879,
五 '*wu* 1060,
十 *shih*, 768,   } Chapter 56.
六 *luh*, 562,
章 *chang* 22,

玄 *hüen* 231, The profound
德 *teh*, 871, virtue.

I.

知 *chi* 53, (*chih*) [Who] knows,
者 *ché* 38, the one
不 *pu* 717, not
言 *yen* 1083, speaks.
言 *yen* 1083, [Who] speaks
者 *ché* 38, the one
不 *pu* 717, not
知 *chi* 53, (*chih*) knows.
塞 *seh*, 728, (*sê*) He shuts
其 *ch'i* 342, his
兑 *tui'* 925, mouth,
閉 *pi'* 676, [and] closes
其 *ch'i* 342, his
門 *măn* 576, (*men*) [sense-] gates.

II.

挫 *ts'o'* 1004, He blunts,
其 *ch'i* 342, his

鋭 *iui'* 302, sharpness.
解 '*chié* 359, He unravels
其 *ch'i* 342, his
紛 *făn* 129, (*fen*) tangles.
和 *ho* 254, He dims
其 *ch'i* 342, his
光 *kwang* 478, brilliancy.
同 *t'ung* 933, He identifies
其 *ch'i* 342, himself
塵 *ch'ăn* 22, (*ch'en*) with the dust.
是 *shi'* 762, (*ssŭ*) This
謂 *wéi'* 1054, is called
玄 *hüen* 231, (*hsüen*) profound
同 *t'ung* 933, identification.

III.

故 *ku'* 434, Therefore
不 *pu* 717, not
可 *k'o* 425, he can
得 *teh*, 872, (*té*) be obtained
而 '*rh* 719, (*err*) and
親 *ts'in* 991, (*ch'in*) be loved
亦 *yi'* 1093, and
不 *pu* 717, not
可 *k'o* 425, can he
得 *teh*, 872, (*té*) be obtained

(Chapter 56.)

而 ',rh 719, (err) and
疎 ,shu 775, be discarded.
不 ,pu 717, Not
可 ,k'o 425, can he
得 teh, 872, (tê) be obtained
而 ',rh 719, (err) and
利 li' 521, interested in profit
亦 yi' 1093, and
不 ,pu 717, not
可 ,k'o 425, can he
得 teh, 872, (tê) be obtained
而 ',rh 719, (err) and
害 hai' 161, be injured
不 ,pu 717, Not
可 ,k'o 425, can he
得 teh, 872, (tê) be obtained
而 ',rh 719, (err) and
貴 kwéi' 484, be honored,
亦 yi' 1093, and
不 ,pu 717, not
可 ,k'o 425, can he
得 teh, 872, (tê) be obtained
而 ',rh 719, (err) and
賤 tsien' 979, (chien) be humiliated.

故 ku' 434, Therefore
爲 ,wéi 1047, it becomes
天 ,t'ien 897, } the
下 hia' 183, (hsia) } world's
貴 kwéi' 484, honor.

第 ti' 879,
五 'wu 1060,
十 shih, 768, } Chapter 57
七 ts'ih, 987,
章 ,chang 22,

淳 ,shun 783, Simplicity
風 ,fung 155, in habit

1.

以 'i 278, With
正 chǎng' 75, (cheng) righteousness [rectitude, justice]
治 chi' 59, (chih) is administered
國 ,kwo 491, the empire.
以 'i 278, With
奇 ,ch'i 344, craftiness
用 yung' 1149, is directed
兵 ,ping 698, the army.
以 'i 278, With
無 ,wu 1059, non-
事 shi' 764, (ssŭ) diplomacy

(Chapters 56-57.)

取 ,ts'ü 1010 (chü) is taken
天 ,t'ien 897,   ⎫
下 ,hia' 183, (hsia) ⎬ the empire
　　　　　　　　⎭
吾 ,wu 1060, I
何 ,ho 215, what-
以 'i 278, by
知 ,chi 53, (chih) know
其 ,ch'i 342, its
然 ,jan 285, being such,
哉 ,tsai 940, indeed?
以 'i 278, It is [by]
此 ,ts'z' 1034, (tzŭ) this [reason].

II.

天 ,t'ien 897,   ⎫
下 ,hia' 183, (hsia) ⎬ In the world
　　　　　　　　⎭
多 ,to 909, the more [there are]
忌 chi" 340, restrictions
諱 hwui' 266, [and] prohibitions
而 ,rh 719, (err) yet
民 ,min 597, the people
彌 ,mi 589, increasingly [the more]
貧 ,t'in 697, become poor.
民 ,min 597, The people
多 ,to 909, the more [they have]

(Chapter 57.)

利 li' 521, sharp
器 ch'i" 349. weapons,
國 ,kwo 491,   ⎫
家 ,chia 351,   ⎬ the state
　　　　　　　⎭
滋 ,tsz' 1029, (tzŭ) the more and more
昏 ,hwun 267, is confused.
人 ,jăn 286, (jen) The people
多 ,to 909, the more [they are]
技 'ch'i 347, artful
巧 'ch'iao 374, [and] cunning,
奇 ,ch'i 344, abnormal
物 wuh, 1065, (wu) things
滋 ,tsz' 1029, (tzŭ) the more and more
起 ,ch'i 347, occur.
法 ,fa 123, Laws
令 ling' 546, [and] orders
滋 ,tsz' 1029, (tzŭ) the more and more
彰 ,chang 23, [are] made manifest,
盜 tao' 868, robbers
賊 ,tsêi 957, [and] thieves
多 ,to 909, the more
有 'yiu 1113, appear.

III.

故 ku' 434, Therefore
聖 shăng' 773, (sheng) the holy

TRANSLITERATION. 237

人 ͵jăn 286, (jen) man
云 ͵yun 1142, says:
我 'ngo 627, I [practise]
無 ͵wu 1059, not
爲 ͵wéi 1047, doing,
而 '͵rh 719, (err) and
民 ͵min 597, the people
自 tsz" 1031, (tzŭ) of themselves
化 hwa' 240, reform.
我 'ngo 627, I
好 'hao 171, love
靜 tsing' 994, (ching) quietude
而 '͵rh 719, (err) and
民 ͵min 597, the people
自 tsz" 1031, (tzŭ) of themselves
正 chăng' 75, (cheng) are righteous.
我 'ngo 627, I [practise]
無 ͵wu 1059, not-doing
事 shi' 764, (ssŭ) business,
而 '͵rh 719, (err) and
民 ͵min 597, the people
自 tsz" 1031, (tzŭ) of themselves
富 fu' 148, become rich.
我 'ngo 627, I [practise]

無 ͵wu 1059, not having
欲 yü' 1139, desires,
而 '͵rh 719, (err) and
民 ͵min 597, the people
自 tsz" 1031, (tzŭ) of themselves
朴 p'u 710, are simple.

第 li" 879,
五 '͵wu 1060
十 shih, 768, } Chapter 58
八 pah, 647,
章 ͵chang 22,

順 shun' 784, Adaptation
化 hwa' 240, to change.

1.

其 ͵ch'i 342, [When] one's
政 chăng' 76, (cheng) administration
悶 măn' 577, (men) is unostentatious,
悶 măn' 577, (men) [quite] unostentatious
其 ͵ch'i 342, one's
民 ͵min 597, people
醇 ͵ch'un 783, are simple,
醇 ͵ch'un 783, [quite] simple.
其 ͵ch'i 342, [When] one's

(Chapters 57-58.)

政 ｡*chăng*' 76, (*cheng*) administration
察 ｡*ch'a* 9, is prying
察 ｡*ch'a* 9, [quite] prying,
其 ｡*ch'i* 342, one's
民 ｡*min* 597, people
缺 ｡*ch'üé* 448, are needy,
缺 ｡*ch'üé* 448, [quite] needy.
禍 *hwo*' 256, Misery
兮 ｡*hi* 179, (*hsi*) alas!
福 ｡*fu* 150 ⎫
之 ｡*chi* 53, (*tzŭ*) ⎬ happiness's
所 *su*' 817, (*shuo*) place
倚 ｡*'i* 279, it supports.
福 ｡*fu* 150, Happiness
兮 ｡*hi* 179, (*hsi*) alas!
禍 *hwo*' 256, ⎫
之 ｡*chi* 53, (*tzŭ*) ⎬ misery's
所 *su*' 817, (*shuo*) place
伏 ｡*fu* 152, it conceals [rests on].
孰 ｡*shu* 780, Who
知 ｡*chi* 53, (*chih*) knows
其 ｡*ch'i* 342, its
極 ｡*chi* 393, limits?
其 ｡*ch'i* 342, It

無 ｡*wu* 1059, not
止 '*chi* 56, (*chih*) ceases [is stopped]

II.

正 ｡*chăng*' 75, (*cheng*) The normal
復 ｡*fu* 151, in turn
爲 ｡*wéi* 1047, becomes
奇 ｡*ch'i* 344, abnormal.
善 *shan*' 752, The good
復 ｡*fu* 151, in turn
爲 ｡*wéi* 1047, becomes
妖 ｡*yao* 1074, unlucky [unpropitious].
人 ｡*jăn* 286, (*jen*) ⎫
之 ｡*chi* 53, (*tzŭ*) ⎬ The people's
迷 ｡*mi* 589, confusion!
其 ｡*ch'i* 342, It [is so]
日 *jih*, 293, daily
固 *ku*' 435, assuredly
久 '*chiu* 413, since long.

III.

是 *shi*' 762, (*ssŭ*) ⎫
以 '*i* 278, ⎬ Therefore
聖 ｡*shăng* 773, (*sheng*) the holy
人 ｡*jăn* 286, (*jen*) man
方 ｡*fang* 132, is square
而 '*rh* 719, (*err*) yet

(Chapter 58.)

TRANSLITERATION.

不 ₍pu 717, not
割 ₍kŏ 428, he injures.
廉 ₍lien 534, [He is] angular
而 '₍rh 719, (err) yet
不 ₍pu 717, not
劌 kwéi' 485, he hurts.
直 chih₍ 70, [He is] upright
而 '₍rh 719, (err) yet
不 ₍pu 717, not
肆 sz' 837, (ssŭ) strict.
光 ₍kwang 478, [He is] bright
而 '₍rh 719, (err) yet
不 ₍pu 717, not
耀 yao' 1078, shining.

第 ti' 879,
五 'wu 1060,
十 shih₍ 768,   } Chapter 59.
九 'kiu 413,
章 ₍chang 22,

守 'sheu 755, To keep
道 tao' 867, reason.

I.

治 chi' 59, (chih) In governing
人 ₍jăn 286, (jen) the people,

事 shi' 764, (ssŭ) [and] in attending
天 ₍t'ien 897, to heaven,
莫 mo' 603, nothing
若 ₍ioh 296, (jê) surpasses
嗇 seh' 728, (sê) moderation.
夫 ₍fu 142, Now
惟 'wéi 1052, consider only
嗇 seh' 728, (sê) moderation:
是 shi' 762, (ssŭ) This
謂 wéi' 1054, is called
早 'tsao 953, early
服 ₍fu 152, habit.
早 'tsao 953, Early
服 ₍fu 152, acquisition
謂 wéi' 1054, is called
之 ₍chi 53, (tzŭ), its
重 chung' 108, (tsung) heaping
積 tsih₍ 986, (chi) [and] accumulating
德 teh₍ 871, (tê) virtue.
重 chung' 108, (tsung) By heaping
積 tsih₍ 986, (chi) [and] accumulating
德 teh₍ 871, (tê) virtue
則 tsch₍ 956, (tsê) then
無 ₍wu 1059, nothing

不 *pu* 717, not
剋 *k'o'* 430, can be overcome.

II.

無 *wu* 1059, [When] nothing is
不 *pu* 717, not
剋 *k'o'* 430, can be overcome,
則 *tseh*, 956, (*tsê*) then
莫 *mo'* 603, no one
知 *chi* 53, (*chih*) knows
其 *ch'i* 342, his
極 *chi* 393, limit.
莫 *mo'* 603, [When] no one
知 *chi* 53, (*chih*) knows
其 *ch'i* 342, his
極 *chi* 393, limit,
可 *k'o* 425, one can
以 *'i* 278, thereby
有 *'yiu* 1113, possess
國 *kwo* 491, the state.
有 *'yiu* 1113, [Who] possesses
國 *kwo* 491,
之 *chi* 53, (*tzŭ*) } the state's
母 *mu* 605, mother [viz., moderation],
可 *k'o* 425, he can

以 *'i* 278, thereby
長 *ch'aug* 27, be lasting
久 *'chiu* 413, [and] enduring
是 *shi'* 762, (*ssŭ*) This
謂 *wéi'* 1054, is called
深 *shăn* 736, (*shen*) having deep
根 *kăn* 317, (*ken*) roots
固 *ku'* 435, [and] a staunch
蒂 *ti'* 881, stem.
長 *ch'ang* 27, [This is] of long
生 *shăng* 743, (*sheng*) life
久 *'chiu* 413, [and] lasting
視 *shi'* 763, (*ssŭ*) insight
之 *chi* 53, (*tzŭ*) [sign of gen.]
道 *tao'* 867, the *way*.

第 *ti'* 879,
六 *luh*, 562,
十 *shih*, 708,   } Chapter 60
章 *chang* 22,

居 *kü* 437, To maintain
位 *wéi'* 1053, one's position

I.

治 *chi'* 59, (*chih*) Govern
大 *ta'* 839, a great

國 ₍kwo 491, state
若 ₍joh, 296, (jê) as
烹 ₍p'ăng 660, (p'eng) one fries
小 'siao 795, (hsiao) small
鮮 ₍sien 800, (hsien) fish.

II.

以 'i 278, [If] With
道 tao' 867, reason
莅 li' 522, one governs
天 ₍t'ien 897, } the empire
下 hia' 183, (hsia) }
其 ₍ch'i 342, its
鬼 'kwéi 482, ghosts
不 ₍pu 717, not
神 ₍shăn 737, (shen) spook.
非 ₍fei 136, Not only
其 ₍chi 737, its
鬼 'kwéi 482, ghosts
不 ₍pu 717, not
神 ₍shan 737, spook.
其 ₍ch'i 342, [but] its
神 ₍shăn 737, (shen) gods
不 ₍pu 717, not
傷 ₍shang 739, harm

人 ₍jăn 286, (jen) the people.
非 ₍fei 136, Not only
其 ₍ch'i 342, its
神 ₍shăn 737, (shen) gods
不 ₍pu 717, not
傷 ₍shang 739, harm
人 ₍jăn 286, (jen) the people
聖 shăng' 773, (sheng) [but] the holy
人 ₍jăn 286, (jen) man
亦 yi' 1093, also
不 ₍pu 717, not
傷 ₍shang 739, harms
人 ₍jăn 286, (jen) the people
夫 'fu 142, Since
兩 'liang 526, both of them
不 ₍pu 717, not
相 ₍siang 790, (hsiang) mutually
傷 ₍shang 739, harm;
故 ku' 434, therefore
德 tch, 871 (tê) virtue
交 ₍chiao 367, unitedly
歸 ₍kwéi, 480, returns
焉 ₍yen 1082, thereto.

(Chapter 60.)

第 *ti'* 879,
六 *luh*, 562,
十 *shih*, 708, } Chapter 61.
一 *yih*, 1095,
章 *chang* 22,

謙 *k'ien* 389, Humility's
德 *teh*, 871, virtue.

I.

大 *ta'* 839, A great
國 *kwo* 491, state,
者 *ché* 38, one that
下 *hia'* 183, (*hsia*) downwards
流 *liu* 549, flows,
天 *t'ien* 897,
下 *hia'* 183, (*hsia*) } [becomes the empire's
之 *chi* 53, (*tzŭ*)
交 *chiao* 367, union,
天 *t'ien* 897,
下 *hia'* 183, (*hsia*) } [and] the empire's
之 *chi* 53, (*tzŭ*)
牝 *p'in* 697, wife [female].

II.

牝 *p'in* 697, The female
常 *chang* 740, always
以 *'i* 278, by

靜 *tsing'* 994, (*ching*) quietude
勝 *shăng* 771, (*sheng*) conquers
牡 *'mu* 588, the male,
以 *'i* 278, [and] by
靜 *tsing'* 994, (*ching*) quietude
爲 *wéi* 1047, she makes [herself]
下 *hia'* 183, (*hsia*) lowly,
故 *ku'* 434, thus
大 *ta'* 839, a great
國 *kwo* 491, state
以 *'i* 278, by
下 *hia'* 183, (*hsia*) stooping
小 *'siao* 795, (*hsiao*) to small
國 *kwo* 491, states,
則 *tsch*, 956, (*tsé*) on that account
取 *'ts'ü* 1010, (*ch'ü*) conquers
小 *'siao* 795, (*hsiao*) the smaller
國 *kwo* 491, states.
小 *'siao* 795, (*hsiao*) Smaller
國 *kwo* 491, states
以 *'i* 278, by
下 *hia'* 183, (*hsia*) stooping to
大 *ta'* 839, great
國 *kwo* 491, states,

(Chapter 61.)

則 tseh, 956, (tsě) on that account
取 'ts'ü 1010, (ch'ü) conquer
大 ta' 839, great
國 ,kwo 491, states.

III.

故 ku' 434, Therefore
或 hwo' 1065, some
下 hia' 183, (hsia) stoop
以 'i 278, to
取 'ts'ü 1010, (chü) conquer,
或 hwo' 1065, others
下 hia' 183, (hsia) stoop
而 ',rh 719, (err) and
取 'ts'ü 1010, (chü) conquer.

IV.

大 ta' 839, Great
國 ,kwo 491, states
不 ,pu 717, not
過 kwo' 490, more
欲 yü' 1139, wish
兼 ,chien 382, [than] to unite
畜 h'ü' 98, (hsü) [and] feed
人 ,jăn 286, (jen) the people.
小 'siao 795, (hsiao) Small

國 ,kwo 491, states
不 ,pu 717, not
過 kwo' 490, more
欲 yü' 1139, wish
入 ju' 299, [than] to enter
事 shi'' 764, (ssŭ) [and] to serve
人 ,jăn 286, (jen) the people.
夫 ,fu 142, Now
兩 'liang 526, both
者 'ché 38, ones,
各 kö' 426, each one in its way
得 teh, 872, (tê) gain
其 ,ch'i 342, they
所 su' 817, (shuo) that which
欲 yü' 1139, they wish.
大 ta' 839, [But] the greater
者 'ché 38, one
宜 ,i 273, properly must
爲 ,wéi 1047, make itself
下 hia' 183, (hsia) lower.

(Chapter 62.)

第 ,ti' 879,
六 ,luh, 562,
十 ,shih, 708, } Chapter 62.
二 ,'rh' 721,
章 ,chang 22,

爲 ,wéi 1047, Practise
道 tao' 867, reason.

I.

道 tao' 867, The rational
者 'chê 38, man [is]
萬 wăn' 1040, the ten thou-sand
物 wuh, 1065, (wu) things
之 ,chi 53, (tzŭ) their
奧 ngao' 625, asylum,
善 shan' 752, the good
人 ,jăn 286, (jen) man
之 ,chi 53, (tzŭ) their
寶 'pao 663, treasure,
不 ,pu 717, the not-
善 shan' 752, good
人 ,jăn 286, (jen) } man's
之 ,chi 53, (tzŭ) }
所 su' 817, (shuo) that which
保 'pao 664, he holds fast to.

II.

美 'méi 586, [With] beautiful
言 ,yen 1083, words
可 'k'o 425, [things] one can
以 'i 278, thereby
市 shi' 762, (ssŭ) sell.
尊 ,tsun 1019, [With] noble
行 ,hing 207, (hsing) deeds
可 'k'o 425, one can
以 'i 278, thereby
加 ,chia 350, accomplish more with
人 ,jăn 286, (jen) the people.

III.

人 ,jăn 286, (jen) A man
之 ,chi 53, (tzŭ) [for] his
不 ,pu 717, not-
善 shăn' 752, goodness
何 ,ho 215, why
棄 ch'i' 349, thrown away
之 ,chi 53, (tzŭ) he
有 'yiu 1113, is?
故 ku' 434, Therefore
立 li' 538, was elected
天 ,t'ien 897, heaven's
子 tsz' 1030, (tzŭ) son

(Chapter 62.)

置 ,chi 60, (chih) [and] were appointed
三 ,san 723, three
公 ,kung 459, ministers.

IV.

雖 ,sui 826, Though
有 'yiu 1113, having
拱 'kung 463, reverently in hand
璧 pi' 691, as a screen [the jade insignia]
以 'i 278, [and] thereto
先 ,sien 799, (hsien) riding with
駟 sz'' 836, (ssŭ) four
馬 'ma 571, horses,
不 ,pu 717, [is it] not
如 ,jü 297, equalled
坐 tso' 1002, by sitting still
進 tsin' 990, (chin) [and] propounding
此 ,ts'z' 1034, (ssŭ) this
道 tao' 867, reason?

V.

古 'ku 432, The ancient
之 ,chi 53, (tzŭ) their
所 su' 817, (shuo) } reason
以 'i 278, } why
貴 kwéi' 484, they esteemed
此 ,ts'z' 1034, (t'zŭ) this

道 tao' 867, reason,
者 'ché 38, that is:
何 ,ho 215, What,
也 'ye' 1079, indeed?
不 ,pu 717, Is it not
曰 yueh, 1130, say that
求 ,ch'iu 416, if sought
以 'i 278, then
得 teh, 872, (té) it is obtained?
有 'yiu 1113, [And] he who has
罪 tsui' 1016, sin
以 'i 278, thereby
免 'mien 594, can be saved?
耶 ,yé 1078, (yeh) [query.]
故 ku' 434, Therefore
為 ,wéi 1047, it becomes
天 ,t'ien 897, } the
下 hia' 183, (hsia) } world's
貴 kwéi' 484, honor.

第 'ti 879,
六 luh, 562,
十 shih, 708, } Chapter 63.
三 ,san 723,
章 ,chang 22,

思 ,sz' 834, Consider
始 'shi 761, the beginning.

I.

爲 ,wéi 1047, Do
無 ,wu 1059, the not-
爲 ,wéi 1047, doing.
事 shi' 764, (ssŭ) Practice
無 ,wu 1059, the not-
事 shi' 764, (ssŭ) practising
味 wéi" 1053, Taste
無 ,wu 1059, the not-
味 wéi" 1053, tasting.
大 ta' 839, Make great
小 'siao 795, (hsiao) the small
多 ,to 909, render many
少 'shao 746, [and] the few.

II.

報 ,pao' 665, Respond
怨 yuen' 1138, to hatred
以 'i 278, with
德 teh. 871, (tê) virtue.

III.

圖 ,t'u 918, Contemplate
難 ,nan 614, a difficulty
于 ,yü 1118, while

其 ,ch'i 342, it
易 i" 281, is easy.
爲 ,wéi 1047, Manage
大 ta' 839, a great thing
于 ,yü 1118, while
其 ,ch'i 342, it
細 si' 790, (hsi) is small.
天 ,t'ien 897, ⎫ The
下 hia' 183, (hsia) ⎬ world's
難 ,nan 614, difficult
事 shi" 764, (ssŭ) affairs
必 ,pi" 692, surely
作 tso' 1005, arise
于 ,yü 1118, from
易 i" 281, easiness.
天 ,t'ien 897, ⎫ The
下 hia' 183, (hsia) ⎬ world's
大 ta' 839, great
事 shi" 764, (ssŭ) affairs
必 ,pi" 692, surely
作 tso' 1005, originate
于 ,yü 1118 from
細 si' 790, (hsi) smallness.

(Chapter 63.)

TRANSLITERATION.

IV.

是 shi' 762 (ssŭ) ⎫
以 'i 278, ⎬ Therefore
          ⎭
聖 shăng' 773, (cheng) the holy
人 jăn 286, (jen) man
終 chung 106, (tsung) to the end
不 fu 717, not
爲 wei 1047, plays
大 ta' 839, the great.
故 ku' 434, Therefore
能 năng 616, (neng) he can
成 ch'ăng 77, (cheng) accomplish
其 ch'i 342, his
大 ta' 839, greatness.

V.

夫 fu 142, Now, as
輕 ch'ing 407, rash
諾 noh, 640, (no) promises
必 pih, 692, surely
寡 'kwa 467, are lacking
信 sin' 807, (hsin) faith,
多 to 909, [so for whom] many things
易 'i 281, are easy,
必 pi' 692, surely
多 to 909, many things

難 nan 614, will be difficult
是 shi' 762, (ssŭ) ⎫
以 'i 278, ⎬ Therefore
          ⎭
聖 shăng' 773, (sheng) the holy
人 jăn 286, (jen) man
猶 yiu 1112, even
難 nan 614, [deems] difficult
之 chi 53, [tzŭ] it.
故 ku' 434, Therefore
終 chung 106, (tsung) to the end
無 wu 1059, he has not
難 nan 614, difficulties.

第 ti" 879, ⎫
六 luh, 562, ⎪
十 shih, 708, ⎬ Chapter 64
四 sz" 836, ⎪
章 chang 22, ⎭

守 'sheu 755, Mind
微 wei 1050, the insignificant

I.

其 ch'i 342, That [which]
安 ngan 620, is at rest
易 i' 281, easily

(Chapters 63-64.)

持 ‚ch'i 64, (chih) is kept quiet.
其 ‚ch'i 342, That [which]
未 wéi' 1052, not yet
兆 chao' 34, has appeared
易 i' 281, easily
謀 'meu 587, (mou) is prevented.
其 ‚ch'i 342, That [which]
脆 ts'ui' 1018, is feeble
易 i' 281, easily
破 p'o' 705, is broken.
其 ‚ch'i 342, That [which]
微 ‚wéi 1050, is scanty
易 i' 281, easily
散 'san 724, is scattered.
爲 ‚wéi 1047, Treat
之 ‚chi 53, (tzŭ) them, [viz., things]
于 ‚yü 1118, while
未 wéi' 1052, not yet
有 'yiu 1113, they exist.
治 chi' 59, (chih) Administer
之 ‚chi 53, (tzŭ) them [viz., things]
于 ‚yü 1118, while
未 wéi' 1052, not yet
亂 luan' 570, they are in disorder.

合 ‚hŏ 217, [Of a growth which] with both arms
抱 pao' 665, can be embraced
之 ‚chi 53, (tzŭ) sign of gen.
木 mu' 607, a tree
生 shăng 742, (sheng) grows
于 ‚yü 1118, from
毫 ‚hao 171, a tiny
末 mo' 604, rootlet.
九 'chiu 413, Of nine
層 ‚ts'ăng 952, (tseng) stories
之 ‚chi 53, (tzŭ) [sign of gen.]
臺 ‚t'ai 847, a tower
起 'ch'i 347, rises
于 ‚yü 1118, from
累 'léi 511, accumulating
土 t'u 920, clay-[bricks], [literally earth].
千 ‚ts'ien 980, (chien) Of ten thousand
里 'li 518, miles
之 ‚chi 53, (tzŭ) [sign of gen.]
行 ‚hing 207, (hsing) a journey
始 'shi 761, (ssŭ) begins
于 ‚yü 1118, with
足 ‚tsu 1014, a foot
下 hia' 183, (hsia) beneath.

(Chapter 64.)

II.

為 ˌwéi 1047, [Who] makes,
者 ˋché 38, the one
敗 ṗai' 648, mars
之 ˌchi 53, (tzŭ) it.
執 chih, 67, [Who] seizes of
者 ˋché 38, the one
失 shih, 769, loses
之 ˌchi 53, (tzŭ) it.
聖 shăng' 773, (sheng) The holy
人 ˌjăn 286, (jen) man
無 ˌwu 1059, not
爲 ˌwéi 1047, makes,
故 ku' 434, therefore
無 ˌwu 1059, not
敗 ṗai' 648, he mars.
無 ˌwu 1059, Not
執 chih, 67, he seizes,
故 ku' 434, therefore
無 ˌwu 1059, not
失 shih, 769, he loses.
民 ˌmin 597, The people
之 ˌchi 53, (tzŭ) in their
從 tsung' 1024, pursuing
事 shi' 764, (ssŭ) business,

常 ˌchang 740, [are] always
于 ˌyü 1118, at
幾 ˌchi 333, the approach
成 ch'ǎng 77, (cheng) of completion,
而 ˌrh 719, (err) yet
敗 ṗai' 648, they fail
之 ˌchi 53, (tzŭ) in it.
愼 shăn' 738, (shen) Be careful
終 ˌchung 106, (tsung) to the end
如 ˌju 297, as well as
始 ˋshi 761, (ssŭ) at the beginning
則 tseh, 956, (tsê) then
無 ˌwu 1059, [they] not
敗 ṗai' 648, fail
事 shi' 764, (ssŭ) in business

III.

是 shi˘ 762, (ssŭ) } Therefore
以 ˋi 278,
聖 shăng' 773, (sheng) the holy
人 ˌjăn 286, (jen) man
欲 yü' 1137, desires
不 ˌpu 717, non-
欲 yü' 1137, desires.
不 ˌpu 717, Not
貴 kwéi' 484, he esteems

(Chapter 64.)

難 ₍nan 614, [of] difficult
得 ₍teh, 872, (tê) obtainment
之 ₍chi 53, (tzŭ) sign of gen.
貨 ₍hwo' 256, the treasures.
學 ₍h'iao 209, (hsiao) He learns
不 ₍pu 717, not-
學 ₍h'iao 209, (hsiao) learned-ness.
復 ₍fu 151, He returns to
衆 ₍chung' 108, all
人 ₍jăn 286, (jên) ⎱
之 ₍chi 53, (tzŭ) ⎰ people's
所 su' 817, (shuo) what they
過 ₍kwo' 490, passed by,
以 ₍'i 278, thereby
輔 ₍'fu 146, he assists
萬 ₍wăn' 1040, the ten thousand
物 ₍wuh, 1065, (wu) things
之 ₍chi 53, (tzŭ) [in] their
自 tsz" 1031, (tzŭ) ⎱ natural self
然 ₍jăn 285, so ⎰ development,
而 ₍'rh 719, (err) but
不 ₍pu 717, not
敢 ₍kan, 312, he dares
爲 ₍wéi 1047, to make.

第 ₍ti' 879, ⎫
六 ₍luh, 562, ⎪
十 ₍shih, 708, ⎬ Chapter 65
五 ₍'wu 1060, ⎪
章 ₍chang 22, ⎭

淳 ₍shun 783, Simplicity
德 ₍teh, 871, virtue.

I.

古 ₍'ku 432, ⎱ In olden times,
之 ₍chi 53, (tzŭ) ⎰
善 ₍shan' 752, Well
爲 ₍wéi' 1047, who practised
道 ₍tao' 867, reason,
者 ₍'ché 38, the ones,
非 ₍féi 136, did not
以 ₍'i 278, thereby
明 ₍ming 599, enlighten
民 ₍min 597, the people,
將 ₍tsiang 967, (chiang) [but] will
以 ₍'i 278, thereby
愚 ₍yü 1120, make simple-hearted
之 ₍chi 53, (tzŭ) them.

II.

民 ₍min 597, The people
之 ₍chi 53, (tzŭ) in their

難	₍nan 614, being difficult	者	'chê 38, things
治	chi' 59, (chih) to govern	亦	yi' 1093, [he is] also [like the ancients]
以	'i 278, [that is] because	楷	'ch'iĕ 362, (chieh) a pattern
其	₍ch'i 342, they	式	shih, 767, [and] a model.
智	chi' 58, (chih) cleverness	常	₍chang 740, Always
多	₍to 909, [have too] much.	知	₍chi 53, (chih) to know
以	'i 278, With	楷	'ch'iĕ 362, (chieh) the pattern
智	chi' 58, (chih) cleverness	式	shih, 767, [and] the mode
治	chi' 59, (chih) to govern	是	shi' 762, (ssŭ) this
國	₍kwo 491, a country	謂	wéi' 1054, is called
國之	₍kwo 491, 'chi 53, (tzŭ) } is the country's	玄德	₍hüen 231, (hsüen) profound teh, 871, (tĕ) virtue.

III.

賊	tseh, 959. (tsê) curse.	玄	₍hüen 231, (hsüen) Profound
不	₍pu 717, Not	德	teh, 871, (tĕ) virtue
以	'i 278, with	深	₍shĕn 736, (shen) is deep
智	chi' 58, (chih) cleverness	矣	'i 279, indeed.
治	chi' 59, (chih) to govern	遠	'yuen 1137, [It is] far-reaching
國	₍kwo 491, a country	矣	'i 279, indeed.
國之	₍kwo 491, ₍chi 53, (tzu) } is the country's	與物	'yü 1125, [It is] to wuh, 1063, (wu) [common] things
福	₍fu 150, blessing.	反	'fan 126, the reverse,
知	₍chi 53, (chih) Who knows	矣	'i 279, indeed.
此	₍ts'z' 1034, (tzŭ) these	乃	'nai 612, Thus
兩	₍liang 526, two	至	chi' 60, (chih) [it] obtains

(Chapter 65.)

于 *yü* 1118, to
大 *ta'* 839, great
順。 *shun'* 784, obedience [followership].

第 *ti'* 879,
六 *luh*, 562,
十 *shih*, 708,   } Chapter 66.
六 *luh*, 562,
章 *chang* 22,

後 *heu'* 175, To put behind
已 *'ki* 337, oneself.

I.

江 *chiang* 362, Rivers
海 *'hai* 160, [and] seas
所 *su'* 817, (*shuo*) } the
以 *'i* 278,   } reason why
能 *năng* 616, (*neng*) they can
爲 *wéi* 1047, become
百 *'pai* 707, of the hundred
谷 *'ku* 453, valleys'
王 *wang* 1043, the kings,
者 *'ché* 38, that [is]
以 *'i* 278, because
其 *ch'i* 342, they

善 *shan'* 752, can
下 *hia'* 183, (*hsia*) lower
之 *chi* 53, (*tzŭ*) themselves.
故 *ku'* 434, Therefore
能 *năng* 616, (*neng*) they can
爲 *wéi* 1047, become
百 *'pai* 707, of the hundred
谷 *'ku* 453, valleys
王 *wang* 1043, the kings.

II.

是 *shi'* 762 (*ssŭ*) }
以 *'i* 278,   } Therefore
聖 *shăng'* 773, (*sheng*) the holy
人 *jăn* 286, (*jen*) man
欲 *yü'* 1137, wishing
上 *'shang* 741, to be above
民 *min* 597, the people;
必 *pi'* 692, surely
以 *'i* 278, in
言 *yen* 1083, his words
下 *hia'* 183, (*hsia*) keeps below
之 *chi* 53, (*tzŭ*) them.
欲 *yü'* 1137, Wishing
先 *sien* 799, (*hsien*) to feed
民 *min* 597, the people,

(Chapters 65-66.)

必 ₁pi' 692, surely
以 'i 278, with
身 ₁shăn 735, (shen) his person
後 heu' 175, (hou) keeps behind
之 ₁chi 53, (tzŭ) them.

III.

是 shi' 762, (ssŭ) ⎫
以 'i 278, ⎬ Therefore
　　　　　　　　⎭
聖 shăng' 773, (sheng) the holy
人 ₁jăn 286, (jen) man
處 'ch'u 94, dwells
上 'shang 741, above,
而 ',rh 719, (err) yet
民 ₁min 597, the people
不 ₁pu 717, not
重 chung' 108, (tsung) feel the burden.
處 ₁ch'u 94, He dwells
前 ts'ien 981, (chien) as a leader
而 ',rh 719, (err) yet
民 ₁min 597, the people
不 ₁pu 717, not
害 hai' 161, suffer harm.
是 shi 762, (ssŭ) ⎫
以 'i 278, ⎬ Therefore

天 ₁t'ien 897, ⎫ the
下 hia' 183, (hsia) ⎬ world.
樂 lö' 554, rejoices
推 ₁t'ui 926, in exalting [him]
而 ',rh 719, (err) and
不 ₁pu 717, not
厭 yen' 1089, tires.
以 'i 278, Because
其 ₁ch'i 342, he
不 ₁pu 717, not
爭 ₁chăng 29, (tseng) quarrels,
故 ku' 434, therefore
天 ₁t'ien 897, ⎫ in the
下 hia' 183, (hsia) ⎬ world
莫 mo' 603, none
能 ₁năng 616, (neng) can
與 ₁yü 1125, with
之 ₁chi 53, (tzŭ) him
爭 ₁chăng 29, (tseng) quarrel

第 ti' 879, ⎫
六 luh, 562, ⎪
十 shih, 708, ⎬ Chapter 67
七 ts'ih, 987, ⎪
章 chang 22, ⎭

(Chapters 66–67.)

三 ,san 723, Three
寶 ,pao 663, treasures.

I.

天 t'ien 897, } In the
下 hia' 183, (hsia) } world
皆 ,chih 358, (chieh) all
謂 wéi' 1054, call
我 'ngo 627, me [viz., my Tao]
大 ta' 839, great,
似 sz" 837, (ssŭ) [but] I resemble
不 ,pu 717, the un-
肖 siao' 795, (hsiao) seeming.

II.

夫 ,fu 142, Now
惟 ,wéi 1049, only
大 ,ta' 839, one is great.
故 ku' 434, because
似 sz" 837, (ssŭ) one resembles
不 ,pu 717, the un-
肖 siao' 795, (hsiao) seeming.
若 joh, 296, (jê) If one were
肖 siao' 795, (hsiao) seeming,
久 'chiu 413, how long would be,
矣 ,'i 279, indeed,
其 ,ch'i 342, his

細 si' 790, (hsi) mediocrity

III.

夫 ,fu 142, Now,
我 'ngo 627, I
有 yiu 1113, have
三 ,san 723, three
寶 ,pao 663, treasures.
持 ,ch'i 64, (chih) I preserve
而 ,'rh 719, (err) and
寶 ,pao 663, treasure
之 ,chi 53, (tzŭ) them.
一 yi" 1095, The first
曰 yueh, 1130, is called
慈 ,ts'z' 1033, (tzŭ) compassion.
二 ,'rh' 721, (err) The second
曰 yueh, 1130, is called
儉 chien' 387, economy.
三 ,san 723, The third
曰 yueh, 1130, is called
不 ,pu 717, not
敢 'kan 312, daring
爲 ,wéi 1047, to be
天 ,t'ien 897, } in the
下 hia' 183, (hsia) } world's
先 ,sien 799, (hsien) foremost

(Chapter 67.)

慈 ₍tsʻz 1033, (tzŭ) [Who is] compassionate,
故 kuʻ 434, therefore
能 ₍năng 616, (neng) he can
勇。 ʻyung 1148, be brave.
儉 chien' 387, [Who is] economical,
故 kuʻ 434, therefore
能 ₍năng 616, (neng) he can
廣。 ʻkwang 478, be generous.
不 ₍fu 717, [Who] not
敢 ʻkan 312, dares
爲 ₍wéi 1047, to be
天 ₍tʻien 897,
下 hiaʻ 183, (hsia) } in the world's
先。 ₍sien 799, (hsien) foremost,
故 kuʻ 434, therefore
能 ₍năng 616, (neng) he can be
成 ₍chʻăng 77, (cheng) perfected
器 chʻi' 349, as vessels
長 ₍chʻang 27, of profit.

IV.

今 ₍chin 398, Now if
捨 ʻshé 748, [people] discard
慈 ₍tsʻz 1033, (tʻzŭ) compassion
且 ʻtsʻié 974, (chʻieh) and
勇 ʻyung 1148, are brave,

捨 ʻshé 748, [if] they discard
儉 chien' 387, economy
且 ʻtsʻié 974, (chʻieh) and
廣。 ʻkwang 478, are generous,
捨 ʻshé 748, [if] they discard
後 heuʻ 175, (hou) being behind
且 ʻtsʻié 974, (chʻieh) and
先。 ₍sien 799, (hsien) go to the front,
死 ʻsz' 836, (ssŭ) they will die
矣。 ʻi 279, indeed.
夫 ₍fu 142, However
慈 ₍tsʻz' 1033, (tʻzŭ) [if] they are compassionate,
以 ʻi 278, thereby
戰 chen' 45, (chan) in battles
則 tseh, 956, (tsê) then they will
勝 ₍shăng 771, (sheng) conquer.
以 ʻi 278, Thereby
守 ʻsheu 755, (shou) in the defence
則 tseh, 956, (tsê) then they will
固。 kuʻ 435, be firm.

V.

天 ₍tʻien 897, Heaven,
將 ₍tsiang 967, (chiang) when about
救 chiuʻ 415, to help
之 ₍chi 53, (tzŭ) them [people],

(Chapter 67.)

以 'i 278, with
慈 ₜts'z' 1033, (t'zŭ) compassion
衞 wéi 1054, will protect
之。 ₜchi 53, (tzŭ) them.

第 li' 879,
六 luh, 562,
十 shih, 708, } Chapter 68.
八 pah, 647,
章 ₜchang 22,

配 p'éi' 672, Comply
天 ₜt'ien 897, with heaven.

1.

善 shan' 752, [Who] well
爲 wéi 1047, excels
士 shi' 762, (ssŭ) as a warrior,
者 'ché 38, the one
不 ₜpu 717, is not
武 'wu 1061, warlike.
善 shan' 752, [Who] well
戰 chen' 45, (shan) fights
者 'ché 38, the one
不 ₜpu 717, is not
怒 nu' 641, wrathful.
善 shan' 752, [Who] well

勝 ₜshăng 771, (sheng) conquers
敵 ₜti 902, the enemy,
者 'ché 38, the one
不 ₜpu 717, is not
爭。 ₜchăng 29, (tseng) quarrelsome.
善 shăn' 752, [Who] well
用 yung' 1149, employs
人 ₜjăn 286, (jen) the people,
者 'ché 38, the one
爲 ₜwéi 1047, renders himself
下。 hia 183, (hsia) lowly.
是 shi' 762, (ssŭ) This
謂 wéi 1054, is called
不 ₜpu 717, not-
爭 ₜchăng 29, (tseng) quarrelling's
之 ₜchi 53, (tzŭ) [sign of gen.]
德。 teh, 871, (tê) virtue.
是 shi' 762, (ssŭ) This
謂 wéi' 1054, is called
用 yung' 1149, the employing
人 ₜjăn 286, (jen) of men's
之 ₜchi 53, (tzŭ) [sign of gen.]
力。 li' 536, ability.
是 shi' 762, (ssŭ) This

(Chapters 67 68.)

謂 *wéi'* 1054, is called
配 *p'éi'* 672, complying
天 *t'ien* 897, with Heaven.
古 *'ku* 432, ⎫
之 *chi* 53, (*tzŭ*) ⎬ Since olden times
極 *chi* 393, [this is] the most perfect [the extremest].

第 *ti'* 879, ⎫
六 *luh* 562,
十 *shih* 708, ⎬ Chapter 69.
九 *'kiu* 413,
章 *chang* 22, ⎭

玄 *hüen* 231, Of the mysterious
用 *yung'* 1149, the function.

I.

用 *yung'* 1149, An expert
兵 *ping* 689, of war
有 *'yiu* 1113, has
言 *yen* 1083, the saying:
吾 *wu* 1060, I
不 *pu* 717, not
敢 *'kan* 312, dare
爲 *wéi* 1047, to become
主 *'chu* 87, a host,

而 *rh* 719, (*err*) but
爲 *wéi* 1047, become
客 *k'ŏ'* 429, a guest.
不 *pu* 717, Not
敢 *'kan* 312, I dare
進 *tsin'* 990, (*chin*) to advance
寸 *ts'un'* 1021, an inch
而 *rh* 719 (*err*) but
退 *t'ui'* 926, withdraw
尺 *ch'ih* 71, a foot.

II.

是 *shi'* 762, (*ssŭ*) This
謂 *wéi'* 1054, is called
行 *hing* 207, (*hsing*) marching
無 *wu* 1059, the not-
行 *hing* 207, (*hsing*) marching,
攘 *jang* 290, threatening
無 *wu* 1059, without
臂 *pi'* 678, (*pei*) arms,
仍 *jăng* 291, (*jeng*) charging
無 *wu* 1059, without
敵 *ti* 902, hostility,
執 *chih* 67, seizing
無 *wu* 1059, without
兵 *ping* 698, weapons.

(Chapters 68-69.)

禍 *hwo'* 256, Evil
莫 *mo'* 603, none
大 *ta'* 839, greater
于 *yü* 1118, than
輕 *ch'ing* 407, making light
敵 *ti* 902, of the enemy.
輕 *ch'ing* 407, By making light of
敵 *ti* 902, the enemy
幾 *chi* 333, we will
喪 *sang* 725, lose
吾 *wu* 1060, our
寶 *pao* 663, treasures.

III.

故 *ku'* 434, Therefore
抗 *k'ang'* 321, [when] matched
兵 *ping* 698, armies
相 *siang* 790, (*hsiang*) mutually
加 *chia* 350, encounter,
哀 *shwai* 785, the weaker [the more compassionate]
者 *chě* 38, one
勝 *shăng* 771, (*sheng*) conquers,
矣 *'i* 279, indeed.

第 *ti'* 879,
七 *ts'ih*, 987,
十 *shih*, 708, } Chapter 70
章 *chang* 22,

知 *chi* 53, Of knowing
難 *nan* 614, difficulty.

I.

吾 *wu* 1060, My
言 *yen* 1083, words [are]
甚 *shăn'* 738, (*shen*) very
易 *i'* 281, easy
知 *chi* 53, (*chih*) to understand,
甚 *shăn'* 738, (*shen*) very
易 *i'* 281, easy
行 *hing* 207, (*hsing*) to practise.

II.

天 *t'ien* 987, } [Yet] in the
下 *hia'* 183, (*hsia*) } world
莫 *mo'* 603, no one
能 *năng* 616, (*neng*) can
知 *chi* 53, (*chih*) understand,
莫 *mo'* 603, no one
能 *năng* 616, (*neng*) can
行 *hing* 207, (*hsing*) practise [them].
言 *yen* 1083, Words

TRANSLITERATION. 259

有 ’yiu 1113, have
宗 ‚tsung 1021, (chung) an ancestor.
事 shi” 764, (ssŭ) Business actions [deeds]
有 ’yiu 1113, have
君 ‚chiün 418, a master,
夫 ‚fu 142,
唯 ’wéi 1052, } Just as
無 ‚wu 1059, he is not
知 ‚chi 53, (chih) known,
是 shi” 762, (ssŭ)
以 ’i 278, } therefore
不 ‚pu 717, not
我 ‚wu 1060, I
知 ‚chi 53, (chih) am known.

III.

知 ‚chi 53, (chih) Who know
我 ‚wu 1060, me
者 ’ché 38, those ones
希 ‚hi 176, (hsi) are rare.
則 tsch. 956, (tsê) On that account
我 ‚wu 1060, I am
貴 kwéi’ 484, honorable.
是 shi” 762, (ssŭ)
以 ’i 278, } Therefore

聖 shăng’ 773, (sheng) the holy
人 ‚jăn 286, (jen) man
被 péi” 669, wears
褐 ‚hö 217, wool [not silk]
懷 ‚hwai 243, [and] hides inside
玉 yü’ 1138, gems.

第 ti” 879,
七 ts’ih, 987,
十 shih, 708, } Chapter 71.
一 yih, 1095,
章 ‚chang 22

知 ‚chi 53, Knowledge’s
病 ping’ 700 disease.

I.

知 ‚chi 53, (chih) To know
不 ‚pu 717, the un-
知 ‚chi 53, (chih) knowable
上 ’shang 741, is high.
不 ‚pu 717, Not
知 ‚chi 53, (chih) to know
知 ‚chi 53, (chih) the knowable
病 ping’ 700, is sickness.

II.

夫 ‚fu 142, Now

唯 'wéi 1052, only
病 ping' 700, by being sick
病 ping' 700, of sickness,
是 shi' 762, (ssŭ) ⎫
以 'i 278, ⎬ thereby
　 ⎭
不 ,pu 717, not
病 ping' 700, we are sick.

III.

聖 shăng' 773, (sheng) The holy
人 jăn 286, (jen) man
不 ,pu 717, not
病 ping' 700, is sick.
以 'i 278, Because
其 ,ch'i 342, he
病 ping' 700, is sick
病 ping' 700, of sickness.
是 shi' 762, (ssŭ) ⎫
以 'i 270, ⎬ therefore
　 ⎭
不 ,pu 717, not
病 ping' 700, he is sick.

第 ti' 879, ⎫
七 ts'ih 987, ⎪
十 shih, 708, ⎬ Chapter 72.
二 'rh' 721, ⎪
章 ,chang 22, ⎭

愛 ngai' 619, To cherish
己 'ki 337, oneself.

I.

民 ,min 597, [When] the people
不 ,pu 717, not
畏 wéi' 1054, are afraid
威 ,wéi 1046, of the dreadful,
大 ta' 839, the great
威 ,wéi 1046, dreadful
至 chi' 60, (chih) will come,
矣 'i 279, indeed!
無 ,wu 1059, Do not
狹 hiah, 186, (hsia) render narrow
其 'ch'i 342, their
所 su' 817, (shuo) place where
居 ,chü 437, they dwell.
無 ,wu 1059, Do not
厭 yen' 1089, make wearisome
其 ,ch'i 342, their
所 su' 817, (shuo) place where

生 shăng 742, (sheng) they live.

II.

夫 fu 142, Now
唯 'wéi 1052, only when
不 ‚pu 717, not
厭 yen' 1089, they are made wearisome,
是 shi' 762, (ssŭ) ⎫
以 'i 278, ⎬ thereby
不 ‚pu 717, not ⎭
厭 yen' 1089, they are wearisome.
是 shi' 762, (ssŭ) ⎫
以 'i 278, ⎬ Therefore
聖 shăng 773, (sheng) the holy
人 ‚jăn 286, (jen) man
自 tsz" 1031, (tzŭ) himself
知 ‚chi 53, (chih) knows,
不 ‚pu 717, [but] not
自 tsz" 1031, (tzŭ) himself
見 chien' 385, he regards.
自 tsz'' 1031, (tzŭ) Himself
愛 ngai' 619, cherishes
不 ‚pu 717, [but] not
自 tsz'' 1031, (tzŭ) himself
貴 kwéi 484, he treasures.

故 ku' 434, Therefore
去 'ch'ü 445, he discards
彼 'pi 674, the latter
取 'ts'ü 1010, (chü) [and] chooses
此 'ts'z' 1034, (tzŭ) the former.

第 ti" 879, ⎫
七 ts'ih, 987, ⎪
十 shih, 708, ⎬ Chapter 73.
三 ‚san 723, ⎪
章 ‚chang 22, ⎭

任 jăn' 289, Daring
爲 ‚wéi 1047, to act.

I.

勇 'yung 1148, Courage,
於 ‚yü 1118, [carried] to
敢 'kan 312, daring
則 tseh, 956, (tsê) then leads to
殺 ‚sha 731, death.
勇 'yung 1148, Courage
於 ‚yü 1118, [carried] to
不 ‚pu 717, not-
敢 'kan 312, daring
則 tseh, 956, (tsê) then leads to

活 ,hwo 258, life.
此 ,ts'z' 1034, (tzŭ) These
兩 'liang 526, two
者 'ché 38, things
或 kwo' 259, sometimes
利 li' 521, are beneficial,
或 hwo' 259, sometimes
害 hai' 161, are harmful.

II.

天 ,t'ien 897, ⎫
之 ,chi 53, (tzŭ) ⎭ Heaven's
所 su' 817, (shuo) what is
惡 wu' 1063, hated [despised by, rejected]
孰 ,shu 780, who
知 chi 53, (chih) knows
其 ,ch'i 342, its
故 ku' 434, reason?

III.

是 shi' 762, (ssŭ) ⎫
以 'i 278, ⎭ Therefore
聖 shăng' 773, (sheng) the holy
人 ,jăn 286, (jen) man
猶 ,yiu 1112, even
難 ,nan 614, deems difficult

之 ,chi 53, (tzŭ) it [the reasons of success and failure].

IV.

天 ,t'ien 897, ⎫
之 ,chi 53, (tzŭ) ⎭ Heaven's
道 tao' 867, reason
不 ,pu 717, not
爭 ,chăng 29, (tseng) quarrels
而 ',rh 719, (err) yet
善 shan' 752, well [in a good way, viz., to perfection]
勝 ,shăng 771, (sheng) it conquers;
不 ,pu 717, not
言 ,yen 1083, it speaks
而 ',rh 719, (err) yet
善 shan' 752, well [in a good way]
應 ,ying 1106, it responds;
不 ,pu 717, not
召 chao' 35, it summons
而 ',rh 719, (err) yet
自 tsz'' 1031, (tzŭ) itself
來 ,lai 498, it comes.
繟 'ch'en* K. v. 27, p. 22b. [It acts] in a lenient [slow]
然 ,jan 285, manner,
而 ',rh 719, (err) yet

*This character ch'en=slow is missing in Williams.

(Chapter 73.)

善 ˏshan' 752, [perfect] good
謀 ˏmeu 587, (mou) [are its] devices.

v.

天 ˏt'ien 897, Heaven's
網 'wang 1044, net
恢 ˏkw'ei 487, is vast,
恢 ˏkw'ei 487, so vast;
疏 ˏshu 775, [it is] wide-meshed
而 ˏrh 719, (erh) and yet
不 ˏpu 717, not
失 shih, 769, it loses.

第 ti' 879,
七 ts'ih, 987
十 shih, 708,   } Chapter 74.
四 sz'' 836,
章 ˏchang 22,

制 chi' 57, To overcome
惑 hwoh, 259, delusion.

I.

民 ˏmin 597, [When] the people
不 ˏpu 717, not
畏 wei' 1054, fear
死 'sz' 836, (ssŭ) death,

奈 nai' 613, in what way
何 ˏho 215, [and] how
以 'i 278, with
死 'sz' 836, (ssŭ) death
懼 chü' 440, [can] one frighten
之 ˏchi 53, (tzŭ) them?
若 joh, 296, (jŏ) If
使 'shi 761, (ssŭ) we make
民 ˏmin 597, people
常 ˏchang 740, always
畏 wei' 1054, fear
死 'sz' 836, (ssŭ) death,
而 ˏrh 719, (erh) but [if]
為 ˏwei 1047, [someone should] make
奇 ˏch'i 344, innovations,
者 'chě 38, that one,
吾 ˏwu 1060, I
得 teh, 872, (tě) take
執 chih, 67, [and] seize
而 ˏrh 719, (erh) and
殺 ˏsha 731, kill
之 ˏchi 53, (tzŭ) him,
孰 ˏshu 780, who
敢 'kan 312, will dare?

常 ,*chang* 740, Always
有 ,*yiu* 1113, there is
司 ,*sz'* 835, (*ssŭ*) an executioner
殺 ,*sha* 731, to kill,
者 '*ché* 38, one
殺 ,*sha* 731, [who] kills.
夫 ,*fu* 142, Now [if a man]
代 ,*tai'* 845, taking the place of
司 ,*sz'* 835, (*ssŭ*) the executioner
殺 ,*sha* 731, to kill,
者 '*ché* 38, of the one
殺 ,*sha* 731, [who] kills,
是 ,*shi'* 762, (*ssŭ*) this
謂 ,*wéi'* 1054, is called
代 ,*tai'* 845, taking the place of
大 ,*ta'* 839, the great
匠 ,*tsiang'* 968, (*chiang*) carpenter
劉 ,*liu* 548, [who] hews.
夫 ,*fu* 142, Now
代 ,*tai'* 845. [who] takes the place of
大 ,*ta'* 839, the great
匠 ,*tsiang'* 968, (*chiang*) carpenter
劉 ,*liu* 548, [who] hews,
者 '*ché* 53, the one,

希 ,*hi* 176, (*hsi*) rare
有 '*yiu* 1113, it is [if]
不 ,*fu* 717, not
傷 ,*shang* 739, he injures
手 '*sheu* 754, (*shou*) his hands.
矣 '*i* 279, [a final particle].

第 ,*ti'* 879,
七 ,*ts'ih*, 987,
十 ,*shih*, 708,   } Chapter 75.
五 '*wu* 1060,
章 ,*chang* 22,

貪 ,*t'an* 853, Greediness'
損 ,*sun* 829, loss.

1.

民 ,*min* 597,   } The
之 ,*chi* 53, (*tzŭ*) } people's
饑 ,*chi* 334, starvation
以 '*i* 278, [comes] from
其 ,*ch'i* 342, their
上 '*shang* 741, superior's
食 ,*chih*, 766, consuming
稅 ,*shui* 782,   } of taxes
之 ,*chi* 53, (*tzŭ*) }

(Chapters 74-75.)

TRANSLITERATION.

多 ,to 909, too much.
是 shi' 762, (ssŭ) ⎫
以 'i 278, ⎭ Therefore
饑 ,chi 334, they starve.
民 ,min 597, The people's
之 ,chi 53, (tzŭ) [sign of gen.]
難 ,nan 614, [being] difficult
治 chi' 59, (chih) to govern
以 'i 278, comes from
其 ,ch'i 342, their
上 'shang 741, ⎫
之 ,chi 53, (tzŭ) ⎭ superiors'
有 'yiu 1113, being
爲 ,wéi 1047, too active [meddlesome].
是 shi' 762, (ssŭ) ⎫
以 'i 278, ⎭ Therefore
難 ,nan 614, it is difficult
治 chi' 59, (chih) to govern.

II.

民 ,min 597, ⎫ The
之 ,chi 53, (tzŭ) ⎭ people's
輕 ,ch'ing 407, making light of
死 'sz' 836, (ssŭ) death
以 'i 278, [comes] from

其 ,ch'i 342, their
求 ,ch'iu 416, seeking
生 ,shăng 742, (sheng) ⎫
之 ,chi 53, (tzŭ) ⎭ life's
厚 heu' 176, (hou) intensity,
是 shi' 762, (ssŭ) ⎫
以 'i 278, ⎭ therefore
輕 ,ch'ing 407, they make light of
死 'sz' 836, (ssŭ) death.
夫 ,fu 142, Now
唯 ,wéi 1052, just [who is]
無 ,wu 1059, not
以 'i 278, on
生 ,shăng 742, (sheng) life
爲 ,wéi 1047, bent,
者 'ché 38, the one
是 shi' 762, (ssŭ) this one
賢 ,hien 197, (hsien) is more moral
于 ,yü 1118, than
貴 kwéi' 484, [those who] esteem
生 ,shăng 742, (sheng) life.

(Chapter 75.)

第 *ti'* 879,
七 *ts'ih*, 987,
十 *shih*, 708,   } Chapter 76.
六 *luh*, 562,
章 *chang* 22,

戒 *kiai'* 360, Beware
強 *k'iang* 366, of strength [viz., of being strong].

I.

人 *jăn* 286, (*jen*) Man
之 *chi* 53, (*tzŭ*) in his
生 *shăng* 742, (*sheng*) life,
也 *yĕ* 1079, (*yeh*) is indeed [auxiliary particle]
柔 *jeu* 294, (*jou*) tender
弱 *joh*, 295, (*jao*) [and] weak.
其 *ch'i* 342, [When] he
死 *'sz'* 836, (*ssŭ*) dies,
也 *yĕ* 1079, (*yeh*) he is indeed
堅 *chien*, 380, hard
強 *ch'iang* 366, [and] stiff.
萬 *wan'* 1040, The ten thousand
物 *wuh*, 1065, (*wu*) things,
草 *'ts'ao* 956, the grass,
木 *mu'* 607, [and] trees
之 *chi* 53, (*tzŭ*) in their

生 *shăng* 742, (*sheng*) life
也 *yĕ* 1079, (*yeh*) are indeed
柔 *jeu* 294, (*jou*) tender
脆 *tsui'* 1018, [and] delicate.
其 *ch'i* 342, [When] they
死 *'sz'* 836, (*ssŭ*) die,
也 *yĕ* 1079, (*yeh*) they are indeed
枯 *k'u* 436, rigid
槁 *'kao* 325, [and] dry.

II.

故 *ku'* 434, Therefore
堅 *chien*, 380, the hard
強 *ch'iang*, 366, [and] stiff
者 *'chĕ* 38, ones [are]
死 *'sz'* 836, (*ssŭ*) } death's
之 *chi* 53, (*tzŭ*) }
徒 *t'u* 919, companions [followers]
柔 *jeu* 294, (*jou*) The tender
弱 *joh*, 295, (*jao*) [and] weak
者 *'chĕ* 38, ones [are]
生 *shăng* 742, (*sheng*) } life's
之 *chi* 53, (*tzŭ*) }
徒 *t'u* 919, companions [followers].

(Chapter 76.)

TRANSLITERATION

III.

是 shi¹ 762, (ssŭ)
以 'i 278, ⎱ Therefore
兵 ₍ping 698, [who in] arms
強 ₍ch'iang 366, are strong,
則 tseh, 956, (tsê) then they will
不 ₍pu 717, not
勝 ₍shĕng, 771, (sheng) conquer.
木 mu¹ 607, [When] trees [are]
強 ₍ch'iang, 366, strong,
則 tseh, 956, (tsê) then they will
共 kung¹ 464, be doomed.
強 ₍ch'iang 366, The strong
大 ta¹ 839, [and] great
處 'ch'u 94, stay
下 hia¹ 183, (hsia) below.
柔 jeu 294, (jou) The tender,
弱 joh, 295, (jao) the weak
處 'ch'u 94, stay
上 'shang 741, above.

第 ti" 879,
七 ts'ih, 987,
十 shih, 708, ⎱ Chapter 77
七 ts'ih, 987,
章 ₍chang 22,

天 ₍t'ien 897, Heaven's
道 tao' 867, reason.

I.

天 ₍t'ien 897, ⎱ Heaven's
之 ₍chi 53, (tzŭ)
道 tao' 867, reason,
其 ₍ch'i 342, it
猶 ₍yiu 1112, resembles
張 ₍chang 22, the stretching
弓 ₍kung 461, of a bow.
乎 ₍hu 224, Oh!
高 ₍kao 324, The higher
者 'chê 38, one
抑 yi" 1093, [it] brings down
之 ₍chi 53, (tzŭ) it.
下 hia¹ 183, (hsia) The lower
者 'chê 38, one
舉 'chü 439, [it] raises
之 ₍chi 53, (tzŭ) it.
有 'yiu 1113, Who have

(Chapters 76–77.)

餘 ,yü 1121, abundance,
者 'ch'ê 38, the ones,
損 'sun 829, [it] diminishes
之 ,chi 53, (tzŭ) them.
不 ,pu 717, Who not
足 ,tsu 1014, have enough
者 'ch'ê 38, the ones,
與 ,yü 1125, [it] gives
之 ,chi 53, (tzŭ) to them.

II.

天 ,t'ien 897, } [That is]
之 ,chi 53, (tzŭ) } Heaven's
道 tao' 867, reason.
損 'sun 829, It diminishes
有 'yiu 1113, [those who] have
餘 ,yü 1121, abundance
而 ',rh 719, (err) and
補 'pu 712, completes
不 ,pu 717, [those who have] not
足 ,tsu 1014, enough,

III.

人 ,jăn 286, (jen) } Man's
之 ,chi 53, (tzŭ) }
道 tao' 867, reason
則 tseh, 956, (tsê) is

不 ,pu 717, not
然 ,jan 285, so.
損 'sun 829, It diminishes
不 ,pu 717, [those who have] not
足 ,tsu 1014, enough
以 'i 278, thereby to
奉 fung' 159, (fêng) serve
有 'yiu 1113, [those who] have
餘 ,yü 1121, abundance.
孰 ,shu 780, Who
能 ,năng 616, (neng) can
有 'yiu 1113, have
餘 ,yü 1121, abundance
以 'i 278, for the purpose of
奉 fung' 159, (feng) serving
天 ,t'ien 897, } the
下 hia' 183, (hsia) } world?

IV.

是 shi' 762, (ssŭ) } Therefore
以 'i 278, }
聖 shăng' 773, (sheng) the holy
人 ,jăn 286, (jen) man
爲 wéi 1047, makes,
而 ',rh 719, (err) yet
不 ,pu 717, not

(Chapter 77.)

TRANSLITERATION.

恃 ₁shi' 761, (shih) claims.
功 ₁kung 460, Merit
成 ₁ch'ăng 77, (cheng) he accomplishes,
而 ',rh 719, (err) yet
不 ₁pu 717, not
處 'ch'u 94, dwells there [is attached to it].
其 ₁ch'i 342, He
不 ₁pu 717, not
欲 yü' 1137, wishes
見 chien' 385, to let be seen [to display]
賢 ₁hien 197, (hsien) his excellence.
耶 ₁yé 1078, Does he? [Sign of interogative sentence.]

第 ti' 879,
七 ts'ih, 987,
十 shih, 708,   } Chapter 78.
八 pah, 647,
章 ₁chang 22,

任 jăn' 289, Trust
信 sin' 807, in faith.

I.

天 ₁t'ien 897,   } In the
下 hia' 183, (hsia)   world

柔 ₁jeu 294, (jou) in tenderness
弱 ₁ioh, 295, (jao) [and] weakness
莫 mo' 603, nothing
過 kwo' 490, can more surpass
于 ₁yü 1118, than
水 'shui 781, water,
而 ',rh 719, (err) And
攻 ₁kung 461, who attacks
堅 chien, 380, the hard
強 ₁ch'iang 366, [and] the strong
者 'ché 38, [of] the ones,
莫 mo' 603, no one
之 ₁chi 53, (tzŭ) of them
能 ₁năng 616, (neng) can
勝 shăng 771, (sheng) surpass [it].
其 ₁ch'i 342, Among things
無 ₁wu 1059, there is none which
以 'i 278, herein
易 i' 281, takes the place
之 ₁chi 53, (tzŭ) of it.
                [The reason is]:
弱 ₁ioh, 295, (jao) The weak
之 ₁chi 53, (tzŭ) being
勝 shăng 771, (sheng) conquerors
強 ₁ch'iang 366, of the strong

(Chapters 77-78.)

柔 ˌjeu 294, (jou) The tender
之 ˌchi 53, (tzŭ) being
勝 ˌshăng 771, (sheng) conquerors
剛 ˌkang 318, of the stiff.
天 ˌt'ien 897, } In the
下 ˌhia' 183, (hsia) } world
莫 mo' 603, there is no one
不 ˌpu 717, [who] not
知 ˌchi 53, (chih) knows [this],
莫 mo' 603, [but] no one
能 ˌnăng 616, (neng) can
行 ˌhing 207, (hsing) practise [it].

II.

故 ku' 434, Therefore
聖 shăng' 773, (sheng) the holy
人 ˌjăn 286, (jen) man
云 ˌyun 1142, declares:
受 sheu' 756, (shou) Who is charged with
國 ˌkwo 491, } the
之 ˌchi 53, (tzŭ) } country's
垢 'keu 330, (kou) sin [moral filth],
是 shi' 762, (ssŭ) this one
謂 wéi' 1054, is called
社 shé' 748, of the altar's

稷 ts'ih, 987, (chi) millet [of the grain sacrifice]
主 ˌchu 87, the master.
受 sheu' 756, (shou) Who is charged with
國 ˌkwo 491, } the
之 ˌchi 53, (tzŭ) } country's
不 ˌpu 717, un-
祥 ˌsiang 792, (hsiang) blessings,
是 shi' 762, (ssŭ) this one
謂 wéi' 1054, is called
天 ˌt'ien 897, } the
下 ˌhia' 183, (hsia) } empire's
王 ˌwang 1043, king.
正 chăng' 75, (cheng) True
言 ˌyen 1083, words
若 joh, 296, (jĕ) seem
反 'fan 126, paradoxical.

第 ti' 879,
七 ts'ih, 987,
十 shih, 708, } Chapter 79
九 'kiu 413,
章 ˌchang 22,

任 jăn' 289, Sustain
契 k'i' 349, contracts.

TRANSLITERATION.

I.

和 ₁hwo 254, [When] reconciling
大 ta' 839, a great
怨 yuen' 1138, hatred,
必 pi' 692, surely
有 'yiu 1113, there will
餘 ₁yü 1121, remain
怨 yuen' 1138, some hatred.
安 ₁ngan 620, Where-
以 'i 278, by
爲 ₁wéi 1047, to make [it]
善 shan' 752, good?
是 shi' 762, (ssŭ) ⎫
以 'i 278, ⎬ Therefore
             ⎭
聖 shăng' 773, (sheng) the holy
人 ₁jăn 286, (jen) man
執 chih, 67, holds
左 'tso 1002, the left side
契 ch'i' 349, of his contract
而 ',rh 719, (err) and
不 ₁pu 717, not
責 tseh, 957, exacts
于 ₁yü 1118, from
人 ₁jăn 286, (jen) others.
有 'yiu 1113, [Who] have

德 teh, 871, (tĕ) virtue
司 ₁sz' 835, (ssŭ) keep
契 ch'i' 349, [their] contract [obligations].
無 ₁wu 1059, [Who] have not
德 teh, 871, (tĕ) virtue
司 ₁sz' 835, (ssŭ) insist on
徹 ch'eh, 42, (chĕ) [their] claims.

II.

天 ₁t'ien 897, Heaven's
道 tao' 867, reason
無 ₁wu 1059, has no
親 ₁ts'in 991, (chin) preference [nepotism, family relation]
常 ₁chang 740, [but] always
與 'yü 1125, helps
善 shan' 752, the good
人 ₁jăn 286, (jen) man.

第 ti' 879, ⎫
八 pah, 647, ⎬ Chapter 80
十 shih, 708, ⎪
章 ₁chang 22, ⎭

獨 tuh, 921, Alone
立 lih, 538, standing.

I.

小 'siao 795, (hsiao) [In] a small
國 ₁kwo 491, country

(Chapters 79–80.)

寡 'kwa 467, [with] few
民 ,min 597, people
使 'shi 761, (ssŭ) let [them]
有 'yiu 1113, have
什 shih, 768, over ten men
伯 ,poh, 707, (ho) [and] hundred men,
人 ,jăn 286, (jen) men
之 ,chi 53, (tzŭ) as their
器 ch'i' 349, officers [vessels]
而 ',rh 719, (err) but
不 ,fu 717, not
用 yung' 1149, use their power.
使 'shi 761, (ssŭ) Let
民 ,min 597, the people
重 chung' 108, esteem
死 'sz' 836, (ssŭ) death
而 ',rh 719, (err) and
不 ,fu 717, not
遠 'yuen 1137, to a distance
徙 'si 789, move.
雖 ,sui 826, Though
有 'yiu 1113, they have
舟 ,cheu 48, (chou) ships
輿 ,yü 1122, [and] carriages,

無 ,wu 1059, they have no
所 su' 817, (shuo) occasion [literally, "place where"]
乘 ,ch'ăng 772, (cheng) to ride
之 ,chi 53, (tzŭ) in them.
雖 ,sui 826, Though
有 'yiu 1113, they have
甲 'chia 355, armors
兵 ,ping 698, [and] weapons
無 ,wu 1059, they have no
所 su' 817, (shuo) occasion
陳 ,ch'ăn 19, (chen) to don
之 ,chi 53, (tzŭ) them.
使 'shi 761, (ssŭ) Let
民 ,min 597, the people
復 ,fu 151, return to
結 chieh, 376, knotted
繩 ,shing 772, (sheng) cords
而 ',rh 719, (err) and
用 yung' 1149, use
之 ,chi 53 (tzŭ) them;
甘 ,kan 310, [let them] delight
其 ch'i 342, in their
食 shih, 766, food;
美 'mei 586, be proud of

(Chapter 80.)

TRANSLITERATION.

其 ₍ch'i₎ 342, their
服 ₍fu₎ 152, clothes;
安 ₍ngan₎ 620, be content with
其 ₍ch'i₎ 342, their
居 ₍chü₎ 437, dwellings;
樂 ₍lŏ'₎ 554, rejoice in
其 ₍ch'i₎ 342, their
俗 ₍su₎ 822, customs.

II.

鄰 ₍lin₎ 541, A neighboring
國 ₍kwo₎ 491, country
相 ₍siang₎ 790, (hsiang) mutually
望 ₍wang'₎ 1045, might be in sight,
鷄 ₍chi₎ 334, Cocks
狗 'keu 329, (kou) [and] dogs
之 ₍chi₎ 53, (tzŭ) their
聲 ₍shing₎ 771, (sheng) voice
相 ₍siang₎ 790, (hsiang) mutually
聞 ₍wăn₎ 1041, (wen) might be heard.
民 ₍min₎ 597, The people
至 ₍chi'₎ 60, (chih) will reach
老 'lao 508, old age
死 'sz' 836, (ssŭ) and die,
不 ₍pu₎ 717, [but] not

相 ₍siang₎ 790, (hsiang) mutually
往 'wang 1044, they will visit
來 ₍lai₎ 498, or come and go.

第 ti' 879,
八 pah, 647,
十 shih, 708,   } Chapter 81
一 yih, 1095,
章 ₍chang₎ 22,

顯 'hien 199, Propounding
質 chih, 68, the essential.

I.

信 sin' 807, (hsin) Faithful
言 ₍yen₎ 1083, words
不 ₍pu₎ 717, are not
美 'mei 586, pleasant.
美 'mei 586, Pleasant
言 ₍yen₎ 1083, words
不 ₍pu₎ 717, are not
信 sin' 807, (hsin) faithful.
善 shan' 752, The good
者 'chĕ 38, ones [i. e., men]
不 ₍pu₎ 717, not
辯 pien' 688, dispute.

(Chapters 80–81.)

辯 *pien'* 688, Who dispute
者 *'chê* 38, the ones
不 *pu* 717, not
善。 *shan'* 752, are good.
知 *chi* 53, (*chih*) The knowing
者 *'chê* 38, ones
不 *pu* 717, not
博 *poh,* 706, (*po*) are learned.
博 *poh,* 706, (*po*) The learned
者 *'chê* 38, ones
不 *pu* 717, not
知。 *chi* 53, (*chih*) know.

II.

聖 *shăng'* 773, (*sheng*) The holy
人 *jăn* 286, (*jen*) man
不 *pu* 717, not
積 *tsi* 986, (*chi'*) hoards.
既 *chi'* 339, Having
以 *'i* 278, thereby
為 *wêi* 1047, worked
人 *jăn* 286, (*jen*) for others;
己 *'chi* 337, he himself
愈 *yü* 1126, the more exceedingly

有。 *yiu* 1113, will acquire.
既 *chi'* 339, Having
以 *'i* 278, thereby
與 *yü* 1123, given
人 *jăn* 286, (*jen*) to the people
己 *'chi* 337, he himself
愈 *yü* 1126, the more exceedingly
多。 *to* 909, will have plenty.
天 *t'ien* 897, } Heaven's
之 *chi* 53, (*tzŭ*)
道 *tao'* 867, reason
利 *li'* 521, benefits
而 *'rh* 719, (*err*) but
不 *pu* 717, not
害。 *hai'* 160, injures.
聖 *shăng'* 773, (*sheng*) The holy
人 *jăn* 286, (*jen*) } man's
之 *chi* 53, (*tzŭ*)
道 *tao'* 867, reason [is]
為 *wêi* 1047, to act
而 *'rh* 719, (*err*) but
不 *pu* 717, not
爭。 *chăng* 29, (*tseng*) to quarrel.

(Chapter 81.)

NOTES AND COMMENTS

NOTES AND COMMENTS.

[The numbers attached to the transcriptions of the Chinese characters commented upon in these notes, indicate their respective places in the passages and chapters under which they are mentioned. References to Sze Ma-Ch'ien's Historical Introduction are made by using the abbreviation S. M. Ch.; references to words in the Tao-Teh-King are simply given by figures denoting the chapter, the section, and the number of the word.]

HISTORICAL INTRODUCTION BY SZE-MA-CH'IEN.

Sze means "trustee," *ma* "horse," and *ch'ien* "to move to distance."

The word *chw'en*, which means as a noun "report" or "tradition," as a verb "to transmit," might in this connexion be better translated "biography."

I.

While we should begin in an enumeration such as this with the smaller and rise to the larger, the Chinese mention first the larger and proceed to the smaller. We should say: Lao-Tze was born in the village of Goodman's Bend, Grinding County, Thistle Province, Bramble State. For further details see pages 3-6 in the first chapter of the Introduction.

The characters *ché* (3) and *jan* (12) "one" and "man" belong together, but in a translation the former has naturally to be dropped. The word *jan*, man, is used in the sense of the English endings *er* (in such words as London*er*) and *ian* (in Washington*ian*).

The word *yé* (13) means "indeed." It is an affirmation which is here used as a final particle, indicating the conclusion of the sentence.

II.

The word *shi* (3) sometimes translatable by "esquire," without being exactly an aristocratic title, is a term of distinction; it is added to family names of prominence.

☞ It would be impolite in Chinese society to address men of distinction by their names, which is a privilege reserved to their most intimate friends only. Appellations are given to young men when they become of age or at the ceremony of graduation. Lao-Tze's appellation *Poh Yang* (7-8), Prince Positive, is apparently a distinction which was given him in his youth by his teachers. Yang is the positive principle, representing the sun, south, and manliness. (See Note to Chapter 42, i. 20).

☞ In addition to appellations, Chinese people receive a title after their death. This posthumous name is intended to characterise the man's life-work. Lao-Tze's posthumous title *Tan* does not mean "long-eared" but "long-lobed," and as long lobes are regarded as a symptom of virtue, it means "a master," or "a teacher," in the sense in which the term applies to a Buddha or a Christ. In all statues of Buddha, the ears have exceedingly long lobes, which according to Asiatic taste is not only a sign of virtue but also a mark of beauty.

The word *chi* (16) is very common in Chinese. It indicates that the following words stand in some relation to prior words It may sometimes be translated by "his, her, its, or theirs," sometimes by placing the preceding noun into the genitive; and sometimes it serves as a pronoun of some preceding substantive, in which case it is translated by "him, her, it, or them." When connecting dependent sentences it may be translated by "that; as; when," etc., without, however, being otherwise an equivalent term of these words.

III.

The term *yü* (8), "with," serves to indicate the indirect object.

IV.

The relative *su* (5) and the pronoun *ché* (7), the ones, belong together.

The word *i* (13) means "to finish," "to pass," and is employed to indicate the perfect tense. It must be distinguished from *chi*, self, which presents the same appearance. Compare Williams, *S. D.*, p. 278 (*i*) with, p. 337, (*chi*).

V.

K'iün (2) *tsz'* (3), "the superior sage," or "the royal philosopher," is a common term in Chinese. It means "the ideal man," and is a synonym of *shang jan,* "the holy man, the saint, the sage." See Introduction pp. 27-29.

The word *shi* (6) means "the right time" or "the right season."

The word *kia* (8) means literally "mounting a carriage."

P'ung (14) is, according to the commentators, a plant growing in the sand and easily carried about in the winds.

The word *lêi* (15) means "to heap," "to gather," "to bind." But the commentators declare that it acquires in this connexion the sense of drifting or being carried about.

VI.

Williams (*S. D.*, p. 1146) defines the word *yung* (14) "to receive," or, as a noun, "face ; mien ; screen."

VII.

The word *k'ü'* (1) "depart" is here causative : "let depart."

The words *tsz'* (2) *chi* (3), "the sir's," stand here in the second person, meaning "sir, your," etc.

The word *k'i* (5) means "the vital principle, air, breath, spirit, mettle." See the translator's article on " Chinese Philosophy " in *The Monist*, Vol. VI., No. 2, pp. 211-214.

The word *seh* (9), color, is used in the sense of showy or stagelike behavior, bland manners, and externalities which are for the eye only.

The position of this sentence cannot be retained in English. It means : "That is what (22) I (21) communicate (24) to (23), the sir (25), [in a way] like (26) this (27), and (28) that is all (29)."

VIII.

☞ Confucius felt much elated at his endeavor to set the world an example of decorous demeanor. He probably expected praise for realising the ideal of propriety, not censure, and was, therefore, greatly dismayed when Lao-Tze denounced his highest aspirations as "proud airs' and "affectations." The basis of Confucian ethics is "filial piety" which inculcates reverence for parents, superiors, and ancestors. Confucius represents belief in tradition. The wisdom of the sages of yore is to him a divine revelation which if questioned would leave the world without any standard of right. Lao-Tze recognises no personal authority whatever, and bases his ethics upon the eternal norm of the

Tao, upon abstract reason, the immutable principles of right, of truth, and goodness. Confucius, unable to grasp Lao-Tze's philosophy, is quite shocked at his condemnation of reverence. The personalities of the sages of yore are to Lao-Tze a matter of the past, their bones moulder in the dust; he considers their words alone as that which still remains of their existence, the value of which he measures by their agreement with the Tao.

Tsz' (5) means "child, boy, philosopher, sage." *Ti* (4) *tsz'* (5), younger followers, means "disciples."

Sheu (20) means any hairy quadruped that is wild; brutes, especially game. (Williams, S. D., p. 756.)

IX.

The word *k'ò* (3) means, as a noun, "power," or "ability;" as a verb, "to be able to be," implying a passive condition. If followed by *i* (4) as here, both words together acquire an active meaning and are commonly translated by "can" or "could." The word *i*, if used as a verb, means "to use, to aid, to serve, to concern oneself with." As a preposition it means "by," "through," "with." (See Williams, S. D., p. 278). Compare the note to Chapter I, i., 2.

X.

The verb *chi'* (1) means "to go to," "to reach" (see xii, 12), when used as a preposition and in connexion with *yü* (2) it may be translated by "as to," "concerning," "with reference to."

The word *'rh* (12) is, as a rule, to be translated by "and" or "but." In this connexion it changes the next following *shàng*, high, into an adverb, viz., "up to" or "upwards."

The word *yé* (24) indicates that the sentence which terminates with it is a question.

XI.

The word *siu* (3) means "to cultivate," "to study," "to practise." (See Williams, S. D., p. 811.)

XII.

Here *chi* (4) (the same as ii., 15 *et alias*) is added to the end of the sentence. It refers to *kiu*, "long time," and we transliterate it by "then."

The word *kwan* (13) means custom-house, toll-gate, boundary, frontier, pass, frontier-pass. (See Williams, S. D., p. 472.)

XIII.

The word *yin* (3) means "to grasp the hand," "to govern." As a noun, "chief or overseer." (Williams, *S. D.*, p. 1102.) *Hi* (4) means "to rejoice." Thus the whole name *Yin-Hi* signifies "he who rejoices being a chief."

K'iang (10) means "to force," "to compel." Here it should be translated "to request earnestly." (See Williams, *S. D.*, p. 366.)

As a verb *wéi* (11) means "to act," "to do." As a preposition, "for the benefit of," "with regard to," "for the sake of." (See Gabelentz, *Anfgr.*, p. 52, § 97, V.)

XIV.

The words *yü* (1) *shi* (2), "to this," mean in their combination "thereupon." (See Gabelentz, *Anfgr.*, p. 55, § 103.)

Shang hia p'ien (8-10) means literally "of a higher and lower," i. e., a former and latter, division (installment). We should say, consisting of two parts.

THE OLD PHILOSOPHER'S CANON ON REASON AND VIRTUE.

King is the title of a book which has been canonised as a standard authority on the subject; it is sometimes translated classical book, or briefly classic, sometimes canon. See the quotation from Legge on page 38.

The ordinal in Chinese is expressed by the noun *ti* which corresponds to the English ending *th*, only that it precedes the number to which it is attached.

The term *chang* means "section" or "chapter."

CHAPTER I.

T'i, in the heading, is a compound of bone and sacrificial vessel. The word means, as a noun, "body;" as a verb, "to embody," "to realise," "to render solid," "to incarnate." (See Williams, *S. D.*, p. 884.)

The word *K'o* (2), as a noun, "power," as a verb, "to be able," is always followed by a passive form, while *K'o i* (see note to S. M. Ch. ix. 3-4) is followed by an active form; accordingly, *k'o tao* means "it can be reasoned," and *k'o i tao* would mean "it can reason."

☞ The sentence i. 1-3 may be translated in various ways. Our version, "The Reason that can be reasoned," is the simplest translation that can be offered, but we might as well translate "the word that can be spoken," or, "the logic that can be argued," or, "the path that can be trodden." To avoid all these difficulties, Chalmers translates "the *tau* (or *tao*) that can be *tau*ed." The word *tao* comes nearest, as explained in the Introduction (pp. 9-10) to the Greek term *logos*, as used in the Fourth Gospel of the New Testament.

The word *fei* (4), "not," differs from *pu*, "not," by being more emphatic. *Pu* is the simple negation, in compounds answering the English *un*- or *in*-, as, e. g., *pu teh*, "unvirtue" (see Chapter 38); *pu shan*, "ungoodness" or "evil" (Chapter 2, ii.), *pu chi* (Chapter 3, vi., 6-7) "ungoverned" or "anarchical," etc. But *fêi* means "by no means," implying a disavowal and an earnest rejection. *Wû* is still another kind of negation which also frequently occurs in compounds, such as *wu ming*, *wu yü*, etc. (See Williams, *S. D.*, pp. 136, 717, and 1059.)

II.

The words *wu ming* (1-2) mean "nameless." *Wu* (see Williams, *S. D.*, p. 1059) means "destitute of," "not having," answering in compounds to the English ending *-less*.

☞ The nameless, or unnameable, *wu ming* (1-2) is not only the undetermined, the abstract, but also the holy, the ineffable. The nameable, *yiu ming* (7-8), is that which can be determined. It is the specific or concrete. For *yiu* see Williams, *S. D.*, p. 1113.

The term *wan wuh* (9-10), the myriad beings, things or creatures (see Williams, *S. D.*, pp. 1040, 1065) means nature in its concrete existence as the sum total of all that exists. (See the first note to Chapter 2.)

The character *chi* (11) is the sign of the genitive. Always follows its noun. (See S. M. Ch. ii. 16.)

The sentence 7-12 means the immanent Tao, as the nameable, which is the factor that shapes the world of concrete realities.

III.

The word *ku* (1), "cause," "reason" (Williams, *S. D.*, p. 434) is commonly used by Lao-Tze to introduce a quotation. It is tantamount to "therefore it has been said," or, "thus you have heard."

The words *wu yü* (3-4), "desireless," and *yiu yü* (10-12) "having desire," or, "desirous," form a similar contrast as *wu ming* and *yiu ming*.

The word *miao* (8) denotes "mysterious" or "spiritual," 'mystery" or "spirituality."

IV.

The word *ché* (3), which is the same as S. M. Ch. i., 3, and ix., 2, etc., makes a noun of preceding adjectives or verbs, like the English word "one," or, "such a one," or, "he who." The two things meant are, presumably, the nameless and the nameable.

CHAPTER 2.

I.

The term *t'ien hia* (1-2), under the Heaven, denotes the world in about the same sense as in English. It means the cosmos and also the people, i. e., mankind at large, and especially the Chinese Empire. The terms *wan wuh* (Chapter 1, ii. 9-10), "the ten thousand things," and *wéi wu*, "the activity of the beings" are synonyms. The former may also be translated by "the whole world"; it is nature as the sum total of concrete existence. The latter is the inherent nature or character of things. Another term for "nature" or "universe" which, however, does not occur in the *Tao-Teh-King*, is *yü ch'eu*, signifying the whole cosmos in space as well as time. *Yü* means "the canopy of heaven," and *ch'eu* "from the beginning till now." See *W. S. D.*, pp. 1126 and 49 ; compare *Le livre des mille mots* (*Thsien-tseu-wen*) by St. Julien, note to words 5 and 6.

The word *i* (11), "that is all," is a final particle indicating the end of a sentence, sometimes translated by "enough," and sometimes omitted. (See Williams, *S. D.*, p. 278.)

II.

☞ That Lao-Tze identifies the origin of evil with the conscious distinction between or the knowledge of good and evil, reminds us of the ideas that underlie the Biblical account of the fall of man. Adam's state before the fall is supposed to be a condition in which he does not know the difference between good and evil.

III.

Existence, *yiu* (2), translates in Buddhist Scriptures the Sanskrit term *bhava*. (See Williams, *S. D.*, p. 1113.) The present passage reminds us of Hamlet's phrase, " to be or not to be."

Shăng (5), "to produce," is here, as indicated by *siang*, "mutually," either passive or must be taken as a reflexive verb The verb *shăng* (such is the pronunciation accŏrding to Williams, *S. D.*, p. 742) was probably pronounced by Lao-Tze *shing*, for it rhymes with *ching*, "to perfect, to form," *hing*, "to shape," and *k'ing*, to incline. The words *hwo* or *ho* (21) and *sui* (25) must also have rhymed in their ancient pronunciation.

IV.

Shi i, (1-2) "this for," is used exactly as our English word "therefore." Subsequently it will be thus translated.

Wu wéi (6-7) is the favorite term of Lao-Tze and contains in one word the fundamental principle of his ethics. (See Williams, *S. D.*, pp. 1059, 1047.)

V.

The particle *yen* (4), "there!" "well!" "why?" is descriptive and characterises the action as enduring or continuously taking place. As a final particle, "truly," "indeed," as an initial particle, "how?" "who is it?" "why?" (See Gabelentz, *Anfgr.*, p. 58, § 109; and Williams, *S. D.*, pp. 1082-1083.)

VI.

Shăng (1), Williams, *S. D.*, p. 742, "to grow," "to beget,' 'to quicken," "to live."

Chü (13), "he dwells in his merit." The term is frequently translated by "attaching oneself to."

VII.

Fu (1), "now," "forasmuch as." (Williams, *S. D.*, p. 142.)

Wêi (2) must frequently remain untranslated; sometimes, as for instance in the sentence quoted on p. 14 from the *Shu King*, i takes the place of the auxiliary verb, "is" or "are." (Williams, *S. D.* p., 1049.)

CHAPTER 3.
III.

Stanislas Julien reads between *sin* (6), "heart," and *pu* (7), ' not," the word *min*, "people," a repetition of the preceding *min*, 3, i. 5 and 3, ii. 8.

Three advices given to rulers, stating what they should *not* do; *pu shang* (3, i. 1-2), "not to exalt;" *pu kwéi* (3, ii. 1-2), "not prize;" and *pu chien* (3, iii. 1-2), "not to look at."

IV.

☞ *Sin* (9), heart, is "the seat of desire," while *fu* (12) (see Williams, *S. D.*, p. 151) which means literally "stomach," is conceived to be "the seat of the mind." As an adjective it means "dear," "intimate," and the most probable interpretation is that the word *fu* is here intended to mean the seat of mental capacities and sensible sentiment, as opposed to *sin*, the seat of desires or passions.

☞ A similar contrast is intended between *chi* (15) and *kuh* (18). The former means "will," "wish," "desire"; the latter, "bone." The former characterises self-willed or head-strong people; the latter, sturdiness, strength, character, or, in a word, backbone.

V.

Chī (5), "to know," is here used in an evil sense; viz., "to be cunning," or "to be crafty." *Wu chi* (4–5) means "not cunning," "unsophisticated;" and *chi ché* (10–11), "the crafty."

Yé (15), "indeed," the particle of affirmation, renders the sentence emphatic.

VI.

The phrase *wei wu wéi* (1–3), "to act with non-assertion," is an irrefutable evidence that *wu wéi* cannot mean "inactivity."

CHAPTER 4.

I.

The characters *pu ying* (7–8) belong together, meaning "never exhausted," or briefly "inexhaustible." For *pu* in the sense of the English *in-* or *un-*, see note to Chapter 1, i. 4.

Whether we take *tao* (1) or *yung* (4) as the subject of *pu ying* (7–8) is indifferent. The sense is in either case the same.

Hu (10), "oh!" "well!" "indeed?" is a particle of exclamation.

☞ The word *Tsung* (15), "ancestor," "patriarch," (St. Julien, "premier aïeul"; Strauss, "Urvater"; "Ahnherr") must be regarded as a synonym of *Ti*, "the Lord or God."

II.

This passage, which is repeated in Chapter 56, is a poetical quotation. The words *fän* (6), "fetter," and *ch'än* (12), "dust," are rhymes.

☞ The words of this passage, *t'ung ch'i ch'ăn* (10-12), "it becomes one with its dust," are, in the translator's opinion, clear, but it is difficult to give an exact translation. It means that the Tao's sameness, its own identity, is preserved even in the smallest and most contemptible of things, viz., in the motes of the dust. The purely formal laws of logic, mathematics and pure mechanics are the same for stars and for molecules.

III.

☞ Two of my Japanese editions read *hwo*, which means "apparently, probably" (Williams, *S. D.*, p. 224), while the two others read *joh*, which means "likely" (*ib.*, p. 296). St. Julien, adopting the isolated reading of his edition G, prefers to read *chang* (eternally), which, however, seems to be the emendation of an ancient copyist. The reading *hwo* gives no sense, and may have slipped in as being to a certain degree a synonym of *joh*. In adopting the reading *joh* (4), we interpret the passage to mean: "it seems in its likeness to remain," that is to say, "it appears to be immutable."

☞ The term *Ti* (13) or frequently *Shang Ti*, meaning 'Lord" or "the highest Lord," is commonly used in Chinese in the same sense as the English term Lord in the Bible. It means God and implies always the personality of God. The context, however, justifies neither the conclusion that Lao-Tze regarded the Tao as a personal Deity, nor that he thought of the Tao and God as two distinct entities. He may and probably did introduce the word *ti* (God), as commonly used and understood by the people neither affirming nor denying his existence, simply stating that Tao, or Reason, or the Logos (viz., the prototype of human reason, those inalienable conditions of all the relations of any possible reality, which logicians and mathematicians formulate in rules that are possessed of an intrinsic necessity and universality) is truly and unequivocally eternal; it is absolutely eternal, while the Lord, supposing him to be a personal being, can only be regarded as relatively eternal. The Tao is prior even to God.

CHAPTER 5.

I.

☞ There has been much discussion about the meaning of grass-dogs. The common explanation suggested by the context of this passage is that grass-dogs or straw-dogs were used for sacrificial purposes, and probably offered as a burnt offering instead of living victims. Such is the traditional interpretation of all the commentators. Plaenckner's interpretation that grass-dogs were revered as a religious symbol (and not sacrificed or burned) is improbable.

II.

☞ This passage is difficult. The commentators explain *jăn* (4) "humane or benevolent," as "having particular affection." Accordingly the sentence would mean, that the sage is not sentimental; he has as little preferences as heaven and earth, where the sun shines on the good as well as the evil, and where both, the good and the evil, are finally doomed to die as grass-dogs are sacrificed. The holy man understands that according to the course of nature man is doomed to die and his life is like a sacrifice. Harlez deviates from the traditional interpretation of the passage by translating: "Si le ciel et la terre étaient sans bonté, ils regarderaient tous les hommes comme des chiens de paille etc." This avoids the difficulty of saying that the sage is not humane; but what sense would the whole chapter have? And is not the idea that heaven shows no partiality a favorite idea of Lao-Tze, who repeats it in another sentence of chapter 79, the construction of which is not subject to the slightest doubt, where he says *T'ien tao wu ts'in*, "heaven's Tao shows no nepotism."

III.

Plaenckner allows his imagination too much play in translating *t'ien ti chi chien*, the space between heaven and earth, by *Weltmenschen* or worldlings.

T'o (7) means a bag, open at both ends, a purse (Williams, S. D., p. 915), and *yoh* (8), a flute or fife (*ib.*, p. 1117). Both words combined are (as Williams states on p. 915) a bellows, or a tube through which potters blow into the fire, and not, as Plaenckner translates, a "bag-pipe."

IV.

This passage is a quotation, and appears to be a proverb. "The man of many words is frequently at his wit's end and will scarcely stick to the truth," for that is here the meaning of the middle path. (See the Introduction pages 31-32.)

Chung (16) means the middle; here it means the golden middle, i. e., the path of virtue and truth.

CHAPTER 6.

I.

Our interpretation of *ku shăn* (1-2), the valley spirit, is set forth in the Introduction on page 32. The quotation is, as Lieh Tse reports, attributed by the commentator T'u-T'au-Kien to Hwang Ti, the yellow emperor.

P'in (8) is the term in natural science to denote the female sex, mother sheep, hens, or mother birds, etc.

III.

The Chinese character following the word *mien* (1) "continually" is the sign of repetition. It means that the previous word, *mien*, should be read twice, and renders the word emphatic. The repetition is frequently translated by "very."

Pu ch'in (7-8), without effort, means it comes natural. It is a synonym of *tsz' jan* in Chapter 17, the two last characters, Chapter 23, i., characters 3-4, etc. *Pu ch'in* means "without external coercion," and *tsz' jan* "in self manner," i. e , according to one's own nature.

CHAPTER 7.

I.

St. Julien reads *t'ien ti ch'ang chiu* instead of *t'ien ch'ăng ti chiu*.

The characters 5 13 are the subject of the following sentence 14 19. The words 5-12 which in themselves form a sentence, are summed up by *che* (13), "that," which in the analogous English construction would be placed at the beginning of the sentence.

Puh tsz' shang (16-18) "not self live," i. e., they live not for the purpose of self ; they are unselfish.

Stanislas Julien reads *ch'ien* for *ch'ang* (21), "long," viz. long and lasting.

II.

The lesson of this chapter, which is summed up in the words : "the sage puts his person behind and his person will be preserved,' reminds us of Christ's word Matth. xxiii. 12, and also Matth. x. 39 (= xvi. 25; Luke, ix. 24 ; xvii. 33; John, xii. 25).

CHAPTER 8.

I.

St. Julien here translates *shan* (6), goodness, as a verb, "to be good, to excel." According to him, we should translate "The water excels in benefiting," etc. The position of *shan* before the verb *li*, makes it an adverb, viz,, "well" or "in a good way." The English "well" has lost its original meaning as an adverb for "good" by frequent use, or at least, is less significant than "in a good way" or "in goodness," wherefore the latter translation has been preferred as coming nearer the sense of the original.

The words *fu chăng* (11-12), "it quarreleth not," reminds us of 1 Cor. xii. 4-7, and of Christ's blessing of the meek (Matth. v. 5).

II.

This sentence reads literally: "It dwells, *ch'u* (1), in the place, *su* (5) which is shunned, *wu* (9), by the multitudes, *chung jan chi* (2-4). The word *su*, however, is the relative pronoun, "he who," or "there where." Thus the sentence reads in smoother English: "It dwells in a place which all the people avoid," etc. This means that water always seeks the lowest elvel. Water, like the hermit, who lives in the wilderness, is distinguished by lowliness, setting an example of unselfish effort.

Chi (8) means to approach, in the sense of coming near in similarity.

III.

Shan (2), "good, or goodness," means when used as a verb "to deem good, to be satisfied with, to love, to prefer, to choose." The subject remains the same as before, viz., "superior goodness."

Yuen (6), "eddies," means a place in the current where the water is in commotion, which here illustrates warmth of sentiment.

The word *shi* (16) is any kind of business, duty, or activity.

Tung (19) (motion or movement) means "in its own course." Goodness and the waves of water move in rhythm (*shi*).

IV.

For *fu wéi* (1-2), "since, whereas," see Chapter 2, vii. 1-2.

CHAPTER 9.

II.

Strauss interprets *t'ang* (4), "hall," as being in contrast to "treasury or safe." Treasures cannot be protected in a public hall which is accessible to anybody. In that case the pronoun *chi* (6) would not refer to *t'ang*, hall, but to *chin yuh* (1-2), treasures.

III.

This passage reminds us of the proverb: "Pride goeth before a fall."

The Way of Heaven or Heaven's Reason *t'ien chi tao* (15–17) must be identified with what Lao-Tze in chapter I. calls *chang tao*, "eternal reason."

CHAPTER 10.

I.

The word *'tsai* (1) means a year, a revolution, but with changed accent *tsai'* it means to contain, to convey, to sustain. (Williams, *S. D.*, p. 941.)

The word *ying* (2) (see Williams, *S. D.*, p. 1107) has given great trouble to the interpreters. As a noun it means "a soldier's camp," as a verb, "to plan, to regulate, to arrange, or to organise." To regulate the soul means to keep it disciplined.

Some commentators replace the word *ying* by *huan*, which means the spiritual soul in contrast to the animal soul. On this basis, Stanislas Julien translates: "L'âme spirituelle doit commander à l'âme sensitive." V. v. Strauss translates: "Wer dem Geiste die Seele einergiebt." Harlez translates: "Traitant convenablement l'être intellectuel qui habite (en soi)."

All these translations are forced and do not justify the interpolation made by the commentators. We prefer to retain the original words and translate them as literally as possible. It gives a better sense than when we interpret the word *ying* in the sense of *huan*. We take the first two words, "sustaining" and "disciplining" as synonymous.

P'oh (3), the animal soul, or the senses, as contrasted to reason. (Williams, *S. D.*, p. 711.)

The words, "by embracing unity one cannot be disintegrated," are explained by the commentators to mean that unity is preserved by the assistance of the Tao. As to becoming free from disintegration, the reader is referred to chapters 22 and 39, where Lao-Tze speaks of embracing unity.

The present passage has given rise among Taoists to the idea that Lao-Tze believed in the possibility of finding an elixir of life.

The common significance of the word *chwen* (9) is "to give special attention to," but some interpreters interpret it to mean "hard to subdue." Stanislas Julien and Victor von Strauss follow this view and translate accordingly. We see no reason for a deviation from the original text.

Some manuscripts add after *'rh* (15) child, the particle of exclamation *hû* (Oh!), which is also introduced between the characters 8 and 9 of this same chapter. Stanislas Julien also adds between characters 13 and 14 the word *joh*, which means "like." Since it is probable that the word "like" suggested by the context has been added by later commentators, we believe that the simpler and terser reading is the more original.

II.

Hüen lan (3-4), "mysterious beholding," or "profound intuition," which means by beholding the mysteries of the Tao. For *lan* see Williams, *S. D.*, p. 502.

III.

天門 *T'ien măn* (1-2), "the heaven gates," are said to be the apertures of the body, the nostrils, the mouth, etc. But since Lao-Tze speaks of the sage if he be in charge of the government, would it not be more natural to understand the sentence in the sense that a wise ruler, if he lets every act of his be reasonable, can open and close the gates of heaven and dispense its bliss?

Two of my Japanese editions and St. Julien read, in place of *wéi tsz'* (6-7), "act as mother bird," *wéi wu tsz'*, "not act like a mother-bird," which, however, gives sense only if construed as a question, viz., "can he in that case not be a mother-bird?" If Lao-Tze had written *wu tsz'*, he would probably have added either *hu* or *tsai*, or some particle of exclamation. We prefer the reading *wei tsz'*.

IV.

These same sentences are repeated in chapter 51

The word *ch'ang* (13) means "long," "to be long," "to cause to be long." In the second sense it means "to prolong life," or "to raise," and also, "to be higher than others," "to excel." The translator is free to interpret the word either as "he excels but does not rule," or "he raises but does not rule."

The character *tsai* (16), "to govern," is derived from the signs "shelter" and "bitter," denoting the slaughtering of animals. It means also "to slaughter; to skin or dress dead animals and prepare for food; to fashion." Thus, the word denotes a method of ruling in the most ruthless sense of the word.

CHAPTER 11.

☞ This chapter is interesting, because it exhibits an instance in which a subtle thinker wrestles with one of the main problems of philosophy. Mankind as a whole is materialistic and appreciates only the amount of things. They know little, or nothing, of the paramount importance of form. They measure, and weigh, and try to express everything (as a modern philosopher, the main representative of agnosticism, has it) in terms of "matter and motion only." They appreciate quantity, not quality. They overlook that configuration, external shape as well as internal structure, are at the bottom of all realities. And form is a quality of existence quite different from either matter or motion. Lao-Tze dimly feels that matter and motion do not explain reality. Nor is there any advantage in masses and quantities. That which gives value to things is their form, and form always involves boundary or limits. He does not state the solution of the problem, but he sees that the partial absence of matter is an essential feature of things that have been shaped into vessels of usefulness; and thus the ancient saying of the Greek sages is verified, "the part is greater than the whole."[1]

CHAPTER 12.

I.

☞ The five colors according to the Chinese are blue, red, yellow, white, and black; the five notes are called *kong*, *shang*, *kid*, *chi*, and *yü*, which correspond to our *c, d, e, g, a,* omitting the fourth and the seventh. See St. Julien's and Strauss's notes to the twelfth chapter.

II.

The word *fang* (17), "checked," denotes an impediment, a hindrance, an obstacle. In the same sense the Buddhists use the term "hindrance" as an equivalent of temptation.

III.

The term *fu* (6) "the inner," which means also stomach and soul, stands here in contrast to the visible, the outer. The same word is used in Chapter 3, iv. 12 in contrast to *sin*, "heart," as the seat of passions.

[1] Literally, "one half is more than the whole," (πλέον ἥμισυ παντός). Hesiod mentions the saying in his ῎Εργα καὶ ἡμέραι, verse 40; and Diogenes Laërtius, L. I. § 11. 75, attributes it to Pittacus.

CHAPTER 13.

I.

This passage presents some grammatical difficulties. Julien translates: "Son corps lui pèse comme une grande calamité!" The commentators, among them Su Chêh, declare that the sentence must be construed not in the order as it stands: "*Kwei ta hwan joh shan*" (esteem grand distress like body "), but "*Kwei shan joh ta hwan*" ("esteeming body [is] like grand distress "). Other translators either overlook or neglect the hint of the commentators. Chalmers translates: "Dignity and disaster are as one's person." Legge: "Honor and calamity [would seem] to be regarded as personal conditions [of the same kind]." Strauss: "Hohheit ist so grosse Plage wie der Körper." Harlez: [Que] la grandeur [soit] une cause de grands soucis comme le corps même [quant à soi même]." The interpretation of Chalmers, Legge, Strauss, and Harlez seems probable enough, but we must consider first that *kwei* is as much here a verb as it is in iv. 2 of the same chapter, where in comment upon the present quotation the phrase *kwei i shan*" ("to esteem as the body") is used. In iv., as much as in i,, the position of the object is at the end of the sentence, which seems odd to us but is natural in Chinese where this transposition possesses much force.

III.

The word *ché* (14) "the one," or "that," changes the whole preceding sentence, viz., "the reason why I have great anxiety," into a noun in somewhat the same way as does the English conjunction "that," which, however, begins the sentence, while the Chinese *ché* stands at the end. In the present case *ché* will naturally remain untranslated.

Wei (14) is used here as a conjunction and may be translated "on that account," or "it is due to the fact that."

IV.

The use of *ché* (8), " the one," changes (as in iii. 14) the preceding clause into a noun which here may be translated by "he," thus: "He (8) who when administering (5) the empire (6-7) esteems it (2) as (3) his own body (4)," etc.

V.

This passage is a repetition of the preceding sentence, except that *kwéi*, "he esteems," is replaced by *ngai*, "he loves." Although all the editions at my disposal and probably all the manuscripts extant contain the repetition, we have not the slightest doubt that it is an interpolation which must at a very early date have slipped into the text. We have preserved the passage in the Chinese text and in the transliteration for the sake of completeness, but we omit it in the translation where it would simply puzzle the reader.

CHAPTER 14.

1.

☞ The fourteenth Chapter has given rise to an interesting theory which was first propounded by the Jesuit missionary M. Abel Rémusat in his essay *Sur la vie et les opinions de Lao-ts'eu* published in the *Mémoires de l'Academie Royale des inscriptions et belles lettres*, Vol. VII. Rémusat claims to have discovered in the *Tao-Teh-King* the name of Jehovah, expressed in the three words, *i* (7), *hi* (14), and *wéi* (21).

The meaning of the three words is as follows:

The word *i* (Williams, *S. D.*, p. 276) means "to level, to equalise, to squat, to be at ease," as an adjective it means "equalising, subtile, placid," and also "colorless as the Taoists say reason is." The original meaning seems to be an indifferent or equalised state of mind, not colored by passions.

The word *hi* (Williams, *S. D.*, p. 176) means "seldom, loose, thin, expectant," and Williams adds: "Deprived of sound as Lao-Tze says reason is."

The word *wéi* (Williams, *S. D.*, p. 1050) means "small, minute, recondite, waning, fading away."

The text of the passage leaves little ubt that we have to translate *i* by "colorless," *hi* by "soundless," and *wéi* by "bodiless," (i. e., the Tao is that which if seized fades away from the touch).

Stanislas Julien devotes in his edition of the *Tao-Teh-King* several pages to a refutation of Rémusat's proposition which seems to be complete; but Victor von Strauss, yielding to his theosophical inclinations, again espouses the lost cause of the French missionary and defends it with great ability.

The meaning of these sentences, which proclaim that the Tao is *i*, *hi*, and *wéi*, is obvious. Reason is distinct from sense-perception; it can neither be seen, nor heard, nor touched by hands. Reason is, as we should say, pure form.

That Lao-Tze should have travelled to Palestine is as unlikely as that Israelites should have travelled to China in the sixth century B. C. There are Jews now living in China (concerning whom see Williams in his work *The Middle Kingdom*, and various notes in the *Chinese Repository*); but they immigrated, according to their own traditions, under the Han dynasty. Should Lao-Tze, after all, have heard of the God of the Hebrews, and should he have intended to speak of him he would certainly have made a clear and unequivocal statement. Nor is there any similarity of sound between the tetragram *jhvh*, which was pronounced *yahveh*, and the three words *i*, *hi*, *wêi*. So long as there is no better evidence than the vague arguments offered by Rémusat and Strauss, we cannot but look upon their theory as fantastical, fascinating though it be.

While we do not hesitate to say that the idea of identifying the characters *i-hi-wêi* with *je-ho-vah* has no foundation whatever, we do not, of course, deny that Lao-Tze's views of the Divinity that shapes our ends, possess in one respect at least a great similarity to Christian doctrines. Both are trinitarian. For further details on Lao-Tze's trinitarianism see the comments on Chapter 42.

II.

☞ The sense of this sentence appears paradoxical, because one would expect that on a superficial consideration a difficult problem might appear clear, but by further inquiry into its deeper complications we will find it obscure. Lao-Tze says the very opposite. He says on a superficial consideration Reason is obscure; its principles do not appear to be clear; but when we inquire into the problem and become acquainted with the depth of its meaning it becomes clear and all obscurity vanishes. The passage reminds us of St. Augustine's saying, that Christianity is like a stream, in which a lamb can wade, while an elephant must swim.

I understand Lao-Tze to mean that the Tao gives food for thought to the immature as well as to the sage. The immature may think that there are no difficulties and that everything is plain, but there are intricacies of which they do not dream; and the sage when pondering on it may be inclined to think that there is no possibility of arriving at a satisfactory solution; but he should not give up, for after all, the Tao is not incomprehensible; it is obviously simple and plain.

Therefore Lao-Tze warns the former, the superficial, that

even to a superficial investigation it will offer difficulties rendering the Tao obscure: and the latter, the profound thinkers, that in spite of all intricacies the Tao is clear throughout.

IV.

Wu chwang (14-15) literally means "the not having form."
The difficulty for Lao-Tze in expressing his thought lies in the fact that the word "form," *chwang* (17), is commonly used as bodily shape and not in the sense of pure form.

VI.

Tao-chi (16-17), the thread of the Tao, is explained by the commentators as the initial thread, which suggests the translation 'cue."

CHAPTER 15.
II.

The guest is reserved in the presence of his host (23-27).
Julien omits the pronoun *ch'i* (25, 37, 42, 47). The omission does not affect the meaning of the passage.

III

Sü (15), Stanislas Julien reads: "Through long stirring."

IV.

The meaning of *sin ch'ing* (15-16) seems doubtful. It may mean "increasingly perfected," or "newly finished," or "stylishly fashioned." For *sin* see Williams, *S. D.*, p. 806; for *ch'ing*, p. 77.

CHAPTER 16.
II.

Tsoh (21), "to invent, to stimulate, to arouse." Here used in the reflective sense: "to rise." (Williams, *S. D.*, p. 1005.)

CHAPTER 17.
I

Stanislas Julien omits *pu* (4), "not," which is contained in one of my Japanese editions. The context requires the negation, and its omission would render the whole chapter unintelligible. The omission of the negation, however, dates back to olden times and the commentators have endeavored to explain the sense as well as they could. Lo Hi Ching says: "The great rulers let the people notice so little of their administration that they knew of them their *mere* existence and nothing more." The similarity of the character *pu*, "not," and *hia*, "inferior," sufficiently accounts for a copyist's mistake.

II.

The word *jan* (16) is used to change the preceding word *tsz* into an adverb, in the same way as the French "ment," or the English "ly," changes adjectives into adverbs. " Selflike," accordingly, means autonomous, independent, free. It implies that they can live according to their own nature, without being interfered with.

CHAPTER 18.
I.

☞ The six relatives are: father, mother, older brother, younger brother, wife, and child. The term "six relatives" means all the members of a family.

Chia (21) is what is within doors : "the household, the family." (Williams, *S. D.*, p. 351.)

CHAPTER 19.
II.

The compound *i wéi* (4-5) means "to consider, to regard, to deem." (Williams, *S. D.*, p. 1047.)

Wan (6), "culture, schooling."

CHAPTER 20.
I.

☞ The Chinese possess two affirmations *wei* (5) and *o* (8); the former is an unequivocal, the latter a hesitating assent. The former is definite and should be used by men and boys. The latter indicates modesty and should be used by women and girls. This distinction is made according to the rules of Chinese propriety, but Lao-Tze deems it unessential.

This interrogative particle (12) at the end of the sentence indicates that the preceding "how much" is to be interpreted in the sense "very little indeed "; while *ho joh* (19-20) may be translated "how greatly."

II.

Su wéi (3-4), viz., that which is an object of the people's fear.

According to the commentators speaking on the words 1-8, the sages must also fear what all the people fear, which is either law and punishments, or the government and rulers, or life and death, or evil in general. Commentator H. (as quoted by Julien) says "the people ought to fear moral evil, especially temptations, viz., "music, pleasures, riches, and luxury." Su Chêh says that while the sage does not attach himself to life, he will nevertheless observe the laws of the country and respect the authorities in power.

The passage *hwang hi ch'i wéi yang tsai!* (9-14) is interpreted by some commentators to mean that the comprehension of the sages is unlimited. Su Chêh explains *hwang* (9) as "extension," and refers the pronoun *ch'i* to "sages," saying that while the intelligence of the masses is limited, the knowledge of the sages is boundless and its potentialities cannot be fathomed. Julien translates: "Ils s'abandonnent au désordre et ne s'arrêtent jamais." Harlez: "O misère qui n'est point encore à son plus haut term." Chalmers: "But alas they will never cease from their madness." Strauss: "Die Verfinsterung, oh dass sie noch nicht aufhört!" Legge: "How wide and without end is the range of questions (asking to be discussed)!"

Williams defines *hwang* (9), p. 250, by "wild, barren, waste; unproductive, deserted; without restraint, reckless; ... blasted; a jungle; a famine, dearth; ... to frustrate." We refer *ch'i* (11), "their," not to sages, but (as grammatically it ought to be construed) to the next preceding noun, which is desolation, and translate: "This desolation, Oh! it has not yet reached its limit."

III.

The word *chao* (33) means a sign which the tortoise shell gives when roasted over a fire for the sake of receiving a favorable omen.

CHAPTER 21.

1.

The word *k'ung* (1) means "a hole, or hollow." It forms the first part of Confucius's name. In the present place, it is explained by the interpreters to mean grand on account of vastness.

The particle *wéi* (13), "then, only; is, or will," is frequently added to complete the sound of a sentence and need not be translated in that case.

The words *hwang* (14), "abstruse," and *hu* (16), "elusive," are difficult to translate. *Hwang* means "wild, unready, not yet done"; and *hu* "to forget, to disregard," or as an adverb, "unexpectedly." Reason is characterised by Lao-Tze as something which is not ready-made, but presents itself as an abstruse problem full of difficulties to be worked out ; and the solution is not a direct answer, not yes or no. It is too intricate to admit a simple statement of its nature.

That the Tao (as stated in 21-23) has in it images reminds one of Plato's ideas.

CHAPTER 22.
I.

There are two forms of *pi* (10), both of which mean "tattered, torn, worn, deteriorated as an old coin." See *W. S. D.*, pp. 675 and 676. St. Julien and one Japanese edition use the simpler form that omits the "kung" (radical 55) underneath.

This chapter reminds us of Isaiah xl. 4, where we read: "Every valley shall be exalted, and every mountain and hill shall be made low: and the crooked shall be made straight, and the rough places plain;" and also of the makarism that those that mourn shall be comforted (Math. v. 4).

CHAPTER 23.
I.

The combination *hi yen* (1-2), " seldom to speak," is commonly translated "to be taciturn."

The phrase *tsz' jan* (3-4) means " in the manner of self," i.e., according to one's own nature, or briefly "natural." See Chapter 17 *et alias*.

Shu Chêh says: "The words of Tao, though they be few, strike home because they are natural."

II.

The Tetzugaku Kwan edition replaces the passages "who pursues his business with virtue, the one," by "the virtue-man," and "who pursues his business with loss, the one," by "the loss-man." The whole passage reads as follows: "Therefore who pursues his business with reason, the one, the reason-man, is identified with reason. The man of loss is identified with loss."

Whether this is a simplification of the other reading, or *vice versa*, whether the more complete version has been rendered more uniform by copyists is an idle question. The sense is the same in either case.

III.

Julien omits the character *loh*, " to rejoice," in the sentences *tao yih loh teh chi* (5-9), *teh yih loh teh chi* (12-18), and *shih yih loh teh chi* (21-27), which appears in all the other texts at my disposal, and translates "Celui qui s'identifie au Tao, gagne le Tao," etc. It appears that the pronoun *chi* at the end of these three passages must be referred to the preceding nouns, *tao, teh,* and *shih* which indicates an anteposition of the object. (About the rules of inversion see Gabelentz, *Anfg.*, pp. 73-75.) We translate therefore "The Tao, in addition, he enjoys to obtain it," etc., etc. To refer *chi* to the sage, viz., to him who identifies himself with Reason, virtue, and loss, is grammatically not impossible, but not probable. We can understand that Lao-Tze personifies the Tao and says that "the Tao enjoys being embraced"; we can even allow that he personifies *Teh,* "Virtue"; but how improbable is a personification of "Loss."

The word *shih* (21), "loss," is conceived by Julien, Chalmers, Strauss, Plänckner, and Alexander in the sense of moral deficiency, which, however, is not warranted by the Chinese and Japanese interpretations of the text. Wang Pi says: "The sage endures everything and can therefore identify himself with everything,"—even with loss.

Chalmers translates "Him who is identified with Tau, (the community) of Tau also rejoices to receive." Strauss agrees with Chalmers in his construction of the Chinese grammar, but he personifies the Tao, saying: "Wer eins wird mit Tao, auch Tao freut's ihn zu bekommen."

CHAPTER 24.
II.

The word *hing* (9), commonly "behavior, elements," etc., is in this connexion explained as "the bodily organism; the system."

The pronoun *chi* (13), "them," refers to offal of food and excrescence in the system (6-9), not directly to the self-approving, self-boasting, and self-glorifying man.

The words *pu ch'u* (18-19), "he does not stay or dwell," mean, the man who has reason, has no use for the self-displaying man: he has nothing to do with him.

CHAPTER 25.
I.

Chalmers translates the words 1-4, "There is something chaotic in nature;" Julien: "Il est un Etre confus;" Harlez: "L'être était indiscernable mais complet;" Strauss: "Es gab ein Wesen unbegreiflich vollkommen." The words *hwun ch'ăng* (3-4) belong together; *hwun* means "mixed as is a turbid current containing all kinds of ingredients," and *ch'ăng* means "in completion."

II.

Ming (16) is the proper name, *tsz* (17) means the title that expresses the character. The distinction is thoughtful and suggestive.

III.

Ch'iang (1), "constrained," may be passive or reflexive, 'should I be constrained," or "should I endeavor."

IV.

Wang (8), "royalty," or "the king," is here apparently used in the sense of *t'ien-tsz'*, "the son of heaven," the guardian of the moral order on earth. As such he is the representative of mankind in general, and in pointing out the interpretation of the four great ones the term *wang*, "king," is replaced by *jan* (v. 1), "man.' That Lao-Tze does not think highly of the sovereign that ruled at his time appears from the concluding paragraph of the following chapter, where he is called "the master of the ten thousand chariots."

V.

The words *tsz' jan* (12-13), "self-like," which are commonly translated by "natural," mean here that "reason follows its own nature," i. e., its standard is intrinsic.

CHAPTER 26.

I.

The expression *pu li tsz' chung* (8-11) is a phrase denoting, "Not to depart from the baggage-waggon," to maintain a grave and composed attitude. *Chung* means "weighty" or "grave."

CHAPTER 27.

I.

The compound *ch'eu ts'eh* (14-15), "computing slips," means abacus or counting machine.

II.

Julien translates the word *sih* (23) by "double," on the authority of one of the commentators who explains it by *chong*, "double." The word *sih* means (1) the lining of garments; (2) stealthy, or to steal; (3) to inherit, etc. We understand the word to mean "the inside," or "that which is not at once seen."

III.

The word *tsz'* (17) means "capital," "wealth," "treasure," "investment," and is used in the same sense as these words are used in English.

CHAPTER 28.

I.

Both words, *k'i* (i. 10 and 14) and *ku* (iii. 10 and 14), mean 'valley" or "river-bed."

II.

The unlimited, or *wu chi* (22-23), is the absolute, i. e., the Tao.

IV.

The word *chi* (5) means literally "vessel;" but as jade becomes useful and acquires value only after having been shaped into a vessel, *chi* is directly used in the sense of "useful person."

Pu san ts'eh wéi ch'i (1-5) may mean, "By scattering simplicity he makes of himself a vessel of usefulness," but the following sentence where the pronoun *chi* (9) can have reference only to *chi* (5), "vessel" or "vessels," indicates that the sage makes of the people vessels of usefulness."

CHAPTER 29.

I.

☞ The proposition, "The state is a divine vessel" (15-18), means in Aristotelian terms the state is φύσει not θέσει; or as Christian teachers of political economy (such men as Stahl) would say, "it is God-created not man-made." Nowadays we should say, "The state is of natural growth according to the eternal laws that condition the evolution of mankind, and not the product of a social contract." (See the author's pamphlet *The Nature of the State*.)

CHAPTER 30.

III.

The word *i* (12) which frequently occurs as a finite particle in the sense "that is all," "that finishes it," is here used as a verb, 'it ends," "it ceases," "it is gone."

CHAPTER 31.

I.

The word *chu* (17), "to dwell," "to attend to," "to be satisfied with," is frequently used in the sense "to be attached to,' "to use," "to employ," "to have dealings with."

II.

Chiün tsz' (1-2), "the master thinker," or "royal philosopher," is a synonym for holy man.

III.

The particle *i* (25) "therefore," is omitted in some editions.

IV.

We have omitted this passage from the translation of the text. It reads as follows:

"In propitious events the left is exalted. In evil events the right is exalted. The assistant army-leader sits to the left. The superior army-leader sits to the right. This indicates that the position of superior power is here as in the arrangement of funeral ceremonies. The slaughter of many multitudes of men must be deplored with sorrow and lamentation, and the conqueror in a battle must be placed according to the funeral ceremonial."

This whole section, and perhaps also the sections ii. and iii., are spurious. Neither is the language Lao-Tze's terse style, nor are the words such as were used in his days. The titles "assistant army leader," or "adjutant general" and "superior army leader" or "chief general" do not occur in any one of the older books and belong unquestionably to a later age. It is probable that some commentator (probably Wang Pi) wrote the passage in explanation of the chapter, and the copyists made the mistake of embodying the gloss into the text.

CHAPTER 32.

I.

The word *pin* (22), "to pay homage," is defined by Williams, "a visitor who comes willingly to pay his respects," "to submit," "to acknowledge," "to come under civilising influences."

II.

The passage *shi chi yiu ming* (1-4) presents some difficulties. Literally it means "In the beginning, when administering (or arranging, governing) [then there is] the having name." Julien translates: "Dès que le tao se fut divisé, il eut un nom;" he explains *chi* as differentiation and interprets the words to mean that the Tao began to divide itself. Legge translates, "As soon as it proceeds to action, it has a name." Harlez, "Quand (le Tao) commença à former (les êtres) il y eut alors des noms." Strauss: "Der da anhebt zu schaffen hat einen Namen." Chalmers leaves us in doubt whether this sentence refers to the Tao. He translates: "If he should ever begin to regulate things with distinctions of names, he would then be getting a name." There seems to be no doubt that Tao must be supplied as the subject of the sentence, for there is a contrast between the unnameable and the nameable. The Tao in itself is unnameable, but it becomes nameable, that is to say determinable as the immanent principle of order in concrete existences, i. e., the Tao is definite as soon as it is practically applied, either in the creation of the world where it appears as cosmic order, or anywhere in logic, arithmetic, mathematics, or any possible system of pure reason. The word *shi*, "at first," "in the beginning," is frequently used in the sense of the Hebrew *bereshith*, and the Greek ἐν ἀρχῇ, viz., in the beginning of the world, but it may also be translated by "at first," "at once," "as soon as." The word *shi* (2), "management," refers mainly to the administration of a civilised government, but may mean any kind of order. Grammatically it would be not impossible to translate: "When in the beginning (1) governments (2) [were instituted], there were (3) names [given to the people]. When names (5) in aduition (6) already (7) existed (8), then (9) in addition (10) [people] would (11) learn (12) where to stop [viz., to refrain their passions] (13). Knowing (14) where to stop (15), that is why (16-17) there are no (18) dangers" (19), i. e., the people would enjoy safety. While this translation would be admissible in any other writer, we must consider that *wu ming* is a favorite and definite expression of Lao Tze's terminology, and the context requires to interpret the passage as a continuation of the first paragraph of the chapter, which brings out the contrast between (1) the absolute Reason, the Tao as it is in itself while it remains nameless, and (2) the applied Reason, the immanent principle of rationality, which is the formative factor of existence.

Tai (19) means "danger" or "risk." The phrase *pu tai* (18-19) is frequently used by Lao-Tze, signifying "a condition of safety." The Tao cannot fail or be exhausted, its possibilities are unlimited.

CHAPTER 33.

III.

Sheu (6), "eternal life," or "longevity," is the first of the five happinesses and is never missing in Chinese congratulations. It touches the Chinese heart perhaps more deeply than ours. The context sufficiently proves that *sheu* does not mean merely "long life," but life eternal, life beyond death.

CHAPTER 36.

The word *wei*, "secret," which occurs in the heading and in ii. 3, means originally "a slight shower of rain." It is interpreted to denote that which is hazy or hidden as in a mist. Julien, Strauss, Legge translate *wei* as a verb, "to enlighten or enlightenment," and *ming* as its object, i. e., "hiding the light." Chalmers translates "secret understanding;" and Harlez, "the understanding of the mysterious."

III.

☞ We translate *wéi ming* (3-4), "the secret's explanation." The secret is that the tender and weak conquer the hard and the strong. The reason is that the tender are growing, while the hard have lost the elasticity of life. Therefore the people ought not to be made warlike; for if they are warlike, if they are familiar with the use of arms, they will soon perish like fish that are taken out of the water.

Li ch'i (9-10), "excellent or sharp tools," always means arms or weapons.

CHAPTER 37.

II.

The word *ting* (17) means "tranquil," "secure," "fixed," "steady," etc. Then "a trance" or "rapture." In Buddhism it denotes the "fixed condition of mind," "peace of soul," "a state of contemplation."

CHAPTER 38.

I.

"Unvirtue" or *pu teh* (3-4) is not merely the absence of virtue but implies the blame of actual immorality. In the same way *pu siang*, "unblessings" (Chapter 78, ii. 17-18), means not a mere absence of bliss but positive curses.

This chapter undoubtedly criticises the Confucian method of preaching ethical culture without taking into consideration the religious emotions. Lao-Tze maintains that genuine virtue does not boast of being virtue, and that the show of virtue actually betrays a lack of virtue. The paradoxical language in which this idea is clothed is characteristic of the old philosopher and will serve to elucidate similar expressions of his, especially his maxim of *wu wéi* as that not-doing by means of which everything can be done.

According to Confucius the highest virtue is justice which doles out rewards to the good and punishments to the bad; but according to Lao-Tze that disposition of heart which meets both the good and the bad with the same goodness is alone true virtue (see Chapter 49 and 63); for even the superior justice as exercised in the imperial courts of the country is full of pretension and self-assertion. The same is true of the rules of propriety and ceremonies which play so important a part in Confucian ethics.

V.

Chang (4), *W. S. D.*, p. 25, is a Chinese measure consisting of 10 *ch'ih* (grasping hands), which is of about 10 feet, reckoned to be 141 English inches. *Chang fu* (4–5) means "husband" (see also *W. S. D.*, p. 142) in the same sense as *fu* alone which otherwise means "any distinguished man," or "one who can help." Finally, *ta chang fu* (3–5) denotes "the great man of affairs;" or "one fit to manage."

The contrast between *heu* (8), "solidity," and *po* (12), "externality" or their covering,, and *shih* (15) "fruit," and *hwa* (19), "flower," sufficiently explains that flower is meant in the sense of mere show.

CHAPTER 39.
V.

Chi shu ch'é wu ch'é (2–6) means literally, "Let (2) go to pieces (3) a carriage (4) it is no [longer] (5) a carriage" (6). *Chi* is a causative auxiliary verb; it means "to go," "to let go," "to let." *Shu*, as a verb, means "to enumerate"; as a noun, "details which are or can be enumerated."

This chapter contains an idea that is more important than may seem at first sight, and may briefly be called the "importance of oneness." A carriage is not the sum total of its parts; its parts must be properly combined into a unity in order to make a carriage. The same is true of heaven and earth, of spiritual beings, of the government, and all other useful institutions.

☞ It is strange that the same simile of a chariot is used in a similar sense in the *Milinda pañha* (the "Questions of King Milinda")[1] for proving both the importance of unities and their absolute non-existence if considered as independent things in themselves, as âtmans or ego-entities. The Buddhist sage Nāgasena says: "My fellow-priests, address me as Nāgasena, but this is an appellation, for there is no âtman [no independent ego-entity] here to be found." The King answers: "If there is no ego-entity, pray tell me who is it who performs acts, who eats, who drinks, who thinks, who keeps the precepts, who commits sins, who acquires merit...? What, then, is Nāgasena? Is Nāgasena the hair? the nails? the teeth? the lungs...? The sensation? the perception? the dispositions? the consciousness?"... When all these questions are denied, the King concludes: "I fail to discover any Nāgasena. Verily now, venerable sir, Nāgasena is an empty sound. You speak a falsehood, a lie: there is no Nāgasena." The Buddhist sage now turns the table and asks the King whether he came on foot or in his chariot. "I came in a chariot," replies the King, whereupon Nāgasena asks: "What is the chariot?" enumerating all its parts. "Is the axle the chariot? the wheels? the box? the yoke? the reins?"... And when Milinda denies these questions, Nāgasena repeats the words of the King, only substituting "chariot" for "Nāgasena"; he says: "Your Majesty, although I question you very closely, I fail to discover any chariot. The word chariot is an empty sound. Your majesty speak a falsehood, a lie. There is no chariot."... The king defends himself, saying: "Venerable sir, I speak no lie; the word 'chariot' is but a way of speaking, a term, an appellation, a name for pole, axle, wheels, chariotbox, etc." Then Nāgasena draws the conclusion, that the unity of a person is just as real as that of a chariot, and yet there is no person in itself, no âtman, no ego in the absolute sense.

The problem of unity has also been treated by Plato in a discussion of the one and many. For quotations, see in the index of Fowett's translation, the references collected *sub voce* "one." Vol. V., p. 479.

[1] See Warren, *Buddhism in Translations*, pp. 124-133, and *Sacred Books of the East*, Vol. XXXV., pp. 40-44.

CHAPTER 41.

II.

The term *ju* (26), "to put to shame," is a common term in the Chinese style of propriety. When we would say, "You have done me the honor," they in their overpoliteness use the word *ju* and say, "You have disgraced yourself."

CHAPTER 42.

II.

The Chinese relative *su* (3), "that which," immediately precedes the verb; we say, "that which is detested by the people," while the Chinese say, *jăn chi su wu* (1-4), "the people's, that which is detested."

☞ The trinity of which Lao-Tze speaks is the *yin* (17), the *yang* (20) and the *ch'i* (22), viz., the negative principle, the positive principle, and the breath of life or the spirit. In their unity they are the *Tao*. The resemblance which this trinity bears to the trinity doctrines in general is no evidence that Taoism has been derived from Brahmanism. Nor is it a triple personality. Lao-Tze's trinity doctrine is quite abstract and philosophical; it may be based upon older teachings, or it may be his own interpretation of the traditional views of the *yang* and *yin*, in combination with the idea of the *ch'i*, all three of which are contained in the *Tao* as the all-comprising Rationality of existence, the divine Logos, the highest unifier, the principle of oneness for all thoughts and things.

The Chinese trinity, being the duality of *yang* and *yin* organised into a higher unity under the harmonious influence of *Ch'i*, is regarded as the source of all existence, and its symbol (which is shown in the adjoined illustration) possesses a deep religious significance for the Chinese heart.

III.

The phrase *chiao fu* (20-21), "a doctrine's father," is explained by the great majority of commentators as "the root of a doctrine," or its "philosophical foundation." Abel Remusat translates, "C'est moi qui suis, à cet égard, le père de la doctrine" (*l. l.*, p. 32). His translation is literally correct, and he either translated the words as he found them or followed Teh Ts'ing (commentator H. of Julien) who is the only one who accepts the literal meaning of the passage. But he explains *fu*, "father," as *mo-to*, "the announcer," literally "wooden bell," which is the bell that was sounded in announcing the arrival of dignitaries. Morrison explains it as the bell that was rung to call the people to service to receive instruction.

CHAPTER 43.

I.

Both words *ch'i* (6) and *ch'ing* (7) mean "to gallop." Two synonyms are frequently used to make the idea emphatic, or, if the sound of one happens to possess too many meanings, to render it unequivocal.

II.

This passage appears absurd, but we must consider that non-existence is the formal aspect which is conditioned by the Tao. The sentence means, "that which has no concrete existence," "the immaterial reality," i. e., the laws of formal relations enter into the impenetrable.

CHAPTER 44.

I.

Lao-Tze apparently means (words 6-10) that hoarded goods invite plunder and thus lead to loss. In our days of an intense utilisation of capital we would say that hoarding is in itself a loss.

CHAPTER 45.

Nishimura, the Japanese editor of the *Tao-Teh-King* regards these passages, i. and ii., as poetry, not as a quotation but as written by Lao-Tze; and he undoubtedly follows a good Chinese authority. The lines sound like verses although the rhymes are very imperfect, at least if we follow the Chinese pronunciation of Williams; but it is not impossible that they may have been good rhymes according to Lao-Tze's own pronunciation. Legge, too, translates them as verses.

CHAPTER 48.

II.

Shi (7) means "business" in the modern sense of the word, denoting "business push and manipulation or artful dexterous management." (See 8, iii., 15.) Here it means "political push, or artifices, diplomacy."

CHAPTER 49.

II.

Legge deems it advisable to change the traditional reading, here replacing *teh* (13), "virtue," by *teh*, "to obtain, to get," and translates "Thus all get good."

CHAPTER 50.

☞ Su Cheh says "Nature knows neither life nor death. Its going forth we call life, and its coming in we call death." The chapter sets forth the idea that there are people who pursue the path of life, others who pursue the path of death, and again others who are now under the sway of life's attractions and now under the doom of death's influence. The sage belongs to none of these three classes of men; he is above life and death, and therefore he has no death-place, i. e., he does not belong to the realm of death; which means he is invulnerable, he cannot be touched by death.

I.

Tu (7) means "a follower" (see *W. S D.*, p. 919) The same phrases "life's followers" and "death's followers" occur a second time in Chapter 76, where there is no doubt about the meaning Accordingly there is little probability here that we must interpret it to mean "ministers of life and of death" in the sense of some unknown mythological beings, or death and life-bringing angels.

Lu-Tze, one of the commentators, interprets the word *yiu* (9), "there are" or "have," in the sense of "and"; accordingly we should translate: "Life's followers are thirteen, death's followers are thirteen, and the death places (or vulnerable spots) of men in their movements are also thirteen." But who are these three times thirteen? The number thirteen does not play any part in Chinese philosophy, religion, and folklore. We are told by some that it means the 5 senses and the 8 apertures; by others the 3 souls, 7 spirits, 1 vital soul (or *ch'i*), 1 yin, and 1 yang. But these explanations are artificial and improbable! Julien, Harlez, and Strauss adopt the interpretation of *shi yiu san* in the sense of thirteen. Chalmers gives the preference to the translation "three in every ten," and Legge follows Chalmers. We have adopted the same interpretation. Three in ten, being repeated three times, makes nine in ten. The tenth in each ten would be the wise, i. e., the sage of whom the next sentence declares that he will not be endangered by rhinoceroses, tigers, or soldiers.

II.

The word *kai* (1), originally "a coarse grass used for thatching houses," then "a covering," is here a particle meaning "now then" or "for." The phrases *kai yüeh*, "now it is said" (quoted by Williams in his *S. D.*, p. 308, first column, line 5) and, as we have it here, *kai wăn* (1-2), "indeed I hear," are of common occurrence. The word *kai* must not be confounded with *ho* (*W. S. D.*, p. 218) which is the same character only without the radical "plants" and means (1) to unite, (2) why not? intimating an alternative.

CHAPTER 53.

I.

The word *shi* (12), "assertion," means originally the hoisting of a banner; then it means "to give, to do, to use, to arrange." it is here used as a contrast to *wu wei*, "non-assertion."

Although this passage appears to be very simple, the translators differ greatly. Their versions are as follows:

Julien: "Si j'étais doué de quelque connaissance, je marcherais dans la grande Voie. La seule chose que je craigne, c'est d'agir."

Chalmers: "Would that I were possessed of sufficient knowledge to walk in the great Tao. Only the administration (of government) is a fearful responsibility."

Strauss: "Wenn ich hinreichend erkannt habe, wandle ich im grossen Tao; nur bei der Durchführung ist dies zu fürchten."

Legge: "If I were suddenly to become known (and put into a position to) conduct (a government) according to the great Tao, what I should be most afraid of would be a boastful display."

Harlez: "Si l'on me chargeait d'une function auxiliaire du gouvernement, ayant alors acquis les connaissances nécessaires, je marcherais dans la grande voie du Tao et je craindrais seulement de me répandre au dehors."

CHAPTER 55.

The word *fu*, "seal," in the heading means originally "Bamboo slips in pairs, made to give one half to each party." Then it means "a seal in two pieces which when joined proves its genuineness by matching." In their sense it is litterally what the Greeks called σύμβολον, a "symbol" (from συν, "together," and βαλλεῖν, "to throw," i. e., "to piece together"). Finally the word acquired the meaning of the impression of a seal, and the warrant of genuineness. As a verb it means to testify, to verify.

I.

The character *tsui* (35), which is explained in the *Kanghi*, Vol. 31, p. 1, as "the privates of an infant," is referred to in *W. S. D.*, p. 821, *sub voce* ,*süen*, "shrivelled, diminished." The character ,*süen* is, according to the *Kanghi*, another mode of writing *tsui*. Baby boys before emptying the bladder are frequently troubled with erections, wich is here misinterpreted as a symptom of vigor.

The character *tsing* (37), consisting of "rice" and "pure,' denotes (1) cleaned rice, then (2) the essence or best of anything; the spirit; and lastly (3) the germinating principle, or the semen of the male.

CHAPTER 56.

III.

The use of '*rh* (5, 11, 16, 22, 26) is causative and progressive in this passage, which literally means "not can he be obtained and then thereby be loved and . . . discarded." Briefly, "he is inaccessible to love, enmity, etc."

CHAPTER 57.

II.

Li ch'i (12–13), "sharp tools, weapons." *Li* means also "useful, profitable." Legge interprets *li* in the sense of "use" and translates "the more implements to add to their profit that the people have, the greater disorder is there in the state and the clan.'

CHAPTER 58.

I.

Chi (32), originally the gable of a roof, means "the extreme the utmost, the final outcome." Here it means "the catastrophe.' *Chi* (32), "the extreme," must not be confounded with *ch'i* (42, i. 22) "the vital principle or breath of life." (See the author's "Chinese Philosophy," No. 30 of the "Religion of Science Library,' p. 24; or *The Monist*, Vol. VI., No. 2, p. 211 ff.) Lao-Tze regards *ch'i* as the third element in the Trinity, which shapes all things. See Chapter 42.

CHAPTER 59.

II.

According to the commentators, *kwo chi mu* (18–20), "the mother of the country," is moderation.

CHAPTER 60.

II.

Julien reads *kwéi* (7), "ghosts," where the texts at my disposal read *shan*, "gods." See the words 16 and 22.

☞ This is a strange chapter as it speaks of ghosts and gods, who otherwise seem to find no room in the philosophy of Lao-Tze. Perhaps Lao-Tze simply assures his followers that so long as the government follows the great Tao, there is no need of fearing either ghosts or gods. But when grievous wrongs are done, superstitions appear and ghost-stories originate, the gods are said to curse the people, while the sages utter prophecies of ill omen and lamentation.

CHAPTER 61.

II.

Some commentators understand *ts'ü* (29) here as passive, "a small country by lowering itself to a great country is taken by the great country. But is this interpretation tenable? If great countries take small countries by stooping, and small countries are conquered by stooping, where is Lao-Tze's lesson about humility?

☞ States in a federative empire, such as was the Chinese empire in the days of Lao-Tze, grow powerful when they serve the common interests of the whole nation. It would be as impossible for great rivers to flow in high mountains as for great states not to be subservient to the universal needs of the people. Streams become naturally great when they flow in the lowlands where they will receive all the other rivers as tributaries. The largest states are not always the greatest states. A state acquires and retains the leadership not by oppressing the other states, but by humbly serving them, by flowing lower than they. This truth has been preached by Christ when he said: "Whosoever will be great among you, let him be your minister; and whosoever will be chief among you, let him be your servant." An instance in the history of China that illustrates Lao-Tze's doctrine, which at first sight appears as paradoxical as all his other teachings, is the ascendancy of the House of Cho, which under the humble but courageous Wu Wang succeeded the Shang Dynasty, whose last emperor, Chow Sin († 1122 B. C.) received the posthumous title Show, the abandoned tyrant. Other instances in history are the rise of Athens in Greece and of Prussia in Germany. Athens's ascendancy began when, in patriotic self-sacrifice, it served the cause of Greece, viz., of all the Greek states; and its decay sets in with the oppressions of the Athenian confederates, i. e., when Athens ceased to serve and began to use the resources of the Ionian confederacy for its own home interests.

Some commentators who find a contradiction in the passage that even the smaller states can conquer the great states by stooping (viz., by serving the interests of the whole empire) translate the second *kwo* (in ii. 31) not as the first *kwo* (in ii. 17) by "they conquer," but by the passive form "they are conquered." It is not probable that Lao-Tze should have used in the same chapter and in the same passage one and the same word in exactly the opposite sense.

III.

This passage reads literally: "The one is low (i. e., he stoops) to conquer, the other is low and conquers." Chalmers and Harlez accept this to be the sense of the passage. There is no reason, when the chapter is viewed in the light in which we interpret it, to put another meaning into the sentence. Julien translates: "C'est pourquoi les uns s'abaissent pour recevoir, les autres s'abaissent pour être reçus." He follows Sin-Kie-Fou who says that *i ts'ü* (4–5) "to conquer," and *'rh ts'ü* (8–9) "to be conquered." Strauss follows Julien. Legge interprets the former *ts'ü* in the sense of gaining power, the latter in the sense of gaining adherents. He translates: "In the one case the abasement leads to gaining adherents, in the other case to procuring favor." This implies a contrast between "gaining adherents" and "gaining favor,' which if it had been intended would have been expressed by different words. The contrast lies in the words *hia i* (3–4) and *hia 'rh* (7–8), which means "it is low through," or "for the purpose of," and "it is low and," etc.

CHAPTER 62.

IV.

Kung (3) means "clasping the hands over the breast, or holding reverently with both hands; bowing."

When speaking to the emperor, imperial ministers of China hold a large jade tablet before their mouths lest their breath should touch the son of heaven. Thus the phrase "holding in both arms for screening" means being an imperial minister. Professor Legge's translation of this passage is hardly tenable.

V.

The word *chê* (8), "that or the one," changes the whole preceding sentence into a noun. In a literal English translation we should change the order of the words and read: "What (9) indeed (10) is the where- (3) for [viz., the reason] of (2) the ancients (1) that (8) they esteemed (5) this (6) reason (7)."

In the place of *yueh* (12), "say," Julien reads *jeh*, "day" (*W. S. D.*, p. 293), and translates, "without seeking it the whole day."

CHAPTER 63.

I.

Julien interprets the words *ta siao to shao* (10–13) as nouns, "the great, the small, the much, the little," and supplies the words "are the same to the sage."

CHAPTER 64.

I.

Julien reads *fang*, "arrest," where we read *wêi* (18), " to do, to manage," and translates "Arrêtez le mal avant qu'il n'existe."

Hö pao chi mu (28–31) means "a tree which is so stout that it can only be embraced with both arms. *Hö* means "together, in union, a pair," *pao* means "to embrace, to hold, to grasp."

Tsu hia (50–51), "the underpart of the foot," means "the space underneath the foot, or a foot measure.

III.

The word *fu* (17), "he returns to," is conceived by Julien to mean "he opposes," and *kwo* (22) as "transgression." He translates the passage "il se préserve des fautes des autres hommes."

CHAPTER 65.

II.

Ch'iê shih (29–30 and 33–34), "standard, or model," is a compound of which both parts mean pattern. *Ch'iê* originally signifies a peculiarly graceful tree, and *shih* is a form or rule set up for imitation. The *ch'iê*-tree was planted upon the grave of Confucius in honor of the great teacher whom the Chinese as a nation, represented by both the government and the schools, officially worship as their highest ideal of propriety and morality.

III.

Julien reads the last sentence "*nai chi ta shun*, omitting *yü* (13), "to," and adding at the beginning of the sentence *yan heu*, "afterwards" (see *W. S. D.*, pp. 285 and 175), viz., "après qu'on a acquis cette vertu." The word *shun* means "to follow, to be a disciple, to obey." The interpretation followership, in the sense of recognition, seems both probable and appropriate. Julien explains the word as submission, which of course the word means in the above sense, and believes the passage means that it will make people submissive, which will bring about a general peace. Accordingly he translates the sentence: "Par elle on parvient à procurer une paix générale."

CHAPTER 66.
I.

The word *chê* (10), "the ones," here again, as usually, sums up the whole sentence and changes it into a noun.

CHAPTER 67.
I.

☞ This passage is difficult because the sense remains doubtful. Some commentators make a stop between *ta* (6), "great," and *sz'* (7), "resemble," others construe *ta* as an adverb, "greatly," belonging to *sz'*, "resemble." According to the former view we should translate: "In the world all say, I greatly resemble the unlikely;" according to the latter: "In the world all call me great; [but] I resemble the unlikely." The latter does not seem to agree with Lao-Tze's modesty; but if we consider that Confucius undertook a long journey to see the philosopher of Cho, we must conclude that he was indeed famous all over China, and the present proposition may be a mere statement of fact. Lao-Tze may have heard the people call him great until he grew sick of it and resented it by calling attention to his awkwardness. We must bear in mind that while Lao-Tze was modest and unassuming, he was at the same time conscious of the grandeur of the Tao which he represented in his philosophising. Therefore we interpret *ngo* (5), "I or me," in the sense of "I as a philosopher," or briefly "my philosophy, my Tao."

The word *siao* (9) means literally "to resemble, to be like;" and *pu siao* accordingly means "the unlike." Following Su-Chêh (or, as the French sinologue spells his name, Sou-tseu-yeou) Julien transliterates the word by "*non-semblable*, c'est à dire différent des êtres, des créatures"; but in the text he translates it "stupid." As in English, the words "likely" and "unlikely" possess the sense which according to the context the Chinese words *siao* and *pu siao* must have, we have retained this most literal translation in the text.

Wang Pî reads *tao* between *ngo* (5) and *ta* (6), an addition which naturally suggested itself. The Ho Shang Kung text reads simply *ngo*. Julien places a period after *ta* (6), "great."

II.

☞ In the first sentence of the chapter the text reads unequivocally *ngo* (i. 5), "I, me, or mine," but in the second sentence the text reads *chi* (ii. 12), "he, him, or his," etc., which is rarely, and only under exceptional conditions, used as a pronoun for the first person. This is the reason why it seemed more appropriate to change the subject. While the first sentence starts with a statement made personally by Lao-Tze of himself, he at once generalises the idea and continues in the third person.

The position of the subject after the predicate is unusual, perhaps for the purpose of emphasising the word *si* (13), "mediocrity."

III.

☞ The word *pao* (5), "treasure," means here moral character and we might translate the title by "the three virtues which constitute a man's worth."

CHAPTER 68.

I.

Shi or *sz'* (3) means now "a literary man," but in early times it meant "a warrior," "a military leader," "a general," in which sense it is also used in the Chinese chess for the figures that represent *tsiang*, our bishops, or the two advisers of the general, our king. See Williams, *The Middle Kingdom*, I., pp. 827–828.

CHAPTER 69.

I.

Plaenckner explains host as aggressor and guest as one who takes the defence.

Plaenckner ridicules Julien for making a coward of Lao-Tze and construes the sentence as follows: "I do not think of allowing myself to be thrown back a whole foot if I have gained an inch." Plaenckner may be a better soldier than Stanislas Julien, but the French professor probably understands Lao-Tze better than the German baron.

II.

Hing wu hing (3-5), "proceeding without proceeding," is analogous to *wéi wu wéi*, "acting non-action." It is difficult to understand how other translators could miss the sense which is quite clear. Julien translates: "C'est ce qui s'appelle n'avoir pas de rang à suivre," and Legge translates "Marshalling the ranks where there are no ranks."

☞ By *pao* (26), "treasure," Lao-Tze means, as indicated in Chapter 67, "moral worth"; and a man's moral worth is constituted first of compassion; hence it is said in the next paragraph, that of two armies the tenderer one will conquer, because its moral worth is superior to the other one.

III.

K'ang ping (2-3) means "well-matched," i. e., equal in physical strength.

CHAPTER 70.

II.

☞ Lao-Tze speaks of the Tao as *tsung* (11), "ancestor," and *chiün* (14), "master," meaning that it is the origin and ultimate authority of his words and deeds. How easily abstract ideas are personified! If Lao-Tze, who otherwise is so explicit in his views of the abstract nature of Reason, personifies the Tao, how natural does it appear to be that the idea of God has been personified among Jews and Christians.

The problem of the idea of God lies at the bottom of all the difficulties which at the present day render religious dogmas objectionable to those who are trained in the school of science. In the face of the fact that the laws of nature are eternal and uncreated —a truth which is universally accepted by all scientists and philosophers of any standing, we can no longer maintain the old view that God is an individual mind, a huge ego-consciousness, a personal being who thinks in syllogisms as we do and arrives at decisions after having taken counsel in his thoughts. If the old anthropotheism alone be the allowable definition of God, the spirit of science must frankly be regarded as atheistic. But is God truly an individual being? We grant that the nature of God must be recognised in his works. God, in a certain sense, must be like his creatures; but certainly he is not like his creatures by being a creature himself, i. e., he can be a concrete, limited being that is only here and not there, that thinks and wills different things at different times. If he were an individual being, he would not be God. If he were concrete, he could not be the allhood, the omnipresence, the universality, the eternity of existence. God has naturally been represented as a man, as a king, as a father; but he is not a human being, not a monarch, not a parent in a literal sense. All these terms are figures of speech, parables, symbols. On the other hand God is not an indefinite generality. He is not concrete, but he is definite. He is that which determines all definiteness in the word. He is the character of the cosmic order with its eternal laws. Thus he is distinct from nature and yet in nature. He is supernatural, because the eternal laws are applicable not only to this actual world, but to any possible world. This view which is the old theism purified of its anthropomorphism, may be called nomotheism, as it identifies God with the eternal and immutable νόμος, the norm of both rationality and existence, of thinking and being, avoids the errors of both the old deism and the old pantheism; it is radical in its admissions to the most radical free thought and at the same time conservative in explaining the significance of the traditional dogmas.

III.

Wool is worn by the common people. The rich, in China, dress in silk.

CHAPTER 71.

I.

☞ *Ping* (8), "malady," is in this chapter used in two senses which in Chinese almost correspond to a similar use of "sick" in English, but the Chinese mean by "being sick of a thing" being grieved at it, rather than loathing it.

CHAPTER 72.

Wéi (4), "the awe-inspiring," or "the authoritative," is a common term to denote majesty. The commentator Tsiao-Hong (as quoted by Julien) says that *wéi*, "majesty," and its homophone *wéi*, "fear," were interchangeably used. Compare also the *K'ang-hi* on the subject.

CHAPTER 73.

IV.

The character *ch'en* (19), "slow," "lenient," "patient," is missing in Williams's *Syllabic Dictionary*. It is found in the *Kanghi*, Vol. XXVII., p. 22b.

V.

This passage reminds us of the Greek proverb ὀψὲ θεῶν ἀλέουσι μύλοι, ἀλέουσι δὲ λεπτά. (Sextus Empiricus, *adv. math.*, ed. Bekker p. 665.) Friedrich von Logau utilised the idea in a *Sinngedicht*.

> " Gottes Mühlen mahlen langsam,
> Mahlen aber trefflich klein.
> Ob aus Langmuth er sich säumet,
> Bringt mit Schärf' er alles ein."

Logau's lines were translated by Longfellow:

> " Though the mills of God grind slowly
> Yet they grind exceeding small.
> Though with patience he stands waiting,
> With exactness grinds he all."

CHAPTER 74.

Sie Hoeï, in comment on this passage, tells the following incident, which is reported by St. Julien, pp. 276-277:

" L'empereur Thaï-tsou-hoang-ti (fondateur de la dynastie des Ming, qui monta sur le trône en 1368) s'exprime ainsi dans sa préface sur le Tao-te-king : Depuis le commencement de mon règne, je n'avais pas encore appris à connaître la voie (la règle de conduite) des sages rois de l'antiquité. J'interrogeai là-dessus les hommes, et tous prétendirent me la montrer. Un jour que j'essayais de parcourir une multitude de livres, je rencontrai le Taote-king. J'en trouvai le style simple et les pensées profondes. Au bout de quelque temps je tombai sur ce passage du texte: 'Lorsque le peuple ne craint pas la mort, comment l'effrayer par la menace de la mort?'

"A cette époque-là l'empire ne faisait que commencer à se pacifier; le peuple était obstiné (dans le mal) et les magistrats étaient corrompus. Quoique chaque matin dix hommes fussent exécutés sur la place publique, le soir il y en avait cent autres qui commettaient les mêmes crimes. Cela ne justifiait-il pas la pensée de Lao-tseu ? Dès ce moment je cessai d infliger la peine capitale; je me contentai d'emprisonner les coupables et de leur imposer des corvées. En moins d'un an mon cœur fut soulagé Je reconnus alors que ce livre est la racine parfaite de toutes choses, le maître sublime des rois et le trésor inestimable des peuples!"

I.

Ch'i (19), "extraordinary," "unusual," "innovations," means here revolution.

CHAPTER 76.

III.

Kung (11) means literally "altogether" (*W. S. D.*, p. 464) and may be translated (as the German *alle*) by "it is gone," "finished,' or "doomed." It is difficult to say how Legge can translate the tree "will fill the outstretched arms (and thereby invites the feller"). Did he perhaps read *kung*, the homophonous compound of radical 32 with *kung*, "all," which means "to hold or take with both hands" (see *W. S. D.*, p. 463; see also Chapter 62, iv. 3), or did he try to interpret the latter by the former?

CHAPTER 77.

I.

☞ While the first sentence is almost literally like Christ's doctrine, "Whosoever shall exalt himself shall be abased," the second sentence is the reverse of the New Testament teaching, that, "Whoever hath, to him shall be given, and he shall have abundance; but whosoever hath not, from him shall be taken away even that he hath." (Math. 13, 12.)

IV.

Hien (18), "virtue," "talent," "excellence"; taking the next rank to *shang*, "holiness," or "saintliness" of the sage. See *IV. S. D.*, p. 197.

CHAPTER 78.

II.

☞ These remarkable verses are perhaps an echo of the legend of *Ti Shun*, which are recorded in the Shu-King, Book II. (*S. B. of the E.*, Vol. III., p. 54), where we read: "In the early time of the Ti when he was living by mount Li, he went into the fields and daily cried with tears to compassionate heaven and to his parents, taking to himself all guilt and charging himself with the wickedness"—viz., of all.

Shê ts'ih (11-12) is the official grain-sacrifice annually offered as a Thanksgiving. *Shê* originally means "the gods of the earth," then the altar of a tutelary god (see *W. S. D.*, p. 748), and *ts'ih* means "millet," which is one of the commonest cereals in China. (*W. S. D.*, p. 987.)

CHAPTER 79.

1.

☞ Contracts were written on two bamboo slips which fitted together, the left one containing the debit or obligations, the right one containing the credit or dues.

The word *ch'ch* (31) means now (see *W. S. D.*, p. 42) "penetrating," "perspicacious"; but during the Cho dynasty it meant 'a tithe" or anything that can be taken with the assistance of the bailiff.

CHAPTER 80.

☞ Plaenckner construes *shi yiu* (5-6), "let there be...," *rh* (12) *pu* (13), "but... not," in the sense "If they had, ... they would not." He interprets the chapter to mean : " In a small country there are always a few people who, if they had the wealth of princes, would not use it ; if they had ships, they would not be able to steer them ; if science returned, they would be satisfied with knotted cords. They are satisfied with eating and drinking, etc. ... Indeed there are neighbors who never take notice of each other, etc." If philological considerations permit this construction, it becomes highly improbable for internal reasons. Herr von Plaenckner translates as he, a child of the nineteenth century, would have Lao-Tze think and write ; but he forgets that Lao-Tze had as strong a belief in the pristine innocence and virtuous simplicity of man as our grandfathers had in the story of the Garden of Eden, and believes that the pristine goodness and happiness could have been preserved if but the pristine simplicity of life had been retained.

1.

Shih (7), composed of man and ten, means "a file of ten soldiers"; and *shih ch'ăng* "a corporal," "a decurion." (See *IV. S. D.*, p. 768.) In the same way *poh* (8), composed of man and hundred, means (1) a hundred men, then (2) the leader of a hundred men, or a centurio. (See *IV. S. D.*, p. 707.) Stanislas Julien reads in place of *poh* its homophone *poh* which is composed of man and white and means "a father's eldest brother," "a senior," "a man of rank," "a chief." Judging from his translation it appears that Strauss adopts the same reading.

☞ The method of writing with knotted cords (*chieh shing*, 42-43) is very ancient and must have been common to all the races of the world at an early period of civilisation. It is mentioned in Herodotus that the Persian king handed a thong with sixty knots, to be used as a calendar for two months, to the Ionians whom he appointed guardians of a bridge over the Danube. The South Sea Islanders keep their records with the assistance of knotted Pandanus leaves and cocoanut fibres, which also serve the purpose of divination. Ratzel mentions in his *History of Mankind*, I., p. 199, that chiefs use them for memoranda to assist their memory and wear them round their neck. The same method of writing has been developed among the Peruvians of South America to a considerable extent where such records of knotted cords are called quipu. There are a great number of Peruvian quipu extant, but the key to their significance is lost. We only know that various colors of the threads were employed to denote various tribes, and also various commodities which had to be delivered as tribute. As numbers the knots denoted units or tens according to the position of the cord. Nor can there be any doubt about it that peculiar twists had their special significance.

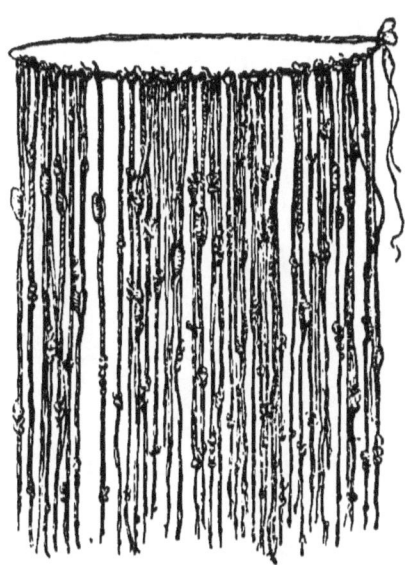

QUIPU OR KNOTTED CORDS FROM PERU.

INDEX

This index, while serviceable for general purposes, is intended to be of special assistance to readers who intend to study the original text. It will be noticed that the *Tao-Teh-King* is rich in synonyms of Lao-Tze's favorite ideas. There are 6 ways of expressing the idea of life everlasting (see *Immortality*), 9 for peace of soul (see *Rest*), 4 for child, 4 for emptiness, 5 for returning or going home, 5 for simplicity, 3 for purity, 3 for form, and 4 for that delicate suppleness which is a symptom of growth and vitality, causing the weak to conquer the strong.

INDEX.

[The figures in parentheses indicate the chapter, section, and place of the Chinese words; while all the other figures refer to the pages of the present edition.]

Absolute, 111, 302.
= 無極 *wu chi*, lit. "without limit" (28, ii. 22-23), 190.
Abundance, 135, 136.
= 有餘 *yu yü* (77, i. 17-18, etc.), 267, 268.
Acquires, he, by giving, 138.
Act but not to strive, 138.
= 為而不爭 *wéi 'rh pu chăng* (81, ii. 30-33), 274.
Adrift, 107.
Agnosticism, 292.
Ahura Mazda, 10.
Alexander, G. G., 45, 300.
Ancestor, 16, 133, 285, 318.
= 宗 *tsung* (70, ii. 11), 259; the Tao as the, 16, (4, i. 15) 153, translated "father," 99.
Angelus Silesius, 25.
Apostle, 21.
Archfather, 16. (Cf. "father of the ten thousand things," 99.)
Aristotelian, 302.
Athens, 313.
Âtman, 307.

Attachment (literally residing in, or dwelling on), 100, 109, 113, 136. (Cf. "calmly he sits."
= 處 *ch'u* (8, ii. 1, translated "dwells in"; 24, ii. 19; 31, i. 17, translated "does [not] rely on"; 77, iv. 13, translated "does [not] linger upon"), 157, 183, 195, 269.
Augustine, St., 295.
Author of all transformations, the Tao as the, 16.

Babe. (See "child.")
Backbone, 98, 285. (Cf. "bone.")
Bad, 121. In Chinese: "not-good" (49, ii. 6-7), 222.
Badness, 98. In Chinese: "not-goodness" (2, ii. 8-9), 149.
Baggage waggon, 119, 301.
= 輜重 *tsz' chung* (26, ii. 10-11), 186.
Beauty, 97.
= 美 *méi* (2, i. 5, 8), 149.

Beginning, 113.
Bellows, 99.
= 槖籥 t'o yoh (5, iii. 7-8) 154.
Benevolence, 99, 116.
= 仁 jăn (5, i. 4, etc.; 38, i. 35, etc.), 153, 154, 206, 207.
Bible, 21.
Bôdhi, 菩提, 10.
Bodiless, 103. (Cf. "incorporeal" and "immaterial.")
= 微 wēi (14, i. 21), 165.
Body, 102, 105.
= 身 shăn (13, i. 9, etc.; 16, iii. 20), 163, 164, 171.
Bone (kuh, 3, ii. 18), 152; translated "backbone," 98.
Bose, Du, Rev. Hampden C., 40, 41.
Bow, 135.
= 弓 kung (77, i. 7), 267.
Brahm, Tao and, 8.
Brahmanism, 308.
Breath, 119.
= 氣 Mentioned three times in the Chinese text: (S.M.Ch., vii. 5; 10, i. 10; 42, i. 22), 143, 159, 214; translated "airs," 95; "vitality," 101; and "breath of life," 119.
Buddha, 3, 7, 278; and Lao-Tze, 39.

Calm. (See "rest.")
Calmly he sits, 110.
Candlin, Rev. George T., 46, 48,
Canon (King), 38, 281.
Capital, 111.
Carpenter, 134.
= 匠 tsiang (74, i. 45, etc.), 264.

Carriage, 117, 306. (See "chariot.")
Causa sui, Spinoza's, 12.
Celebrations, 124.
= 祭祀 tse' sz' (54, ii. 3-4), 230.
Chalmers, 44, 45, 293, 298, 300, 304, 305, 310, 311, 314.
Change, 126.
Chang-Liang, 39.
Chariot, 117, 306-307.
= 車 ch'ê (39, v. 4, etc.), 211. In another place (11, i. 11) this same word is translated "wheel," 101.
Chariots, ten thousand, 110.
Chen-Tsai (i.e., True Ruler), 16.
Chih, the extreme. (Cf. "perfection.")
Ch'i (also transcribed Chih), the robber, 22, 36, 37, 308, 312.
Ch'i, the vital principle; also transcribed k'i. (See breath.)
Chief vessels, 131.
Child, has several Chinese equivalents:
= 赤子 ch'ih tsz' (55, i. 7-8), 232, 312; translated "little child," 124.
= 孩 hai (20, iii. 39; 49, iii. 24), 175, 228. In English: 106, 122.
= 子 tsz' (52, i. 17, etc.), 227. In English: 123.
= 嬰兒 ying 'rh (10, i. 14-15; 20, iii. 35-36; 28, i. 22-23), 159, 175, 190; translated "[become like a] little child," 101; "a babe [that does not yet smile]," 106; "a child's estate," 111.

INDEX.

Children, treats as (*hai*), 122, 223,
Cho, 95.
Chords, knotted, 137, 323.
Christ, 3, 7, 15, 313.
Ch'ü-Jhren, 4, 95.
Chwang-Tze, 7, 12-16, 19, 22, 27, 36, 37, 38.
Classic (*King*), 38, 281.
Clear. (See "pure.")
Colorless, 103.
= 夷 *i* (14, i. 7), 165.
Commoners, 117.
Compassion, 131, 132.
= 慈 *ts'z'* (60, iii. 12, etc.), 254, 255.
Completeth, it, 136.
= 補 *pu* (77, ii. 8), 268.
Completion, 104. (See "perfection.")
Confucius, 34, 35-38, 95, 96, 279, 280, 298, 306, 315, 316.
Contentment (sufficiency), 120, 121. (See "Rest.")
= 足 *tsu* (44, iii. 2; 46, ii. 13, etc.), 217, 219.
Cosmic order (literally "administration"), 113.
= 制 *chi* (32, ii. 2), 198.
Cosmos, 282.
Crafty, the, 98.
= 知者 *chi ché* (3, v. 10-11), 152; translated "one who knows," 114, 125; (33, i. 6-7; 56, i. 1-2), 199, 234; translated "the wise," 138; (81, i. 17-18), 274.
Curse, 136.
= 不祥 *pu siang*, lit. "unbliss" (78, ii. 17-18), 270.

Danger, implies no, 105, 113, 120, 123. (Cf. "immortality.")
Death, 122, 134.
Death-place, 310.
Deeds, 133.
Deficient corresponds to two Chinese terms:
= 曲 *ch'ü*, lit. "crooked" (22, i. 1; iv. 5), 178, 180. In English: 108.
= 不足 *pu tsu*, literally "not enough" (77, i. 22-23, etc.), 268. In English: 136.
Delicate, 135, 136. (See "weak.")
Depleteth those who have abundance, 135.
Depth not obscure, 103.
Desire, 106; moderation of, 120.
= 欲 *yü* (19, ii. 21; 46, heading), 174, 218.
Desireless, 97, 98, 114, 126.
= 無欲 *wu yü* (1, iii. 4; 3, v. 7; 34. ii. 15-16; 57, ii. 27-28), 148, 152, 200, 237.
Dignity (see "baggage-waggon"), 46, 110, 301.
Disgrace, 102. (See also "humiliation.")
= 辱 *ju* (13, i. 2, etc.), 163.
Divine vessel, 112. (See "vessel.")
= 神器 *shăn ch'i* (29, i. 17-18), 192.
Douglas, Robert K., 4, 5, 7, 8, 39 footnote.
Dreadful, 133.
= 畏 *wéi* (72, i. 4), 260.
Duration, 120.

Eckhart, Master, 24,

Economy, 131.
= 儉 *chien* (67, iii. 15, etc.), 254, 255.
Editions of the Tao-Teh-King, 42.
Eitel, Ernest John, 45.
Elixir of life, 39, 290.
Empire. (See "world," *t'ien hia*.)
Empty, has several Chinese equivalents:
= 虛 *hü* (3, iv. 7; 5, iv. 1), 151, 154; translated "he empties," 98; and "empty," 99.
= 沖 *ch'ung* (4, i, 2; 45, i. 12), 152, 218. In English: 99, 120.
= 曠 *kwang* (15, ii. 40), 168. In English: 104.
= 窪 *wa* (22, i. 7), 179. In English: 108.
Enlightened (Enlightenment), 104, 111, 114, 115, 123, 125.
= 明 *ming* (16, ii. 16; 23, ii. 15; 27, ii. 24; 33, i. 8; 36, ii. 4; 52, iii. 15; 55, ii. 8), 170, 179, 188, 199, 203, 228, 233.
Er, Lao-Tze's proper name, 3, 8, 95.
Essence (spirit), 107,
= 精 *tsing* (21, i. 38, etc.), 178.
Eternal, 104, 125.
= 常 *ch'ang* (16, ii. 12, etc.; 55, ii. 4), 170, 233.
Eternal Reason, 97.
= 常道 *ch'ang tao* (1, i. 5-6), 147.
Evil, 104. (Cf. "bad.")
= 凶 *hiung*, (16, ii. 22), 170.

Executioner, 134.
= 司殺者 *sz' sha ché* (74, i. 31-33, etc.), 264.
Extreme, the. (See "perfection," and "absolute.")
External, 116.
= 薄 *po* (38, v. 12), 207.

Faith, 105, 109, 116, 122.
= 信 *sin* (17, ii. 2, etc.; 23, iii. 28, etc.; 38, iv. 5; 49, iv. 15, etc.), 171, 182, 207, 222.
Father of the ten thousand things, 99,
= 萬物之宗 *wan wuh chi tsung* (4, i. 12-15), 152-153.
Favor, 102.
= 寵 *ch'ung* (13, i. 1, etc.), 163.
Feast, 106.
= 大牢 *ta lao*, (20, iii. 7-8), 175.
Feeble, 129.
Filial devotion, 106.
Fish (*yü*), 115; (*sien*), 127.
= 鮮 *sien* (60, i. 7), 241.
= 魚 *yü* (36, iii. 1), 203.
Flower, 116.
= 華 *hwa* (38, iv. 19, etc.), 207, 208.
Forever and aye, 100. (Cf. "immortality.")
Form, has several Chinese equivalents:
= 狀 *chwang* (14, iv. 15, etc.), 166. In English: 103.
= 容 *yung* (21, i. 4), 177. In connexion with *k'ung teh chi* translated "vast virtue's form," 107.
= 象 *siang* (35, i. 3; 41, ii.

53), 201, 213. In combination with *ta* translated "Great Form," 114, 119. (See also 11, 292, 296.)

Foundation, 119.
= 父 *fu*, lit. "father" (42, iii. 21), 215; meaning here the [doctrine's] father-hood, viz., its philosophical foundation, 119.

Force, 118. (See "function.")
Forces, 122.
Fourth Gospel, 13.
Function, 99, 101, 132.
= 用 *yung* (5, heading; 11, heading, i. 13, etc., here translated "utility"; 40, heading, i. 10, here translated "force"; 45, i. 6 and 14, here translated "work"; 69, heading), 153, 160, 161, 211, 218, 257.

Gabelentz, 43, 300.
Gem (jewel), 101, 118, 133.
= 玉 *yuh* (9, ii. 2; 39, iv. 12; 70, iii. 15), 158, 211, 259.

Genuine, 107, 124.
= 眞 *chăn* (21, i. 42, here translated "pure"; 54, ii. 14), 178, 230.

Ghost, 127.
= 鬼 *kwéi* (60, ii. 7, etc.), 241.

Giving, by, he acquires, 138.
God, Tao prior to, 13; Philo's conception of, 21; the Bible on, 21; Tao and, 16, 285, 286. (See "Lord," "father," "Ancestor," and "mother.")

Goodness, 98, 100, 111, 121, 137.
= 善 *shan* (2, ii. 3, etc.; 8, i,

2; 27, i. 1, etc.; 49, ii. 1, etc.; 81, i. 9, etc.), 149, 156, 187, 188, 222, 273, 274.

= 德 *teh*, lit. "virtue" (63, ii. 4), 246; translated "goodness," 129. (See also "requite" and "virtue.")

Gossip, 99.
= 多言 *to yen* (5, iv. 9-10), 154.

Government, 18; administration of, 115. (See "cosmic order.")

Grass-dogs, 286. (See "straw-dogs, 99.)

Gravity. (See "baggage waggon"), 46, 110, 301.

Great, reason obliterated, 105; I call it the, 109; four things are, 110; great rivers, 114; make the small, 129; all call me, 131.
= 大 *ta* (18, i. 1, etc.; 25, iv. 3, etc.; 34, ii. 32, etc., 63, iv. 8, etc.; 67, i. 6), 172, 185, 201, 247, 254.

Great form, 114. (See "form.")
Great state, 128.
= 大國 *ta kwo* (61, i. 1-2, etc.), 242.

Great Tao, 114, 123.
= 大道 *ta tao* (34, i. 1-2; 53, i. 9-10, etc.), 200, 229.

Guest, 104, 132, 296.
= 客 *k'oh* (15, ii. 27; 69, i. 12), 168, 257.

Happiness, 126.
= 福 *fu* (58, i. 19, etc,), 238.
Happy, so happy! 106.

= 熙熙 *hi hi* (20, iii. 3-4), 175.
Harlez, C. De, 44, 287, 290, 293, 298, 300, 304, 305, 310, 311, 314.
Harm, 115.
= 害 *hai* (35, i. 10), 201.
Hatred, 129, 136.
= 怨 *yuen* (63, ii. 2; 79, i. 3, etc.), 246, 271.
Heart (the seat of desire), 98, 106, 121, 122, 285.
= 心 *sin* (3, iii. 6, etc.; 20, iv. 22; 49, i. 5, etc.), 151, 176, 222.
= 人心 *jan sin*, "man's heart is subject to error," 14, 19.
= 道心 *tao sin*, "the rational heart," is the disposition of the saintly man, 14.
Heaven's net, 134. (See "Comments," 320.)
Heaven's way, 101.
Heaven's reason, 12, 101, 121, 134, 135, 137, 138.
= 天之道 *t'ien chi tao* (9, iii. 15-17; 47, i. 11-12; 73, iv. 1-3; 77, ii. 1-3; 79, ii. 1-2; 81, ii. 19-21), 158, 220, 262, 268, 271, 274.
Herodotus, 323.
High, it brings down the, and lifts up the lowly, 135.
Hoard, 138. (See also "treasure.")
= 積 *tsi* (81, ii. 4), 274.
Holy man, abides by non-assertion, 98; empties the people's heart, 99; exhibits no benevolence, 99; puts his person behind, 100; embraces unity' 108; does not depart from dignity, 110; is a good saviour, 110; abandons pleasure, 112; does not make himself great, 114; prognosticates, 121; possesses not a fixed heart, 121; universalises his heart, 122; practises non-assertion, 126; does not venture to play the great, 129; does not make, 130; wears wool, 133; is sick of sickness, 133; knows himself but does not display himself, 133; regards it as difficult, 134; acts but claims not, 136; hoards not, 138.
= 聖人 *shăn jăn* (2, iv. 3-4; 3, iv. 3-4; 5, ii. 1-2; 7, ii. 3-4; 22, ii, 3-4; 26, ii. 3-4; 27, ii. 3-4; 28, iv. 6-7; 29, iii. 3-4; 34, iii. 3-4; 47, ii. 3-4; 49, i. 1-2, etc.; 57, ii. 35-36; 63, iv. 3-4; 64, ii. 9-10, etc.; 70, iii. 10-11; 71, iii. 1-2; 72, ii. 11-12; 73, iii. 3-4; 77, iv. 3-4; 81, ii. 1-2), 150, 151, 154, 156, 179, 186, 188, 191, 192, 201, 220, 222, 236, 247, 249, 259, 260, 261, 262, 268, 274.
Home he turneth, 20, 111.
Homewards, 20, 118. (See also "the returning.")
= 反 *fan* (40, i. 1), 211.
Horace, 29.
Ho Shang Kung, 317.
Host, 132, 296.
Humiliation, 120. (See also "disgrace.")
= 辱 *ju* (44, iii. 4), 217.

INDEX. 333

Humility, 108, 128. (See also "lowliness.")
= 謙 *kien* (22, heading; 61, heading), 178, 242.
Human reason, 12, 14, 19. (See "man's reason.")
Hundred families, 99, 105, 122.
= 百姓 *pai sing* (5, ii. 6-7; 17, iii. 10-11; 49, i. 7-8), 154, 172, 222.
Hwang Ti, the yellow emperor, 288.

Identification, 97, 99, 125.
= 同 *t'ung* (1, v. 1; 4, ii, 10; 56, ii. 10, etc.), 148, 153, 234.
Identity, 286.
Images, 103, 299. (Cf. "form.")
= 象 *siang* (14, iv. 19, etc.), 166.
Immaterial breath, 119. (Cf. "bodiless" and "incorporeal.")
= 冲氣 *ch'ung ch'i* (42, i. 21-22), 214.
Immortality, has several Chinese equivalents :
= 不殆 *pu tai*, lit. "implies no danger," viz., it is lasting and inexhaustible, (16, iii. 21-22; 32, ii. 18-19; 44, iii. 7-8; 52, i. 28-29), 171, 198, 217, 227. In English: 105, 113, 120, 123.
= 長久 *ch'ang chiu* (7, i. 2 and 4; 44, iii. 11-12), 155, 217; translated "endure and be lasting," 100, and "duration," 120.
= 壽 *sheu*, life eternal, lit.

"longevity," 114. In Chinese: (33, iii. 6) 200.
= 常 *ch'ang*, the eternal, 104, 123. In Chinese : (16, ii. 12, etc.; 52, iii. 23), 170, 228.
= 綿々 *mien mien*, (6, iii. 1-2), 155; translated "for ever and aye," 100.
In addition there are such word-combinations as : *ch'ang shǎng*, "live eternally" (7, i. 21-22), 150; translated "endure," 100.
Imperfect, 120.
= 缺 *ch'üeh* (45, i. 4), 218.
Inaccessible, 125.
= 不可得 *pu k'o teh* (56, iii. 2-4, etc.), 234, 235.
Incorporeal, 109. (Cf. "bodiless" and "immaterial.")
= 寥 *liao* (25, i. 11), 184.
Ineffable (lit. "no name"), 113, 115. (See "nameless.")
= 無名 *wu ming* (37, i. 28-29, ii. 1-2), 204.
Inexhaustible, has two Chinese equivalents :
= 不可既 *pu k'o chi* (35, ii. 28-30), 202. In English: 115.
= 不盈 *pu ying* (4, i. 7-8), 152. In English : 99.
Intensity, 123, 135.
= 厚 *heu* (50, i. 37; 75, ii. 10) 224, 265.
Intrinsic, 301.
Intuition, 101, 124.
= 覽 *lan* (10, ii. 4), 159.
Isaiah, 21, 23 24, 299.

Jade table, 128, 314.
= 璧 *pi* (62, iv. 4), 245.

Jehovah, 294.
Jewels. (See "gem.")
Jews in China, 295.
Julien, Stanislas, 10, 30, 42, 44, 284, 288, 290-291, 293-294, 296, 298-301, 303, 305, 310, 311, 313-320, 322.

K'anghi, 45; referred to: 4, 5, 6, 9, 11, 16, 20, 232, 262, 312, 320.
K'i, 279. (See "breath" and "Ch'i.")
King (a classical or canonical book), 38, 281, 301.
Knotted cords, 137, 323.
= 結繩 *chieh shing* (80, i. 42-43), 272.
K'u-Hien (Thistle district), 4, 6, 95.
Kwong Ki Chin, author of dictionary, 45.

Lao-Tze, his personality, 3-6; his philosophy, 9-16; his ethics, 17; Taoism and, 30-41; and Confucius, 34; Buddha and, 39; 278-280, 282, 316.
Learned, 138. (Cf. "crafty.")
Learnedness, 106, 121.
= 學 *hioh*, (20, i. 2; 48, i. 2), 174, 221.
Legge, 7, 15, 38, 44, 293, 298, 304, 305, 309-311, 314, 321.
Li, Lao-Tze's family name, 95.
Life for ever, 114. (See "immortality.")
Life's follower's, 310.
Life's intensity, 122.

Likely, the, 131.
Long-lobed, 278.
Lo Hi Ching, a commentator, 296.
Logau, 320.
Logos, 10, 21, 282.
Longevity, 305. (See "immortality.")
Longfellow, 320.
Lord, 99, 285, 286,
= 帝 *ti* (4. iii. 13), 153.
Lowliness, 21, 117, 131, 132,135.
= 下 *hia* (39, iv. 9; 66, i. 14, etc.; 68, i. 23; 77, i. 13), 210, 252, 256, 267.
Lowly, who excells in employing men is, 132; lifts up the, 135.
Lu-Tze, a commentator, 310.

Makes, mars, 112, 130.
Manhood, 111.
= 雄 *hiung* (28, i. 3), 189.
Man's Reason, 136.
= 人之道 *jăn chi tao* (77, iii. 1-3), 268,
Master, 16, 103, 110, 133.
= 君 *chiün* (26, i. 8; 70, ii. 14), 186, 259.
= 士 *shi* (15, i. 5), 167.
Master of Mankind, 112.
= 人主 *jăn chu* (30, i. 4-5), 193.
Master of the ten thousand chariots, 110.
= 萬乘之主 *wan shăng chi shu* (26, iv. 3-6), 186.
Mayers, W. Fr. 39, 43 footnote.
Mediocrity, 131.
Metal (*tsing*=spirit, manliness, semen), 125, 312,

Middle-path, 99.
= 中 *chung* (5, iv. 16), 154.
Milinda pañha, 307.
Military expert, 132.
Mind, 99, 117. (Cf. "spirit.")
Model, has two Chinese equivalents:
= 式 *shih* (22, ii. 10; 28, ii. 10, etc.; 65, ii. 30, etc.), 179, 190, 251. In English: 108, 111, 130, 315.
= 正 *chang* (39, ii. 35), 209. In English: 117.
Moderation, 127.
= 嗇 *seh* (59, i. 7, etc.), 239.
Morrison, 309.
Mother, 107.
= 母 *mu* (20, vi. 22), 177.
Mother-bird, 101, 111, 291. The word reminds us of the expression "hen" in Matt. xxiii. 37 and Luke xiii. 34.
= 雌 *tsz'* (10, iii. 7), 159; translated "womanhood" (28, i. 6), 189.
Mother, mysterious, 99.
= 玄牝 *hüen p'in* (6, i. 7-8, etc.), 155.
Mother of the ten thousand things, 97.
= 萬物之母 *wan wu chi mu* (1, ii. 9-12), 147.
Mother of the country, 127.
= 國之母 *kwo chi mu* (59, ii. 18-20), 240.
Mother of the world, 109, 123.
= 天下母 *t'ien hia mu*, lit. "the mother of the underheaven," (25, ii. 9-11; 52, i. 7-9), 184, 227.
Motion's master, 110.

= 躁君 *tsao chiün* (26, i. 7-8) 186.
Music, 115.
= 樂 *lö* (35, ii. 1), 202.
Mysterious, 124, 132.
Mysterious mother. (See "mother.")
Mystery, 97.
= 玄 *hüen* (1, v. 4, etc.), 148
Mystics, 24.

Nāgasena, 307.
Nameable, 97, 113.
= 有名 *yiu ming* (1, ii. 7-8; 32, ii. 3-4), 147, 198.
Name, viz., proper name, 95.
= 名 *ming* (S. M. Ch., ii. 4) 141.
Nameless, 97, 113, 119, 282.
= 無名 *mu ming* (1, ii. 1-2 32, i. 3-4; 41, iii. 3-4), 147 197, 213-214.
Natural, 288. (See "selflike.")
Nature, 283.
Nave, 101.
Negative principle, 119.
= 陰 *yin* (42, i. 17), 214.
Nishimura, Japanese editor of Lao-Tze, 43, 309.
Nobody, 117, 119.
Non-action, 19, 21; not inactivity, 18-21.
Non-assertion (non-action), 10; the holy man abides by, 98; he acts with, 98; he can practise, 101, 112; Reason always practises, 115; superior virtue is, 116; the advantage of, 119; he arrives at, 121; practise, 126; assert 129.

= 無爲 *wu wéi* (2, iv. 6–7;
3, vi. 2–3; 10, ii. 13–14; 29,
heading; 37, i. 3–4; 38, i.
20–21; 43, iii. 5–6, etc.; 48,
i. 16–17, etc.; 57, ii. 39–40;
63, i. 2–3), 150, 152, 159,
191, 204, 205, 216, 221, 237,
246.
Non-existence, has several Chinese equivalents :
= 無 *wu* (2, iii. 3; 11, heading, i. 9, etc.; 40, ii. 11), 149,
160, 161, 211; translated
"not to be," 98; translated
"the non-existent," 101, 102,
118.
= 無有 *wu yiu* (43, ii. 1–2),
216. In English : 119.
= 無物 *wu wuh* (14, iv. 10–
11), 166. In English : 103.
Not, 282.
Not dare to come to the front
in the world, 131.
= 不敢爲天下先 *pu kan
wéi t'ien hia sien* (67. iii.
18 23, etc.), 254–255.

Obligation, 137.
= 契 *ch'i* (79, i. 18, etc.), 271.
Obliterated, 105.
= 廢 *féi* (18, i. 3), 172.
Oceans, 107, 114, 131. (See also
"sea.")
= 海 *hai* (20, v. 23; 32, iii.
13; 66, i. 2), 176, 199, 252.
Omen, 106.
One. (See "identification.")
Oneness, 117; translated
"unity," 101, 103, 108, 119.
= 一 *yi* (10, i. 5; 14, ii. 12; 22,
ii. 6; 39, i. 4, etc.; 42, i. 3,

etc.), 159, 165, 179, 208, 209
214.
Orphans, widows and nobodies
117, 119.
= 孤寡不穀 *ku kwo pu ku*
(39, iv. 18–21; 42, ii. 6–9),
210, 214–215.
Outcast people, 110.
= 棄人 *ch'i jăn* (27, ii. 11–
12), 188.
Outcast things, 111.
= 棄物 *ch'i wuh* (27, ii. 19–
20), 188.
Own. (See "self.")

Palace, 124.
People, 98, 101, 105, 106, 124,
126, 127, 130, 131, 133, 134,
135, 137.
= 民 *min* (3, i. 5, etc.; 10, ii.
9; 19, i. 5, etc.; 53, ii. 6; 57,
ii. 7, etc., iii. 9, etc.; 58, i.
6, etc.; 65, i. 10, ii. 1; 66,
ii. 7, etc.; 72, i. 1; 74, i. 1,
etc.; 75, i. 1, etc.; 80, i. 4,
etc.), 151, 152, 159, 173, 229
236, 237, 238, 250, 252, 253,
260, 263, 264, 265, 272.
People, common, 106.
= 俗人 *su jăn* (20, v. 4–5,
etc.), 176.
Perfection, has several Chinese
equivalents :
= 成 *ch'ing*, lit. "completion" (45, i. 2; 51, i. 11, etc.),
218, 225, 226; translated
"perfection," 120; translated
"complete," 122
= 至 *chi* (55, i. 39, etc.), 233;
(i.e., "maturity") 125.
= 極 *chi* (16, i. 3; 68, i. 42),

169, 257. Translated "completion," 104; and "highest," 132. This word is an important term in Chinese philosophy, and is, as such, commonly translated "the extreme"; but Lao-Tze uses the word only in its popular acceptance as "the extreme," i. e., "highest point," and also with the negation "having no existence" in the sense of "absolute." (See "absolute.")

Person, 100, 120, 124. (See also "body.")

= 身 *shăn* (7, ii. 7, etc.; 44, i. 3 etc.; 54, ii. 10, etc.), 156, 217, 230, 231.

Philo, 21, 22.

Pittacus, 292.

Plaenckner, 45, 287, 300, 317, 322.

Plato, 307; Tao similar to the conception of "ideas," 10; his ideas, 299.

Pleasure, 112.

Positive principle, 119.

= 陽 *yang* (42, i. 20), 214.

Po-Yang, Prince Positive, 3, 95, 278.

Precedence (precedes), 99, 109, translated "comes to the front," 100, 131; translated "to lead," 131.

= 先 *sien* (4, iii. 15; 7, ii. 16; 25, i. 5; 66. ii. 14; 67, iii. 23, etc.), 153, 156, 184, 252, 254, 255.

Prince Positive, Poh Yang, 2, 278.

Profound virtue, 101, 123, 130.

= 玄德 *hüen teh* (10, iv. 19–20; 51, iii. 15–16; 65, ii. 37–38, etc.), 160, 227, 251.

Propriety, 95, 116.

Prussia, 313.

Prying, 126.

Psalmist, 21, 23.

P'ung-plant, 279.

Pure, purify, purity, have several Chinese equivalents:

= 清 *ts'ing* (15, iii. 8; 39, ii. 5, etc.; 45, iii. 7), 168, 208, 218; translated "clear," 104; "pure," 117; "purity," 120.

= 淨 *tsing* (45, iii. 8), 218; translated "clearness," 120.

Quarrel (strive), 100, 108, 131, 138.

= 爭 *chang* (8, i. 12; 22, iii. 20, etc.; 66, iii. 37; 81, ii. 33), 157, 180, 253, 274.

Quiet, 98. (Cf. "rest.")

= 安 *ngan* (3, heading), 151.

Quipu, 332.

Race horses, 120.

Ratzel, 323.

Reality, 122.

Reason, that can be reasoned, 97; is empty, 99; water is near to, 100; of the ancients, 103; "heavenly" means, 104; when obliterated, 105; its nature eluding, 107; the man of reason identified with, 108–109; one who has, 109; defined as "the Great," 109; Heaven's standard is, 110; one who assists with,

112; as absolute (eternal), 113; its relation to the world all-pervading, etc., 114; the great, 114; is tasteless, invisible, etc., 115; practises non-assertion, 115; homeward, the course of, 118; a superior scholar and, 118; begets unity, 119; the world and, 120; prognosticating, 121; he diminishes who seeks, 121; quickens all creatures, 122 (cf. 114, the same is said of the sage in ch. 2 and 10); becomes the world's mother, 123; walk in the great, 123; is very plain, 124; who cultivates, 124; non-diplomacy and, 126; if the empire is managed with, 127; is the ten thousand things' asylum, 128, well versed in, 130; strives not, 134 and 138; like stretching a bow, 135; man's and heaven's, 136; shows no preference, 137; to benefit, 138; 282, 286, 295, 298.

= 道 *tao* (1, i. 1, etc.; 4, 1. 1; 8, ii. 10; 14, vi. 4, etc.; 15, iv. 3; 16, iii. 15, etc.; 18, i. 2; 21, i. 6, etc.; 23, ii. 5, etc.; 24, ii. 3, etc.; 25, ii. 20, etc.; 30, i. 2, etc.; 32, i. 1, etc.; 34, i. 2; 35, ii. 10; 37, i. 1; 40, i. 3; 41, i. 4, etc.; 42, heading, i. 1; 46, i. 4, etc.; 47, i. 12; 48, i. 6; 51, i, 1, etc.; 53, i. 13, etc.; 60, ii. 2; 62, i. 1; 65, i. 5; 73, iv. 3; 77, heading, i. 3, etc.;

79, ii. 2; 81, ii. 21, etc.), 147, 152, 157, 166, 167, 169, 170, 172, 177, 181, 183, 184, 185, 193, 194, 197, 198, 200, 202, 204, 211, 212, 213, 214, 219, 220, 221, 225, 226, 229, 241, 244, 250, 262, 267, 268, 271, 274.

Reason, human, 12, 14; heaven's, 12.

Reason of the ancients, 103.

= 古之道 *ku chi tao* (14, vi. 2-4), 166.

Reason's clue, 103,

= 道紀 *tai chi* (14, vi. 16–17), 167.

Reason's light, 123.

= 明 *ming* (52, iii. 15), 228.

Reason's standard, intrinsic, 110. Cf. "selflike."

Reconciled, 136; translated "harmony," 125.

= 和 *hwo* (55, i. 48; 79, i. 1), 233, 271.

Recuperate, 108.

= 全 *chüen* (22, i. 3), 179.

Relatives, the six, 297.

Rémusat, Abel, 4, 294, 308.

Repetitions in the Tao-Teh-King, enumerated in the footnote, 33–34.

Resolute, 112.

Requital, his methods invite, 112. (See also 121–122.)

= 還 *hwan* (30, i. 16), 193.

Requite hatred with goodness, 129.

= 報怨以德 *pao yuen i teh* (63, ii. 1–4), 246.

Rest, has several Chinese equivalents:

INDEX. 339

= 恬淡 *t'ien tan* (31, iii. 1–2), 195; translated "quietude and peace," 113.
= 靜 *tsing* (16, i. 5, ii. 4; 26, i. 5; 37, ii. 12; 45, iii. 4; 61, ii. 4), 169, 170, 186, 205, 218, 242; translated "quietude," 104, 110, 116, 120, 128.
= 安 *ngan* (15, iii. 11; 35, i. 11), 168, 201; translated: "still," 104; and "rest," 115.
= 平 *p'ing* (35, i. 12), 201; translated "contentment," 115.
= 泰 *t'ai* (35, i. 13), 202; translated "comfort," 115.
= 湛 *tsan* (4, iii. 1), 153; translated "calm," 99.
= 寂 *tsih* (25, i. 9), 184; translated "calm," 109.
= 燕處 *yen ch'u* (26, iii. 5–6), 186; translated "calmly he sits," 110.
Return to its root, 104.
= 歸根 *kwei kan* (16 heading, ii. 1–2), 169, 170.
Return home, 103, 106, 108, 111, 114, 123.
= 歸 *kwei* (20, iv. 7; 22, iv. 16; 34, ii. 23), 175, 180, 201.
= 復歸 *fu kwei* (14, iv. 7–8; 28, i. 19–20, etc.; 52, iii. 12–13), 166, 189, 190, 228; translated, "again and again it returns home," 103.
Returning, the, 109. (See also "homeward.")
= 反 *fan* (25, iii. 15), 185.
Rhinoceros, 122.
= 兕 *sz'* (50, ii. 11), 224.

Riedel Dr. Heinrich, 46.
River-valley has several Chinese equivalents:
= 江 *chiang* (32, iii. 12; 66, i. 1), 198, 252; translated "rivers," 114, 131.
= 谿 *k'i* (28, i. 10), 189; translated "river," 111.
= 谷 *ku* (6, i. 1; 15, ii. 44; 28, iii. 10, etc.; 32, iii. 9; 39, ii. 16; 41, ii. 22; 66, i. 8, etc.), 154, 168, 190, 198, 208, 213, 252; translated "vale" or "valley," 99, 104, 111, 117, 118, 131, 288; translated "creeks," 114.
Root has two Chinese equivalents:
= 根 *kăn* (6, ii. 9; 16, heading; 26, i. 4), 155, 169, 186; English version: 100, 104, 110.
= 本 *păn* (39, heading; iv. 6, etc.), 208, 210. English version: 117.
Roving-plant, 95. Cf. "P'ung.

Sacrificial celebrations, 124.
Sages, great, 105.
Same. (See "identification.")
Sameness, 286.
Saved, 123, 129, 131.
= 救 *chiu* (52, ii. 20; 67, v. 3), 228, 255.
Saviour, 110, 111.
= 救人 *chiu jăn* (27, ii. 7–8), 188.
Scheffler, Johannes, 25.
Scholar, 118. (See also "master."

= 士 *shi* (41, i. 2, etc.), 212.
Schopenhauer, 22.
Scotus Erigena, 24.
Sea, 107. See "ocean." (20, v. 23), 176.
Self has several Chinese equivalents:
= 身 *shăn*, (9, iii. 13), 158; translated "one-self," 101. (See "body.")
= 私 *sz'* (7, ii. 21, etc.), 156; translated "own self," 100.
= 自 *tsz'* (7, i. 17; 32, i. 21, etc.; 57, ii. 10, etc.; 73, iv. 17), 155, 197, 237, 262; translated "for themselves," 100; "of themselves" or "of itself," 113, 126, 134.
= 不自生 *pu tsz' shăng* (7, i. 16-18), 155; translated "not live for themselves," 100.
Self assertion, 123.
= 施 *shi* (53, i. 12), 229.
Self-displaying, 108, 109.
= 自見 *tsz' chien* (22, ii. 12-13; 24, i. 9-10), 179 183.
Self-like = 自然 *tsz' jan*, is translated:
"Independent," "free," 105 (17, iii. 15-16), 172.
"Intrinsic," 110 (25, v. 12-13), 186.
"Natural way" or "development," 108, 130 (23, i. 3-4; 64, iii. 28-29), 180, 250.
"Spontaneous," 123, 297, 301 (51, ii. 13 14), 226.
Sense-gates, 125.
Sextus Empiricus, 320.
Sharp tools, 115. Cf. "weapons."
Shu-King, quoted, 14-15, 321.

Sick of sickness, 133, 319.
Significant spirituality, 111.
= 要妙 *yao miao* (27, iii. 32-33), 189.
Silence (not talk), 98, 119, 125. (See also "taciturn.")
= 不言 *pu yen* (2, iv. 11-12; 43, iii. 10-11; 56, i. 3-4), 150, 216, 234.
Simple corresponds to various Chinese equivalents:
= 質 *chih* (41, ii. 36), 213; translated "simple," 118.
= 樸 *p'u* (15, ii. 39; 19, ii. 17; 28, heading), 168, 174, 189; translated "unseasoned wood," 104; transl'd "pure," 106; translated "simplicity," 111.
= 朴 *p'oh*, (28, ii. 22, etc.; 32, i. 5; 37, i. 31, etc.; 57, iii. 32), 191, 197, 204, 237; translated "simplicity," 111, 112, 113, 115, 116, 126.
= 素 *su* (19, ii. 15), 173; translated "simple," 106.
= 愚 *yü* (S. M. Ch., vi, 17; 65, i. 13), 143, 250; translated "stupid," 95, and "simple-hearted," 130.
Sin, 136.
= 垢 *keu* (78, ii. 8), 270.
Simplicity, 105, 112, 113, 115, 116, 126.
Sin Kie-Fou, 314.
Solid, opposite of externality, or thinness, 116. (See also "intensity.")
= 厚 *heu* (38, v. 8), 207.
Son of heaven, 301.
Sons and grandsons, 124.

INDEX. 341

= 子孫 *ʻszʼ sun* (54, ii. 1-2), 230.
Soul (animal soul), 101.
= 魄 *ṗʻoh* (10, i. 3), 159.
Soul (lit. "abdomen" or "stomach"), 98, 102, 285.
= 腹 *fu* (3, iv. 12; 12, iii. 6), 151, 162.
Soundless, 103.
= 希 *hi* (14, i. 14), 165.
Spinoza's *causa sui*, 12.
Spirit in the sense of spiritual beings, 99; transl'd "mind," 117; translated "spook," 127.
= 神 *shăn* (6, i. 2; 39, i. 11, etc.; 60, ii. 9, etc.), 154, 208, 209, 241.
Spirit, pure, in the sense of the essential of existence, 107. (See "essence.")
= 精 *tsing* (21, i. 38, etc.), 178.
Spirituality (spiritual), 97, 103, 111.
= 妙 *miao* (1,iii. 8, etc.; 15, i. 8, 27, iii. 33), 148, 167, 189.
Spontaneous, 123. (See "self-like.")
Spurious, 303.
Stammer, 120.
= 訥 *no* (45, ii. 12), 218.
Standard, 120, 315. (Cf. "model.")
= 正 *chang* (45, iii. 12), 218.
State, 302.
Still, 104. (See also "rest.")
Stoop, 128. (See "lowliness.")
= 下 *hia* (61, ii. 15, etc.), 242, 243.
Stout, 129.

St. Paul, 23.
Strauss, Victor von, 15 footnote, 45, 289, 290, 293, 294, 298, 300, 304, 305, 310, 311, 314.
Straw-dogs, 99.
= 芻狗 *tsʼu keu* (5, i. 9-10, etc.), 153, 154.
Strive, 131, 138. (Cf. "quarrel," 100, 108.)
= 爭 *chăng* (8, i. 12, ete.; 22, iii. 20, etc.; 66, iii. 29, etc.; 81, ii. 13), 157, 180, 253, 274.
Su Chéh, 293, 299, 310, 316.
Sufficiency, 114, 120. (See "content.")
= 足 *tsu* (33, i. 19; 44, iii. 2), 199, 217.
Superior, benevolence, 116.
= 上仁 *shang jăn* (38, i. 34-35), 206.
Superior justice, 116.
= 上義 *shang i* (38, ii. 1-2) 206.
Superior man, 113; translated "noble man," 95.
= 君子 *chiün tszʼ* (S. M. Ch. v, 2-3, etc., 31, ii. 1-2, etc,), 142, 143, 195.
Superior virtue, 116.
= 上德 *shang teh* (38, i. 1-2), 205.
Supple, 135. (See "weak.")
Surface not clear, 103.
Suzuki, Teitaro, 46.
Sze-Ma-Ch'ien, 6, 7, 36, 43, 95, 277.

Taciturn, 108. (Cf. "silent.")
= 希言 *hi yen* (23, i. 1-2), 180.

T'ai Chi, the great extreme, 15. (Cf. "Breath.")
Tan, 95, 278.
Tanaka, K., 46.
Tao, and Brahm, 8; the meaning of the term, 9; as "purely formal," 10; as the absolute, 10; similar to Plato's term "idea," 10; two kinds of, 11; prior to God, 13; personified, 16; the world-mother, 16, 97, 123; the ancestor, 16, 133; the master, 16, 133; the author of all transformations, 16; and God, 16; personified, 318; also 282, 286.
Tao Teh-King, its authenticity, 6; editions of the, 42.
Taoist literature, 38.
Tasteless, 115.
= 無味 *wu wei* (35, ii. 14-15), 202.
Taxes, 135.
Teh Ts'ing, a commentator, 308.
Tenderer, 132. (See "weak.")
Tenderness, 101, 115, 123, 125, 135, 136. (Cf. "delicate," "supple," and "weak.")
= 柔 *jeu* (10, i. 12; 36, ii. 5; 52, iii. 6; 55, i. 24; 76, i. 5, etc.; 78, i. 3, etc.), 159, 203, 228, 232, 266, 267, 269, 270.
Tetzugaku Kwan, 43, 299.
Thaï-tsou-hoang-ti, founder of the Ming dynasty and admirer of Lao-Tze, 320.
Three things a unity, 103. (Cf. "trinity.")
Tiger, 122.
= 虎 *hu* (50, ii. 12, etc.), 224.
Ti-Shun (Emperor Shun), 321.

Tools, sharp, 115.
Tolstoi, 25, 26.
Tranquillity. (See "quietude.")
Treasure, viz., moral character, 317.
Treasures, 131, 132.
= 寶 *pao* (67, heading, iii. 5; 69, ii. 26), 254, 258.
= 多藏 *to ts'ang* (44, ii. 6-7), 217; translated "hoarded wealth," 120.
Trinitarianism, 295.
Trinity, 119, 308, 312. (Cf. 10
= 三 *san* (42, i 9, etc (Cf. "yang," "yi, 'ch'i," also "breath," and 'col
True man, definition of th 2 not hurt, 28; Lao Tze the, 29.
Tsiao Hong, 319.
Types, 107. (See also "form
= 象 *siang* (21, i. 23), 177.

Ugliness, 97.
= 惡 *wu* (2, i. 10), 149.
Unexpressed, 116. (See "nameless" and "ineffable.")
Unity, 101, 103, 117, 119, 290, 306, 307. (See "oneness.")
Universe, 283.
Unknowable, 133.
= 不知 *pu chi* (71, i. 1-2), 259.
Unlike, 316.
Unlikely, 131, 317.
Unnameable, 97, 103.
Unreason, 113, 124, 125.
= 不道 *pu tao* (30, iii. 7-8, etc.; 55, ii. 24-25, etc.), 194, 233.

= 非道 *fei tao* (53, ii. 35-36), 229.
Unseasoned wood. (See "simple.")
Unsophisticated, 98, 101.
= 無知 *wu chi* (3, v. 4-5; 10, iii. 13-14), 152, 160.
Unvirtue, 17, 116, 282.
= 不德 *pu teh* (38, ii. 3-4), 208.
Usefulness, 107.
= 以 *i* (20, vi. 5), 176.
Utility, 101, 118, 120, 132. (See "function.")

Vacuity. (See "empty.")
Valley. (See "river-valley.")
Valley spirit, 99.
= 谷神 *ku shǎn*, (6, i. 1-2), 154.
Vessel (frequently used in the sense of "useful man"), 102, 112, 119.
= 器 *ch'i* (28, iv. 5; 29, i. 18; 41, ii. 45), 191, 192, 213.
Virility, 125.
Virtue, 17; the noble man of perfect, 95; reason and, 96; profound, 101; vast, 107; one who pursues his business with, 108, 109; will be sufficient, 111; superior, 116; resembles a vale, 118; is good, 121; is faithful, 122; feeds all creatures, 122; is genuine, overflowing, etc., 124; who in all its solidity possesses, 124 (cf. "child"); will be combined, 127; profound, 130; those who have, 137; denounced, 105, 106, 116.
= 德 *teh* (S. M. Ch., vi. 14; xi. 5; xiv. 13; 10, iv. 20; 21, i. 2; 23, ii. 15, etc.; 18, i; 19, i; 28, i. 16, etc.; 38, i. 2, etc.; 41, ii. 20, etc.; 49, i. 13, etc.; 51, i. 4, etc.; 54, ii. 12, etc.; 55, i. 2; 60, ii. 38; 63, ii. 4; 65, ii. 38, etc.; 79, i. 25, etc.), 143, 145, 160, 172, 173, 177, 181, 189, 190, 205, 205-208, 212, 222, 225, 226, 227, 230, 231, 232, 241, 246, 251, 271. In the phrase "*pao yuen i teh*" it has been translated "goodness," 129. (Cf. "requite.")
Vital principle, 279. (Cf. "ch'i" and "breath.")
Vitality (immaterial breath), 101, 119. (Cf. "breath.")
Vitiation, risks no, 120. (See "danger" and "immortality."
Vulgarity, 105.

Wang Pi, 303, 317.
War-horses, 120.
Warlike, 132.
Wars, 112, 113.
= 軍 *chün* (30, ii. 10), 193.
Water, 24, 100, 136.
= 水 *shui* (8, i. 4, etc.; 78, i. 8), 156, 269.
Weak or weakness, has several Chinese equivalents:
= 柔 *jeu* (76, i. 6, etc; 78, i. 3, etc.) 266, 267, 269, 270; mostly translated "delicate" and frequently used with its

synonyms *joh* (76, i. 5-6; 78, i. 3-4), 266, 269; and *tsui,* "supple" (76, i. 19-20), 266. In English: 135, 136.
= 弱 *joh* (3, iv. 13; 36, i. 11, etc.; 40, i. 6; 78, i. 4, etc.), 151, 203, 211, 269. In English: 98, 115, 118, 136.
= 脆 *tsui* (76, i. 20), 266; translated "supple," 135.
= 衰 *shwai* (69, iii. 6), 258; translated "tenderer," 132.
Weakest, 119. (See also "weakness.")
= 至柔 *chi jeu* (43, i. 4-5), 216.
Wheel, 101. (See "carriage.")
Widowers, 117, 119.
Williams, S. Wells, 45, 295, 317; referred to throughout the Notes and Comments.
Without desire, the people, 98. (Cf. "desireless.")
Without effort, 100.
= 不勤 *pu ch'in* (6, iii. 7-8), 155.
Womanhood, 111. (The same word as "motherbird.")
Word, (Tao as Logos), 10, 282.
Words, alone extant, 95; have an ancestor, 133.
Work, 120. (Cf. "function.")
World, has two equivalents in our text:
= 萬物 *wan wuh,* lit. "the 10,000 things," (1, ii. 9-10; 2, v. 1-2; 4, i. 12-13; 5, i. 6-7; 8, i. 8-9; 16, i. 7-8; 32, i. 18-19; 34, i. 9-10, etc.; 37, i. 14-15; 39, ii. 21-22; 40, ii. 3-4; 42, i. 12-13, etc.; 51, i. 15-16; 62, i. 3-4; 64, iii. 25-26; 76, i. 12-13), 147, 150, 152, 153, 156, 169, 197, 200, 201, 204, 208, 209, 211, 214, 225, 244, 250, 266. In English: 97, 98, 99, 100, 104, 113, 114, 115, 117, 118, 119, 122, 128, 130, 135.
= 天下 *t'ien hia,* lit. "under heaven" (see Notes 283) (2, i. 1-2; 13, iv. 6-7, etc.; 22, ii. 8-9, etc.; 25, ii, 9-10; 26, iv. 11-12; 28, i. 8-9, etc.; 29, i. 4-5, etc.; 30, i. 11-12; 31, iii. 29-30; 32, i. 8-9; 35, i. 4-5; 37, ii. 13-14; 39, ii. 33-34; 43, i. 1-2, etc.; 45, iii. 10-11; 46, i. 1-2; 47, i. 5-6; 48, ii. 2-3, etc.; 49, iii. 4-5; 52, i. 1-2, etc.; 54, ii. 42-43, etc.; 56, iii. 37-38; 57, i. 13-14, etc.; 60, ii. 4-5; 61, i. 6-7; 62, v. 23-24; 63, iii. 11-12, etc.; 66, iii. 19-20, etc.; 67, i. 1-2, etc.; 70, ii. 1-2; 77, iii. 20-21), 148, 164, 165, 179, 180, 184, 187, 189, 190, 191, 193, 196, 197, 201, 205, 209, 216, 218, 219, 220, 221, 223, 227, 231, 235, 236, 241, 242, 245, 246, 253, 254, 255, 258, 268; sometimes translated "the empire," 97, 103, 108, 109, 110, 111, 112, 113, 114, 116, 119, 120, 121, 122, 123, 124, 125, 126, 127, 128, 129, 131, 133, 136.
World-honored, 125, 129.
World's formation, the, 107.
= 衆甫 *chung fu,* lit. "of all

things the organisation" (21, i. 57–58), 178.

World's mother, has two Chinese equivalents:

= 天下母 *t'ien hia mu*, lit. "the mother of the underheaven," (25, ii. 9–11; 52, i. 7–9), 184, 227. In English: 109, 123. (Cf. 16.)

= 萬物之母 *wan wuh chi mu*, lit. "the mother of the ten thousand things" (1, ii. 9–12), 147. In English: 97.

Yang, 278, 308. (See "positive principle.")

Yea, 106.

= 唯 *wéi* (20, i. 5), 174. (See also p. 297.)

Yes, 106.

= 阿 *o* (20, i. 8), 174. (See also p. 297.)

Yin, 308. (See "negative principle.")

Zoroastrian, 10.

A MONTHLY MAGAZINE

Devoted to the Science of Religion, the Religion of Science, and the Extension of the Religious Parliament Idea.

THE OPEN COURT does not understand by religion any creed or dogmatic belief, but man's world-conception in so far as it regulates his conduct.

The old dogmatic conception of religion is based upon the science of past ages; to base religion upon the maturest and truest thought of the present time is the object of *The Open Court*. Thus, the religion of *The Open Court* is the Religion of Science, that is, the religion of verified and verifiable truth.

Although opposed to irrational orthodoxy and narrow bigotry, *The Open Court* does not attack the properly religious element of the various religions. It criticises their errors unflinchingly but without animosity, and endeavors to preserve of them all that is true and good.

The current numbers of *The Open Court* contain valuable original articles from the pens of distinguished thinkers. Accurate and authorised translations are made in Philosophy, Science, and Criticism from the literature of Continental Europe, and reviews of noteworthy recent investigations are presented. Portraits of eminent philosophers and scientists are published, and appropriate illustrations accompany some of the articles.

Terms: $1.00 a year; $1.35 to foreign countries in the Postal Union. Single Copies, 10 cents.

THE MONIST

A QUARTERLY MAGAZINE OF

PHILOSOPHY AND SCIENCE.

THE MONIST discusses the fundamental problems of Philosophy in their practical relations to the religious, ethical, and sociological questions of the day. The following have contributed to its columns:

Prof. Joseph Le Conte,
Dr. W. T. Harris,
M. D. Conway,
Charles S. Peirce,
Prof. F. Max Müller,
Prof. E. D. Cope,
Carus Sterne,
Mrs. C. Ladd Franklin,
Prof. Max Verworn,
Prof. Felix Klein,

Prof. G. J. Romanes,
Prof. C. Lloyd Morgan,
James Sully,
B. Bosanquet,
Dr. A. Binet,
Prof. Ernst Mach,
Rabbi Emil Hirsch,
Lester F. Ward,
Prof. H. Schubert,
Dr. Edm. Montgomery,

Prof. C. Lombroso,
Prof. E. Haeckel,
Prof. H. Höffding,
Dr. F. Oswald,
Prof. J. Delbœuf,
Prof. F. Jodl,
Prof. H. M. Stanley,
G. Ferrero,
J. Venn,
Prof. H. von Holst.

Per Copy, 50 cents; Yearly, $2.00. In England and all countries in U.P.U. per Copy, 2s 6d; Yearly, 9s 6d.

CHICAGO:

THE OPEN COURT PUBLISHING CO.,

Monon Building, 324 Dearborn St.,

LONDON: Kegan Paul, Trench, Trübner & Co.

CATALOGUE OF PUBLICATIONS

OF THE

OPEN COURT PUBLISHING CO.

COPE, E. D.
   THE PRIMARY FACTORS OF ORGANIC EVOLUTION.
      121 cuts. Pp., xvi, 547. Cloth, $2.00, net.

MÜLLER, F. MAX.
   THREE INTRODUCTORY LECTURES ON THE SCIENCE OF THOUGHT.
      With a correspondence on "Thought Without Words," between F. Max Müller and Francis Galton, the Duke of Argyll, George J. Romanes and others. 128 pages. Cloth, 75 cents. Paper, 25 cents.
   THREE LECTURES ON THE SCIENCE OF LANGUAGE.
      The Oxford University Extension Lectures, with a Supplement, " My Predecessors." 112 pages. 2nd Edition. Cloth, 75 cents. Paper, 25c.

ROMANES, GEORGE JOHN.
   DARWIN AND AFTER DARWIN.
      An Exposition of the Darwinian Theory and a Discussion of Post-Darwinian Questions. Three Vols., $4.00. Singly, as follows:
      1. THE DARWINIAN THEORY. 460 pages. 125 illustrations. Cloth, $2.00.
      2. POST-DARWINIAN QUESTIONS. Heredity and Utility. Pp. 338. $1.50.
      3. POST-DARWINIAN QUESTIONS. Isolation and Physiological Selection. Pp. 181. $1.00.
   AN EXAMINATION OF WEISMANNISM.
      236 pages. Cloth, $1.00. Paper, 35c.
   THOUGHTS ON RELIGION.
      Edited by Charles Gore, M. A., Canon of Westminster. Third Edition, Pages, 184. Cloth, gilt top, $1.25.

RIBOT, TH.
   THE PSYCHOLOGY OF ATTENTION.
   THE DISEASES OF PERSONALITY.
   THE DISEASES OF THE WILL.
      Authorised translations. Cloth, 75 cents each. Paper, 25 cents. *Full set, cloth, $1.75, net.*

MACH, ERNST.
   THE SCIENCE OF MECHANICS.
      A CRITICAL AND HISTORICAL EXPOSITION OF ITS PRINCIPLES. Translated by T. J. MCCORMACK. 250 cuts. 534 pages. ½ m., gilt top. $2.50.
   POPULAR SCIENTIFIC LECTURES.
      Second Edition. 382 pages. 50 cuts. Cloth, gilt top. Net, $1.00.
   THE ANALYSIS OF THE SENSATIONS.
      Pp. 208. 37 cuts. Cloth, $1.25, net.

GOODWIN, REV. T. A.
   LOVERS THREE THOUSAND YEARS AGO.
      As Indicated by the Song of Solomon. Pp. 41. Boards, 50c.

HOLYOAKE, G. J.
   ENGLISH SECULARISM. A CONFESSION OF BELIEF.
      Pp. 146. Cloth, 50c., net.

CORNILL, CARL HEINRICH.
   THE PROPHETS OF ISRAEL.
      Popular Sketches from Old Testament History. Pp., 200. Cloth, $1.00.
   THE RISE OF THE PEOPLE OF ISRAEL.
      See *Epitomes of Three Sciences*, below.

BINET, ALFRED.
   THE PSYCHIC LIFE OF MICRO-ORGANISMS.
      Authorised translation. 135 pages. Cloth, 75 cents; Paper, 25 cents.
   ON DOUBLE CONSCIOUSNESS.
      Studies in Experimental Psychology. 93 pages. Paper, 15 cents.

WAGNER, RICHARD.
A PILGRIMAGE TO BEETHOVEN.
A Novelette. Frontispiece, portrait of Beethoven. Pp. 40. Boards, 50c

WEISMANN, AUGUST.
GERMINAL SELECTION. As a Source of Definite Variation.
Pp. 73. Paper, 25c.

NOIRÉ, LUDWIG.
ON THE ORIGIN OF LANGUAGE. Pp. 57. Paper, 15c.

FREYTAG, GUSTAV.
THE LOST MANUSCRIPT. A Novel.
2 vols. 953 pages. Extra cloth, $4.00. One vol., cl., $1.00; paper, 75c.
MARTIN LUTHER.
Illustrated. Pp. 130. Cloth, $1.00. Paper, 25c.

HERING, EWALD.
ON MEMORY, and THE SPECIFIC ENERGIES OF THE NERVOUS SYSTEM. Pp. 50. Paper, 15c.

TRUMBULL, M. M.
THE FREE TRADE STRUGGLE IN ENGLAND.
Second Edition. 296 pages. Cloth, 75 cents; paper, 25 cents.
WHEELBARROW: Articles and Discussions on the Labor Question
With portrait of the author. 303 pages. Cloth, $1.00; paper, 35 cents.
EARL GREY ON RECIPROCITY AND CIVIL SERVICE REFORM.
With Comments by Gen. M. M. Trumbull. Price, 10 cents.

GOETHE AND SCHILLER'S XENIONS.
Selected and translated by Paul Carus. Album form. Pp., 162. Cl., $1.00

OLDENBERG, H.
ANCIENT INDIA: ITS LANGUAGE AND RELIGIONS.
Pp. 100. Cloth, 50c. Paper, 25c.

CARUS, PAUL.
THE ETHICAL PROBLEM.
90 pages. Cloth, 50 cents; Paper, 30 cents.
FUNDAMENTAL PROBLEMS.
Second edition, enlarged and revised. 372 pp. Cl., $1.50. Paper, 50c.
HOMILIES OF SCIENCE.
317 pages. Cloth, Gilt Top, $1.50.
THE IDEA OF GOD.
Fourth edition. 32 pages. Paper, 15 cents.
THE SOUL OF MAN.
With 152 cuts and diagrams. 458 pages. Cloth, $3.00.
TRUTH IN FICTION. Twelve Tales with a Moral.
Fine laid paper, white and gold binding, gilt edges. Pp. 111. $1.00.
THE RELIGION OF SCIENCE.
Second, extra edition. Price, 50 cents. R. S. L. edition, 25c. Pp. 103.
PRIMER OF PHILOSOPHY.
240 pages. Second Edition. Cloth, $1.00. Paper, 25c.
THREE LECTURES: (1) The Philosophy of the Tool. Pages, 24. Paper, 10c. (2) Our Need of Philosophy. Pages, 14. Paper, 5c. (3) Science a Religious Revelation. Pages, 21. Paper, 5c.
THE GOSPEL OF BUDDHA. According to Old Records.
4th Edition. Pp., 275. Cloth, $1.00. Paper, 35 cents. In German, $1.25.
BUDDHISM AND ITS CHRISTIAN CRITICS.
Pages, 311. Cloth, $1.25.
KARMA. A Story of Early Buddhism.
Illustrated by Japanese artists. 2nd Edition. Crêpe paper, 75 cents.

GARBE, RICHARD.
THE REDEMPTION OF THE BRAHMAN. A Tale of Hindu Life.
Laid paper. Gilt top. 96 pages. Price, 75c. Paper, 25c.
THE PHILOSOPHY OF ANCIENT INDIA.
Pp. 89. Cloth, 50c. Paper, 25c.

EPITOMES OF THREE SCIENCES.
1. The Study of Sanskrit. By *H. Oldenberg.* 2. Experimental Psychology. By *Joseph Jastrow.* 3. The Rise of the People of Israel. By *C. H. Cornill.* 140 pages. Cloth, reduced to 50 cents.

The Religion of Science Library.

A collection of bi-monthly publications, most of which are reprints of books published by The Open Court Publishing Company. Yearly, $1.50. Separate copies according to prices quoted. The books are printed upon good paper, from large type.

The Religion of Science Library, by its extraordinarily reasonable price, will place a large number of valuable books within the reach of all readers

The following have already appeared in the series:

No. 1. *The Religion of Science.* By PAUL CARUS. 25c.
2. *Three Introductory Lectures on the Science of Thought.* By F. MAX MÜLLER. 25c.
3. *Three Lectures on the Science of Language.* By F. MAX MÜLLER. 25c.
4. *The Diseases of Personality.* By TH. RIBOT. 25c.
5. *The Psychology of Attention.* By TH. RIBOT. 25c.
6. *The Psychic Life of Micro-Organisms.* By ALFRED BINET. 25c.
7. *The Nature of the State.* By PAUL CARUS. 15c.
8. *On Double Consciousness.* By ALFRED BINET. 15c.
9. *Fundamental Problems.* By PAUL CARUS. 50c.
10. *The Diseases of the Will.* By TH. RIBOT. 25c.
11. *The Origin of Language.* By LUDWIG NOIRÉ. 15c.
12. *The Free Trade Struggle in England.* By M. M. TRUMBULL. 25c.
13. *Wheelbarrow on the Labor Question.* By M. M. TRUMBULL. 35c.
14. *The Gospel of Buddha.* By PAUL CARUS. 35c.
15. *The Primer of Philosophy.* By PAUL CARUS. 25c.
16. *On Memory,* and *The Specific Energies of the Nervous System.* By PROF. EWALD HERING. 15c.
17. *The Redemption of the Brahman.* A Tale of Hindu Life. By RICHARD GARBE. 25c.
18. *An Examination of Weismannism.* By G. J. ROMANES. 35c.
19. *On Germinal Selection.* By AUGUST WEISMANN. 25c.
20. *Lovers Three Thousand Years Ago.* By T. A. GOODWIN. 15c.
21. *Popular Scientific Lectures.* By ERNST MACH. 35c.
22. *Ancient India: Its Language and Religions.* By H. OLDENBERG. 25c.
23. *The Prophets of Ancient Israel.* By PROF. C. H. CORNILL. 25c.
24. *Homilies of Science.* By PAUL CARUS. 35c.
25. *Thoughts on Religion.* By G. J. ROMANES. 50 cents.
26. *The Philosophy of Ancient India.* By PROF. RICHARD GARBE. 25c.
27. *Martin Luther.* By GUSTAV FREYTAG. 25c.
28. *English Secularism.* By GEORGE JACOB HOLYOAKE. 25c.
29. *On Orthogenesis.* By TH. EIMER. 25c.

THE OPEN COURT PUBLISHING CO.
324 DEARBORN STREET, CHICAGO, ILL.

LONDON: Kegan Paul, Trench, Trübner & Co

www.ingramcontent.com/pod-product-compliance
Lightning Source LLC
Chambersburg PA
CBHW030258240426
43673CB00040B/999